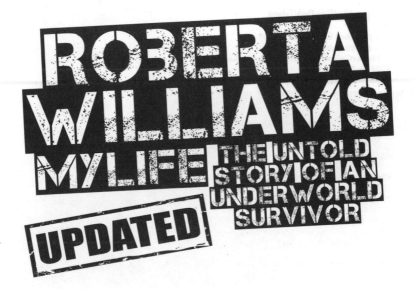

ROBERTA WILLIAMS

MY LIFE

THE UNTOLD STORY OF AN UNDERWORLD SURVIVOR

UPDATED

HarperCollins*Publishers*

HarperCollins*Publishers*
25 Ryde Road, Pymble, Sydney, NSW 2073, Australia
31 View Road, Glenfield, Auckland 0627, New Zealand
A 53, Sector 57, Noida, UP, India
77–85 Fulham Palace Road, London, W6 8JB, United Kingdom
2 Bloor Street East, 20th floor, Toronto, Ontario M4W 1A8, Canada
10 East 53rd Street, New York NY 10022, USA

National Library of Australia Cataloguing-in-Publication data:

Williams, Roberta, 1969-
    Roberta Williams : my life / Roberta Williams, Michael Gleeson.
    ISBN: 978 0 7322 8953 9 (pbk.)
    Williams, Roberta, 1969-
    Divorced women – Victoria – Biography.
    Abused women – Victoria – Biography.
    Adult child abuse victims – Victoria – Biography.
    Women prisoners – Victoria – Biography.
    Organized crime – Victoria – Melbourne.
    Gangs – Victoria – Melbourne.
    Other Authors/Contributors: Gleeson, Michael, 1969-
306.893092

Cover design by Brendon Cook
Cover images: Roberta Williams faces court for tax evasion by Kristian Dowling/Getty Images;
    Carl and Roberta Williams © Newspix
Typeset in Sabon by Kirby Jones
Printed and bound in Australia by Griffin Press
70gsm Classic used by HarperCollins*Publishers* is a natural, recyclable product made from wood grown in sustainable forests. The manufacturing processes conform to the environmental regulations in the country of origin, Finland.

5 4 3 2   10 11 12 13

To my dad, I'll always love you

*To my beautiful children, Tye, Danielle, Breanane
and Dhakota, with love from Mum*

CONTENTS

CHAPTER 1

I'M ROBERTA

First things first: my name is Roberta Williams. Some people call me Bert. A few call me Billy. No-one calls me Bobby. You might think you know me because you have seen me on TV on the news or in that cartoon, *Underbelly*. But you don't know me. Not yet, anyway. I'll tell you who I am and how I came to be the woman you know swearing like a wharfie on the TV.

I suppose what you really want to know is how did I end up married to Carl Williams? How does anyone end up married to someone like Carl Williams? I get asked that question a bit. Not as often as I get asked what Carl was really like and what it was like living with him during all the bullshit of the so-called Gangland Wars, but I get it a fair bit. People also always want to know what it was like in that period, they want to know how I met Carl and what I thought when people started dropping dead all over

Melbourne. They also want to know why I didn't leave him. So I'll tell you.

There is a short answer to those questions and a long one. The short answer is I loved him. Simple as that. I loved Carl Williams. He might have had some people killed but he treated me better than any other man ever did. Sounds strange, doesn't it, that a bloke who everyone was shit-scared of because he was some 'gangland killer' treated me better than any other bloke I'd ever met before in my life. But it's true, Carl was a gentleman. He was the first man who didn't abuse me, so to me he wasn't a killer, he was just Carl — big fatty boombah Carl — and I loved him. I probably still do in a lot of ways, to tell the truth, but that doesn't mean I want to be with him anymore. We are over, and in more ways than one I am *over* Carl. Back then we were like two best friends who ended up together and got married when we should have known we were better off just staying really good friends.

As to why I never left Carl the short answer is that I did leave him. Not straight away, I know, and it was as much because he was rooting around as anything else, but I did break up with him. The reason I didn't leave him earlier, in the middle of all the bullshit, is the same as the first one: I loved him. And at the time things were out of control. It wasn't like I could just decide one day to step out of that life. It wasn't that simple.

The truth is that at the time people were being killed every other week in Melbourne we *were* in the middle of a 'war'. It wasn't like the police and the media described it, it was more about drug dealers fighting than gangs, but it was really personal between us and the Morans and the so-called Carlton Crew, and it *was* a war. For Carl it was a choice between watching the people around him get killed or doing something about it. Carl did something about it. Who wouldn't have done what we did in the same situation?

I know some people won't like the fact that I am writing a book about this but I think why not? Haven't I got a right to tell my side of the story? I am not making anyone buy this book. If it's alright for someone who wasn't involved in all the bullshit to guess what happened and make a whole lot of stuff up for a TV series about it, then it must be alright for someone who was in the middle of it to write about it and put the record straight. I want to tell it the way it was and some people won't like that, but too bad — it is what it is.

I didn't set out to live life this way. I didn't want to marry someone who ended up in jail for murder. I didn't want to be in the middle of a drug war. My whole life has been about dealing with shit when it happens and trying to survive as best I can for my kids. I look at my life now and break it into parts — before Carl and after Carl. In fact you could make that three parts — before Carl, with Carl and after Carl, because life could never be the same after living with Carl Williams. Each part of my life explains the next part, so to understand how I came to be in the middle of all the madness that happened you have to understand where I came from.

From what I can gather, people think I had a pretty normal life and I met up with this crazy bloke and pushed him into doing all this stuff. But that is bullshit, it wasn't like that at all. Firstly, my life before Carl was not what you would call normal. I will tell you about it, not because I want your sympathy but because I know a lot of people want to understand what happened and how it happened.

I'm looking back at my life now partly to explain it to myself. One ex-copper wrote about me in another book that you could 'take the girl out of Frankston but you couldn't take Frankston out of the girl'. I am not sure what he was trying to say by that. I don't think I'm a trashy person, I try and be the best person I can be. Given where I have come from and knowing some of the people I knew when I was growing up, I could easily have ended up being a heroin addict and not cared about my kids, but I chose to care for them and bring them up the best way I knew how.

Now I see my past was wrong, but I can't change that. Like I said, I don't want sympathy, I just want to explain how it was. This is how it was.

CHAPTER 2

HAPPY FAMILY

I never knew my dad. He died after a truck crash and fire when I was eight months old. I often wonder how different life might have been if I had known him. I like to think Dad would have made life better — I have no doubt he would have, because it couldn't have been much worse.

Not having known him I have tried to piece together what the family knew of him. Mum never told us much. I sent away for his birth certificate a few years ago and when I received it it was like a whole story tumbled out of that one piece of paper. The little bits of his life I discovered made me embarrassed for how much I didn't know about him. I didn't even know his name — well, not his real names anyway. My grandparents' names were Giuseppe and Giuseppa — similar names — and my father had three names: Emanuel, Giovanni and some other woggy name. I knew his surname, because that was mine, Mercieca. I had obviously kept that. He was born in Malta and came out here when he was fifteen. He was a deckhand on a ship — he was working on ships to get to Australia.

He met my mum when they were both young. I am not sure where or how, but they met. Mum was just an Aussie girl, she was born here and so were her parents, but her grandparents were German. They had lived in Leeton, New South Wales but the whole family moved down to Melbourne at some stage. She met Dad and they got married when Mum was three months' pregnant with my eldest brother, Michael. I was the youngest of the seven kids Mum and Dad had together. I know, seven. It's a lot but I don't think it was that uncommon back then to have a lot of kids. Not in Maltese families, anyway. They had them all pretty quick — there is just eighteen months between each of us. I might as well list us off here: Michael, then Susan, Sharon, who passed away in 2007 from cancer, then Josephine, Laurie, Michelle and me. I was born at the Royal Women's in Carlton on 23 March 1969.

Eight months later, on 22 November 1969, a careless driver in another truck lost control and smashed into my dad's truck. The whole truck exploded in flames and Dad was trapped in the cabin. The other driver ran away and when they got Dad to hospital they said he had burns to 97 per cent of his body. All he could do was recite his kids' names and dates of birth. You'd never imagine anyone could survive that but he did, for five days. Without all the technology they have now he still hung on for five days. They must have been five agonising days. Eventually he died of heart failure because I don't think his body could cope with the pain of the burns. It must have been hell.

I was only eight months old so I never really had a dad. Surely none of the scum Mum took up with afterwards counted as dads or father figures. Or even men. They were dogs. Not one of them behaved like a human being, not one of them looked at Mum's kids and gave them anything but abuse. The saddest thing about it is that even though I never knew him, I loved my dad to death. I have shed many tears for this man I never really met. I just miss him with all my heart. Maybe it was because of the arseholes that Mum started seeing after Dad died that I built up in my mind what my real dad would have been like and what he would have done to these fucking arseholes if he were alive and saw what they did to his kids.

Mum never gave us any background about Dad. It was like when he died she just moved on and didn't want to talk about him anymore. I only heard bits and pieces about him and sort of grew up not knowing anything about this person I loved to death. It probably made it easier to love him so much, because she didn't tell us anything. Being so young I almost made him into the person I wanted him to be. I remember Mum telling me once that when I was born Dad would hold me and say I was the most beautiful thing he'd ever seen and kept kissing me. I think of that a lot and it makes me happy because there's not a day goes by that I don't think about him and wish he was here. I know it sounds simple to say that our lives would have been better had he lived, because anything else could have happened, but when you think that Mum was suddenly a single mother with seven kids, the youngest just eight months old, you have to think it would have been a lot easier for everyone if her husband was still alive. I can't imagine that all the shit that happened later would still have happened if Dad was alive.

It would have been different in other ways too. For instance, I would have been brought up speaking Maltese, and I probably would have married some Maltese guy, probably a concreter or brickie or something, and had a stable life and a working class family. It was what I've dreamed of since but one man's carelessness destroyed our whole life. People don't understand that. I know people say Carl killed people and I was living with him when he did it, but that was different — they were drug dealers and they were trying to kill us. Dad did nothing wrong and was killed because of someone else's stupidity.

The driver of the other truck lost his licence for seven years and paid a fine of a couple of hundred dollars. Me, and my brother and sisters all got paid compensation by the TAC — the Victorian government's Transport Accident Commission, which pays compensation to victims of road accidents — or whatever it was called then, when I was eighteen and then again when I was twenty-one. It made me feel weird to get money knowing it was because my dad died.

Mum met another bloke pretty much straight away and had another baby, my younger brother Robert. I don't even want to tell you her new partner's name. It was Theo Van something and he was a Dutch car salesman. I know, a car salesman *and* Dutch — it's like a double whammy. My mum had gone out with him when she was younger, before she met my dad, so she didn't muck around finding him again when Dad died. I think my mum was a bit of a skank when I look back at everything.

We were living in Rosella Avenue, Altona North, at the time. Theo used to abuse us even though we were really little. I don't remember the abuse very well but my oldest brother Mick has told me that when I was about two I went up to Theo one day and called him 'Daddy', because I suppose I didn't know any different — I must have thought he was my dad because he was around all the time. And he backhanded me, saying, 'I'm not your fucking daddy.' Mick and he got in a fight and Mick bashed him up. I mean, what kind of a piece of shit does that to a kid?

Theo used to hit us and be really nasty — he refused to speak to me at all and I was still just a toddler. My brother said that one night he came in and Theo was smashing his knife and fork on the table and yelling at Mum, saying, 'Shut these fucking kids up,' because he couldn't stand it. So to keep him, she allowed him to hit us when he was angry, probably because we were loud. I mean, there were eight of us by then and you can imagine the noise with a baby, a three-year-old and a four-year-old among them. I love the noise of children in the house, I love that playing and laughing and mucking around, and that would have been us. But Theo hated it. We weren't his kids and he hated having to put up with the noise, so given a choice Mum chose him and kicked us out of the house or let him beat us.

I hate Mum for that as much as I hate Theo for hitting us. I probably hate her more for it because not only would she let Theo hit us, she used to lay into us herself. Michelle and I were the youngest and Mum used to beat us really badly. I remember the electric jug cord would detach from the kettle and she'd whip me with that. I remember when I was three or four years old I used to wet the bed because I was so terrified, and I would change the sheets myself and put them in the wash because I knew she'd hit me if she found the bed wet and had to change it.

Michelle and I used to have a bath together when we were little and Mum would hold our heads under the water sometimes. We used to say to each other, 'Next time she does it, we'll pull the plug out of the bath' and things like that. Because it was so crazy we'd try and make a joke of it so it wasn't so mad. I'm still terrified of the water. I'm also terrified of being in confined spaces because we used to have to hide under the bed or in the wardrobe so she wouldn't find us and hit us. Michelle was always fantastic and always tried to protect me, like when we ran to hide under the bed she would always push me under first to make sure I was OK when Mum was chasing us. Anything at all would set Mum off, like when we'd have a shower, she'd make us have two minutes in the shower and get out and dry the shower with the towel. It's almost embarrassing to say now.

I look back at what my mum did in horror. When I was four years old and I had head lice, she washed my hair with kerosene and put me in the bath and just left it in. It stung like you have no idea. I was screaming and she knew I was in pain but she just left me. How could anyone do that? Sometimes if I yell at my kids I'll break down and cry because I think, 'This is *her*. What am I doing, yelling at my kids?' I've broken the cycle now because I've forced myself to never, ever, hit my kids. It's not fucking normal to hit your children. It took years to get the fear of Mum and being abused out of me.

Mum got with Theo when I was two and she had my younger brother Robert to Theo when I was four. But when Robert was born Theo moved out and got his own place in Footscray and every weekend my mum just used to leave the rest of us kids at home and take Robert over to Theo's place. Every week she would just leave us kids to fend for ourselves from Friday until Monday. Sharon, Mick and Susan were older and sort of did their own thing, so there was just Josephine, Laurie, Michelle and me in the house all weekend. I was four and Josephine was the eldest — she would have been nine, nearly ten, at the time — and Mum would just leave the four of us there. On Sunday nights we'd walk to the bus stop at the shops on Millers Road and meet my mum and we'd walk home.

Josephine always made the food in the house, even when Mum was there. We couldn't afford takeaway food and for school we'd be lucky to get a Vegemite sandwich. I remember mostly we'd eat sausages and mashed potatoes, and one-pan dinner. Oh my God, I cooked that stuff once a few years ago just to see what it was like. Honestly, I nearly vomited. I thought we must have been starving to eat that shit. We had no choice of Macca's or pizza or anything.

A treat was when my sister Sharon brought home a pizza. Shaz used to hang around the shops on Millers Road and she was friends with everyone. Some of the time someone would give her a pizza and she would bring it home for all of us and it was like, 'Oh, my God!' Sharon always tried to do whatever she could for us. She used to break into the canteen at the school over the road and steal ice-cream and stuff and bring it home for us just to give us all a treat because we never had anything. I know it sort of sounds pathetic now, breaking into the canteen to get ice-creams, but she was doing it for her little brothers and sisters, not like some street skank. Sharon had to take on the role of the parent and she tried to protect us all. When she passed away, everyone felt it hard.

So first of all Theo got sick of us kids and moved out to his own place in Footscray, then he got sick of Mum too. They split up and he said to her, 'If I give you $500, I don't want to see you again. I don't want you coming back asking for maintenance for Robert and I never want to see you or the fucking kid again.' That was the kind of bloke he was and that was the last we had to do with him. Mum didn't really want that — she wanted him — but I suppose the five hundred bucks thirty-something years ago would have been a lot of money to her so she took the cash.

Sharon was getting in a bit of trouble in Altona at the time so we moved across town to Seaford. I remember the first night we stayed there they put me in a cot and I was five years old. They didn't set it up properly and the bottom fell out. We always used to laugh about it, my big sister

Sharon and I. The house was a four-bedroom place on Seaford Road, which is a busy road.

Mum always played favourites with the kids. I know some people will say that all kids think their parents like one of their brothers or sisters more than them, but with Mum it was true — and she was open about. Josephine and Robert were her favourites. I don't know why, what us other kids did that she loved them and not us. She had eight kids all up but she loved Josephine and Robert the most. In fact you could say she only loved Josephine and Robert. For instance, Josephine always had her own bedroom. When we moved to Seaford Road she was the only one to get her own bedroom while the rest of us slept in bunks.

At first Robert slept in Mum's bed with her, then he used to sleep with my sister, Josephine. He was a sooky little shit. I never liked him. I hated him because he took away what I thought should have been mine, the love of my mother. Even though she was a crazy bitch and beat us, for some reason you still want your mother to love you. I don't know, maybe it was thinking that if she loved you more she wouldn't hit you. And she was our mother, you are supposed to love your mum. So we wanted her affection but she wouldn't give us any. She gave that to Robert — and Josephine — and I always hated his guts for that. It's horrible to say, but I fucking hated him.

Growing up we never had toys or dolls or anything because there was never enough money for that stuff for us kids. I don't remember ever having a doll but my sister Josephine always had them. I wondered later if I was just remembering wrong and maybe we did all get things, so I asked Sharon about it and she said no, that was how it was — Mum used to send away for dolls for Josephine and buy her everything, and we got nothing. When she died Mum left Josephine and Robert all the money in her will.

Josephine didn't even look like Mum. If you see us all together, my sister Sharon, my brother Laurie and me are the spitting image of each other. And my sister Josephine is totally the odd one out. Michelle looks like Mum's side of the family. Poor Susan was always just ugly, and Robert looked like his fucking ugly father.

Susan was the one who later went on TV and said we had such a great life growing up. It was such bullshit. I don't know how you can see your mum holding your sisters' heads under the water in the bath or whipping their arses with an electric cord and say it was a great happy childhood. I don't know how you could have watched us kids being locked out of the house and say it was a happy family. Theo must never have beaten her like he beat Sharon, Michelle and me. The rest of us spoke about it after she did that TV bullshit and asked each other how she could sit there and tell story after story about how great our lives were and what great stuff Mum had done. It's horrible to think that she told lies, but isn't that what happened with that Schapelle Corby and her family? People say some strange things about their families on those shows. The problem with Susan was, she didn't just say it once, she repeated it later on in the newspapers.

I said a few things back about her in the newspaper at the time that she made her comments, and it became a bit of a daily soap opera for a while. I will talk more about her later in the book because I want to tell you about all this other stuff that happened before I get to that.

Despite what Susan said, life was not normal for us growing up. It mightn't have been that bad for Josephine and Robert, and maybe Susan thought it was OK, but for the rest of us it was just shit. I must say, though, that Mum even got sick of Josephine on one occasion and kicked her out. I was about ten or eleven, and Mum was kicking Josephine out of the house and Sharon had her car full of Josephine's stuff. I was in one of the bedrooms and Mum was yelling and screaming at me and going nuts. She was throwing Josephine's stuff out when she suddenly grabbed me and tried to pin me down. She had a bottle of nail polish remover and she was fighting me with one hand and trying to pour nail polish remover in my eyes with the other. She was screaming and yelling and completely out of control.

Sharon came to the window and was yelling at me saying, 'Quick, get out, Bertie, get out.' I was halfway out the window and Mum was pulling at my hair and holding my arms, trying to pour the nail polish remover in my eyes, and I was fighting her. Sharon was outside ripping me the other way, like we were in some kind of tug-of-war with Mum, and pulled my tracksuit pants right off.

Shaz was able to overpower Mum and she just wrenched me out the window. It was terrifying — it's one thing I'll never forget. I remember the clothes I was wearing, I remember what Shaz was wearing, and Mum. I remember the look on Shaz's face, she was just so scared for me and angry at Mum, and I remember Mum's eyes were just wild — she was completely out of control. I was ten or eleven years old, for fuck's sake. What could a ten-year-old have done that was so bad? I had no idea why she was trying to pour nail polish remover in my eyes. I think now that it was probably the closest thing to hand that she could use to hurt me with.

I look at my daughter Dhakota now and she's around that age and I just think, my God, I couldn't imagine her going through that or anyone harming her. I remember at the time it freaked us out, but it was the sort of weird shit we grew up with. Shaz would probably have been just eighteen then and she had a flat, I think, and I stayed there for a couple of days. I couldn't stay there for good so eventually I had to go home again. I was ten after all.

Mum never left a key out for us to get into the house. If she wasn't home she would just leave us locked out. I remember that on my eighth birthday I came home from school and no-one was home so I went out and roamed the streets and hung around Frankston for a while, and came home late and still there was no-one home. So I sat on the doorstep until 10.30 pm when Mum finally arrived. She didn't say anything, just went inside. If she remembered it was my birthday, she didn't say so, but that year was actually the first time she ever gave me anything for my birthday — it was a necklace, with matching earrings and a ring. It's the only time I ever remember getting a birthday gift from her. I can't say for certain that I never got anything else, because maybe when I was really little she gave me a present and I don't remember it, but that was the only time I ever remember getting a birthday present. It wasn't wrapped or anything — she just put it on the table and didn't even say much other than 'this is for you' or something. It was a day or two after my birthday and she had left me sitting on the doorstep, so maybe she remembered and bought something.

I doubt she felt bad about leaving me locked out because she used to do that all the time. Some nights she would just lock us all out in the back yard, although often Josephine and Robert were allowed inside. It would be nearly midnight before we could come back in. We'd sit together in the back yard till all hours of the night, in winter too, when it was freezing cold. The next morning we'd go off battered and bruised with fuck-all for lunch and we were meant to concentrate and get down to work. I didn't care less about school, I just couldn't wait till I was old enough to get out and do my own thing. But on the night of my birthday, I suppose I'll give her the benefit of the doubt and say maybe being locked out was the reason I got a present that year.

At birthdays we never normally got presents — I suppose when you are broke and you have so many kids you would be buying birthday presents every other week — but at Easter we always got Easter eggs. I remember one year she bought me this bunny. It was a fluffy bunny and it had a wagon on the back made out of cardboard with four eggs in it. I loved that bunny, because I never had toys or dolls or anything like that growing up and that was the first and only time I got one. At Christmas time she always tried to buy things for us and some years she would take us to the Royal Melbourne Show, but that was only between the boyfriends. It was always like, 'get a new partner and fuck the kids off'. It was like the kids only got in the way of her being with a bloke, so she would just try and piss us off.

I remember some nights lying in bed in pain and not being able to move. I've had broken bones since and I've thought 'it's the same pain'. I'd go to school and they'd ask me where the bruises came from and I'd say I fell over; it's like an abused child actually defending the abuser, and it's wrong. I tell my children now, 'If anyone hits you, tell the teacher, or tell the counsellor or tell somebody, ring 000 and tell them. Tell someone who will help you. It's not right.'

Mum used to get sick of me and just kick me out at times, so when I was about eight or nine I used to befriend people who had kids. I always loved kids. I'd always hang out with single parents or junkies or something and in return for a place to stay I'd look after their babies for them like I had my own live doll. I remember one day I was staying with a druggie called Jackie and her kid, Sonia. I was bathing Sonia in a laundry trough because they didn't have a bath and all of a sudden I dropped her under the water. I was only like a baby myself but I didn't panic, I just picked this kid out of the water before she drowned and kept bathing her and fixing her up and getting her dressed. I loved kids, but I should never have been looking after them at that age. Sometimes I used to come home to Mum's house pushing a pram with the kids and the bags of clothes in it — I'd try to get a foot in the door because I was caring for somebody else, but she'd kick me out and so I'd go and stay at these junkies' houses.

I used to catch the train from Seaford to Frankston two stations away and I'd hang out with other kids and go to Myer where we'd shoplift our clothes. I think the staff probably knew, but they didn't do anything about the shoplifting. You could walk into Myer and whack jeans under your jeans and walk out. We were in Myer so often, one time they asked my sister and me to model bathers for them. So we modelled their bathers one day and we got to keep their clothes whether they knew it or not! We'd go to Safeway to steal food. I used to go to the one at the end of Seaford Road, on the corner with the Nepean Highway, and shoplift Peppermint Crisps and cans of Fanta, and I used to eat until I vomited. Because I never got anything much to eat it was like 'get it in while you can' and I would bolt the food down and keep eating until I was sick.

I wasn't stealing for the thrill of it or to sell it or anything. I'd steal the clothes to wear and the food to eat. I was supposed to be going to Seaford Primary School at the time, but I was never there because I hated school and used to wag and just roam the streets. The teachers were pretty mean. I remember the sports teacher, Mr Edmonds, always saying, 'You're never going to amount to anything — why do you even bother coming to school?' But I remember there was an art teacher who was beautiful to me. She was married to another teacher and she was so kind and caring and knew that I was having hard times, so she used to try and be really nice. By the time I was in Grade 6 I was a ward of the state.

Funnily enough, given that people might think of me as some tough kid hanging out on the street, I was bullied at school. I used to get in punch-ups at high school, but not at primary school. At primary school I was the one being bullied. I remember this thumping big girl used to pick on me and call me Scarface because I had a scar on my face from where Mum hit me with something. Other kids would say, 'At least I've got a dad ...' and in the end I'd get so angry I'd retaliate and then I'd be seen as the naughty one. I didn't care enough to complain that they had started it and been mean to me. It was a case of the dumb rebellious kid being pushed to the back of the class while the smart one is pushed forward.

Not everyone was awful, though. Like I said, there was the art teacher, and there was this lady, Mrs O'Neil, who lived on the corner of our road and Railway Parade. I can honestly say she used to love me. We lived five houses down from her and I used to talk to her from when I was really small. She had a nectarine tree and she used to pick them and bring them down for us and I used to go to her house and make her toasted muffins with melted cheese on them, and lamingtons. When I was in Allambie Youth Training Centre, that disgusting state-run home for children in Burwood, I remember she moved to a farm with deer and she used to say to my mum that she wanted me to go and stay with her because she thought she could help me, but my mum never wanted anything good for me, obviously, so she didn't tell me about it at the time because it would have been an 'out' for me.

Mum got a new partner pretty quickly after we moved to Seaford — I told you she was a bit of a skank — and he was Maltese as well. His name was Joe and he was as bad as Theo — he used to hit me and he hated my guts. One time he smashed my head against the toilet bowl so badly that my ears bled. I think I was maybe seven or eight years old. It was just over a dumb thing. Like all kids, I never wanted to do the dishes so I would hide, and this time I hid in the bathroom and he found me and smashed my head into the toilet bowl. Fucking arsehole.

He would always backhand me but he never sexually abused me. Neither did Theo, but they both beat the shit out of me. The thing was, afterwards I hated Mum more than them because we were hers and it was her responsibility to protect us, but she just let them do whatever they wanted to us as long as they stayed with her. The bitch. I never had any positive males in my life. My brother Mick was in and out of jail when he was young. Mick was really close to my dad and when Dad died Mick went to the hospital with Mum and saw the burns and it just sent him off a bit. The first time he got in trouble he stole money from milk bottles, but he has pretty much straightened himself out now and he has his own transport company, driving semi-trailers.

Eventually Mum had enough of me. I tried to stay with Mick for a while and then Shaz, but they couldn't keep me forever. When I was eleven Mum rang the police and said I was uncontrollable and they had to come and take me away.

Which they did. They made me a ward of the state. Well, it wasn't surprising — I *was* out of control. Why would you want to be around when your mum and her boyfriends are beating you up? So Mum just packed my stuff up in a cardboard box — there wasn't much of it — and she and Josephine carried it to the footpath. Everyone else had more or less gone by then. Robert and Josephine were there, and Laurie, but Laurie was quiet. I know I was a handful, I am not saying it would have been easy to handle me because I've spoken to doctors since and they diagnosed me with ADD, which I had then and probably still have now, but do you really kick your kid out of the house at eleven?

I rang my brother Mick and he came and got me and I stayed at his house for a while. Then my sister Shaz took me in and I stayed at her place. I'd roam the streets to keep out of her way so she didn't get sick of me too, and the police would pick me up and lock me up. I was in and out of Allambie Youth Training Centre through this time and Shaz would visit me and take me out for Christmas and things like that. I was never locked up for major crimes or anything. I was locked up because I was a ward of the state and some of the time, later on, I was locked up for little stuff like shoplifting or minor assaults.

I was always really tight with my sister Shaz but since she died in 2007 Mick and I have become closer. He has really become the man of the family. My younger brother Robert and I started to build a relationship later on but we didn't speak for a long time because of a dispute over a property deal.

Later, when Carl was in jail and I was absolutely broke — there were days when I didn't have $10 to buy milk and bread for my kids — I rang Robert. I begged him for money telling him I had nowhere to go and no money for food. I said, 'My kids have done nothing to you; at least help them if you won't help me.' He brought me a lousy $2000 and that was the last I've seen of him. He's that sort of person — just like my mother and his father.

I wouldn't have thought many people at the time would have wanted to get into a dispute with Carl Williams, because by then he had a bit of a reputation in Melbourne and not many people would have wanted to cross him. I know Purana — the police task force set up to investigate the gangland murders — approached Robert and said, 'You want to be careful because you might come across Carl one day and jack a bullet in the head.'

Robert got a bit wary after that but I think it worked for the jacks because I reckon Robert helped set Carl up for them. The day Carl got arrested in Beaconsfield Parade, St Kilda, he had been having lunch with Robert in Acland Street. Carl had organised the lunch with him, but no-one knew they were going to be there — no-one. Carl had a few drinks with him before getting in his car and driving off. He was arrested within minutes. Clearly the jacks had been tipped off. It was all a bit suss, because after he was arrested Carl also realised that an undercover jack had walked into the café, presumably to confirm it was definitely Carl in there.

At the time all I knew was that Carl was late and not answering his phone so I rang Robert, because I knew he was supposed to be with Carl, to ask him where Carl was — I thought Carl might have been killed — but Robert wasn't answering his phone.

Sometimes I reflect on how my life unfolded and all the shit that happened and I think a lot of it can be traced back to that stupid truck accident. I don't reckon a lot of the shit that happened later would have happened if Dad had been around. I think sometimes that maybe I should have given Mum more sympathy because Dad died and left her with seven kids, but then I remind myself that that does not give her the right to abuse her kids and let other people hurt them. I look back now and wonder how many broken bones I had in that time that just healed on their own. More than anything I wonder what it would have been like if some dickhead hadn't driven into Dad's truck.

CHAPTER 3

ALLAMBIE

I still remember my mum's face as the police car drove away. She was standing at the door of the house on Seaford Road with Josephine next to her and they watched as the police carried the boxes of my stuff to the car and loaded me in the back seat. When they drove off I was crying and looking out the window at her and she just looked coldly at me and said nothing. She just turned and went inside. I might as well have been someone sitting on a bus driving by for all she cared.

Back then it was all dealt with by the police and the courts. I'll never forget the judge, his name was Jones, and he was an old dog of a bloke who looked at me like I was scum or something revolting he had stood in. He made me a ward of the state and sent me to Allambie girls' home. I have often thought about it since, how I was taken away and put into custody by police because my mum could not deal with me or cope with all of her kids, so *I* was the one taken away by the jacks. What about her? Isn't the real crime that a mother treats her kids like shit? No police came around to lock her up for the way she treated her kids. No-one was putting her in front of a judge and saying you have been treating your kids like shit and now they are all in trouble. No, they took the kids away one by one and told a twelve-year-old girl it was her fault her mum couldn't control her and sent her to a jail for kids. I mean, how fucked is that?

I vividly remember the day I arrived at Allambie. They made you take a shower when you got there and they gave you Wella Balsam shampoo and conditioner to wash your hair. Ever since then I've never been able to stand the smell of that stuff because it reminded me of that place. I sobbed my heart out that night because I just wanted to go home. As bad as home was it wasn't a fucking prison like Allambie. I remember sobbing all night the first night thinking, 'What have I done?' and, 'It must be all my fault,' but now I just think how wrong that all was. The truth was this: I was put in a prison and treated like a criminal for doing nothing other than having had a shit mum who didn't want me anymore.

That first night they brought in this little kid who was four years old and I'll never forget it. His mother didn't want him because her boyfriend didn't want him around. Sound familiar? And this poor little kid just lay on his bed and sobbed his heart out. It still breaks my heart to think about him lying there abandoned and crying. He was just like me but he was four years old. I was so upset about what had happened to me but seeing that boy I remember thinking I would try and comfort him and help him because it made me feel better too. This kid whimpered and cried his heart out but he cuddled into me and hung on like I was the only person left in the world.

It just makes me sick. The older I am and the more kids I have had myself, the more outraged and disgusted I am at my own mother's behaviour. My mum had eight kids so she obviously liked the idea of having kids, she just didn't like being a mother, or didn't know how to be a mother. I tell my kids these stories now, and I don't want to scare them but I also want them to know that life is not easy, you have to fight the fight every day. You have to go to school and make something of yourself. I didn't go to school and I know how much harder that makes things.

That first night in Allambie I was honestly afraid. I was like a little kid left in the middle of the ocean. Fuck I was scared. But I had to keep going, and I think that's where my defensive skills were learned. I remember I smoked cigarettes at eleven. Allambie rang Mum and Michelle made her give permission for me to smoke in there. I smoked my little lungs out. I only stopped later when I got pregnant with Danielle.

That first time I think I was in Allambie for about six months before I had to go back to court and they put me in a foster home. The first one I went to the couple were both drunks and they used to bash each other all night. I'd hear them yelling and screaming and fighting and I used to lie in my bed, terrified. I was lying there scared shitless that he was going to get drunk and get through fighting with her and come in to me and start touching me. He never did, but I didn't give him much of a chance because I took off pretty quickly. I just ran away, I couldn't deal with it. Back then Human Services didn't really give a fuck where they placed you — they've changed now, I think, but back then they didn't care — so I'd run away every time and they'd find me and send me back to Allambie and the whole stupid cycle would start again.

Sometimes I'd go back to Mum's for a weekend but then she'd just boot me out and I'd end up on the streets again anyway. At one stage I stayed with my sister Sue, but she kicked me out too because she had a boyfriend who didn't want me there. You'd reckon she'd have learned from Mum but she just did the same thing. She was getting paid by Human Services for me to be there as a foster kid but Susan would take the money and wouldn't let me sleep there so I'd stay in the bus stop opposite her house.

I met my best friend Lisa at this time and her parents used to let me stay with them. They were good friends to me then and we're still really close now. Her family were great to me, they always wanted people to give me a go. So I'd stay there but I'd also roam the streets and get in fights and all sorts of minor trouble. Each time I'd just get sent straight back into care.

I didn't go to school much after that. I got kicked out of a few high schools in between being put in and out of Allambie and being sent back home to Mum a few times. I never made new friends at school because I was never there long enough. I could never bond because I never had stability in my life and I think I was wary of people. I got kicked out of three different high schools in the Seaford–Frankston area because I would get in fights. I say now that it was like I was searching for home but couldn't find it.

One night I met up with my friend Kelly from down the road and we decided to piss off and run away together. My brother Laurie lived in Seaford at that stage so we went to his house and stole two towels off his clothesline just to be a pain in the arse and we hitchhiked to Perth for no apparent reason. We were twelve or thirteen at the time but we got there, all the way to Perth, and we never ate anything for three days. We finally got a lift on this dairy truck full of yoghurt and the driver gave us some. I rang David MacKenzie, my social worker, from Perth and told him I wanted to come back. We hadn't eaten for days. He organised for me to be extradited back to Melbourne.

My mum came to a meeting at Allambie after this and I remember when she left I thought to myself, 'Why don't you take me with you?' I was sobbing at the gate. Unbeknown to me she could have said to them, 'I want my daughter home,' and they would have let me go with her, but she didn't say anything of the sort. In the meeting with them she just said to leave me there. Come Christmas, my sister Sharon came and picked me up and took me out for the night and I had Christmas with them, but the next day they took me back. I hated it. I used to cry my guts out every day.

There was one section at Allambie where the girls thought they were rough and tough, and I used to just want to be by myself. They'd take me swimming in the pool instead of going to school because I could never sit still long enough to do school work and I would just disrupt the rest of the class so they stopped even bothering. One time we had a lock-down and they went through everyone's rooms looking for weapons and stuff. I'd stolen a butter knife from the kitchen for some stupid reason and they came in and ripped us out of bed and reckoned we were going to use the knife as a weapon. Some kid must have known I had the knife and told them. I think we thought we were tough and took the knife because it would make us look even tougher.

I got transferred to Winlaton after that. When I was in Allambie I thought it was like prison, but that was until I got to Winlaton, which is a youth prison — then I realised by comparison Allambie was a home. I was thirteen then and that was hard because there were some pretty tough older girls in there. There was a section of Winlaton called Goonyah or something, and that's where there were bars up on the windows and the girls were locked in all the time. In my section the doors were only locked at night.

I was there for about three months before I was allowed to leave. Back then you didn't have to prove you had somewhere to go, or have someone come and vouch for you, you just had to say, 'I am going home to Mum's,' and they would let you go. So I would tell them I was going to Mum's and when I got out I would just roam the streets. I would make my way down to Frankston and find my mates and sleep in the empty trains where they parked them just outside Frankston station overnight. We were just mates. I wasn't into boys or anything at all at the time. We used to all cuddle up and sleep because we had nowhere to go and the trains kept us dry and warm. In summer we'd sleep on the beach a bit. We also used to sit by the creek in Frankston and drink Cinzano until we were virtually sick. It was just an escape, I guess, something to do to break the boredom.

We used to go along the Nepean Highway picking magic mushrooms and take them back to this flat and we'd boil them up. We'd drink it and sit around hallucinating all day. We'd also take carsick tablets because they'd make you hallucinate too if you had enough of them. I was getting a bit of money at the time by buying blocks of hash and cutting them up and selling to my mates. A lot of kids in this situation end up on heroin but I never really did the heavy drugs like that. Most other girls who are living rough end up in prostitution too, but I never ever did any of that shit either. You can judge people however you want but from the life I was in I never ended up a junkie and I never ended up a prostitute.

By the time I was fourteen I was staying with different people here and there and being returned to Winlaton whenever I got caught. If you were arrested on an assault charge or something they'd take you to Winbirra, which was the youth remand centre. That was tough — you'd have to file in outside the kitchen every morning and wait until you had permission to go in and sit down in the dining room. After meals you'd have to clean the whole kitchen. It was all stainless steel and if you didn't scrub it until you could see your reflection in the benches and stuff, you'd get locked in your room for ages and lose privileges. You could only eat breakfast, lunch and dinner at set times and there was nothing to eat between meals. We'd all sit in this recreation room the whole day filling in time between meals. I can honestly say that was the hardest time of my life, being in Winbirra. I was bored and lonely.

When I was about sixteen I would be put into a hostel when they caught me on the street, instead of Winlaton or Winbirra. I'd only have to go to Winbirra if I had committed a crime. I was given weekend leave and I used to try and go home to my mum but I'd only be there a few hours before she'd kick me out. I wanted to make it work with her, but it never did. I am not saying she was entirely to blame because I know I must have been pretty hard to handle.

At the hostel we'd have to try and find a job during the day or do classes — anger management and shit like that. It never did me much good, but I think I've learned over the years how to deal with situations. Most of my 'background' charges (charges classed as young offender under eighteen) were for assaults — just punch-ups, no stabbings or shit like that — because I had a lot of aggression and I just didn't give a fuck what happened. I would walk up to people and pick a fight for no reason. I'd go up to people who were just doing their everyday thing and I'd pick a fight and punch them up. Boys, girls, adults, I didn't care. The police would know straight away who had done it and normally where I was, and they'd come and get me. I think a lot of the jacks kind of saw me as a troubled kid and used to try and help. Some of them would be nasty, of course, and I'd provoke them.

When I was sixteen I got a job at a childcare centre. Back then they used to smack kids in crèches and the owner of the crèche thumped kids and told me to smack them if they were naughty. I just couldn't do that. After all I'd been through, I wasn't going to hit somebody's child. So I had a big fight with them and quit. They begged me to come back because they said I was good with the kids.

The last day I actually went to school I was in Form 2 (Year 8). I was in and out of the homes and roaming the streets in between, but at one stage I got another job at a supermarket. You had to be fifteen and I was too young but I lied and I got the job. For some reason I went back to my mum to tell her, because I think I thought that if I had a job and was earning money she might look at me as though I was more mature, and if I was giving her money she might let me stay. It didn't work. She rang the supermarket and lagged me in about my age. So I lost that job and wound up back on the street.

One time I was due up in court on another assault charge but the day before I got another job at a crèche. Back then they just let you spend time with the kids to see how you got on with them and they'd give you the job. I was there for ten minutes and the lady said, 'You've got the job, start tomorrow.' And I thought, 'Fuck, I've got court tomorrow,' so I asked to start the day after and she said, 'No worries.' I went to court the next day thinking that if I had a job they would give me a break and try to let me see if I could sort things out, but they didn't care; they sent me back to Winlaton for three months. Needless to say I lost the job.

Out of Winlaton I'd just roam the streets and sleep in the trains and break into a few houses looking for food. I'd never break in to take stuff and sell it or anything, I was just hungry. I used to sit there and eat out of their fridges and leave. I wasn't the sort of kid to take property for the sake of it. I had one youth worker, David Mackenzie, who was fantastic. We bonded really well. He knew my family from my brother, so he knew what my mum was like and he really tried to help me.

One night I was hanging out with my mates — my gang — in the car park of the Frankston Bayside shopping centre and we were hooning around the streets jumping on cars. I jumped from the bonnet to the boot of this car but I skidded off and smacked my arm on the ground. I went to my brother's house and he took me to hospital where they x-rayed it. They found it was broken and put it in plaster. I remember thinking it'd give me an 'in' with my mum so I went home but she just belted me and booted me out again. I went to Mick's and stayed there.

When I was old enough not to have to stay at the hostel I rented a flat in Frankston on the Nepean Highway. I was only sixteen and a bit and I had no furniture — nothing at all — so I bought a clock radio and I used to sit on the floor and listen to the radio and watch the minutes and hours tick by. I didn't know it then but now I realise I was suffering bad depression. I used to just sit in the dark in this flat with all the curtains closed listening to the clock radio. Never having never owned anything before, even having a clock radio was a big deal. I went to the Salvos and they gave me a bed, a couch and a fridge. I thought I was Queen, it was like everything to me. I went and bought myself a sheet and a blanket and slept on this bed and thought I was in paradise. I had my own space where no-one could kick me out and I didn't have to answer to anyone.

I met my first son's dad — he wasn't a very nice person — and I soon fell pregnant. At seventeen, I was just a baby myself and I know we didn't plan to have a kid or anything, but I remember I was stoked that I was going to be a mum because I would be able to have something of my own to properly look after and love. And I suppose finally I would have someone that would love me back. But this arsehole bloke used to bash me up really badly. One night when I was six months pregnant he bashed me so badly I was rushed to hospital. He wouldn't ring the ambulance because he knew he might get into trouble with the jacks so he just left me.

When I fell pregnant I'd rung my mum to tell her and she was surprisingly good about it. She was really supportive and helpful early on, so when I got bashed I rang her to ask what to do. She told me to go to hospital, which I did, and when I got there they found I was actually in labour. I was freaking out because I knew I wasn't supposed to have the baby until 28 February and it wasn't even Christmas yet. I might only have been a kid and the dad was a prick but I wanted this baby and I was shit-scared.

They used these steroids to stop my contractions and they kept me in hospital on a drip because I wouldn't eat. I couldn't eat. I was so stressed and had been bashed so badly I just couldn't eat food and the baby was getting sick. I improved a bit and at Christmas I was allowed to go out, so I went to Mum's. That night my baby's dad and I rowed and he bashed me again and I ended up back in hospital. They were trying to give me steroids again to stop the labour but this time they couldn't stop it. It wasn't a bad labour but it lasted a long time. The baby was still two months prem so I was terrified of what it all meant.

On the 29th they came to me and said, 'Tomorrow you're going to have to have the baby. We don't know if the baby will survive. We've got the helicopter ready because we can't really cater for a baby so small here and it might have to be airlifted to the Mercy.' I was freaking out because I didn't know what the fuck was going on. I was only seventeen years old and nobody explained anything. I was so naive about boys and sex and stuff. I didn't even know what my period was because Mum had never told me. Here I was just seventeen and I was about to have a baby and they were telling me they didn't know if it would survive. I didn't know if it was going to be really painful or if I could die too, but at the time I didn't really care because I was just shitting myself that my baby might die.

Back then they gave you an enema before they induced you — which was disgusting — then on 30 December they put the stuff in the drip and I went into strong labour. My mum and my sister Josephine waited outside. The baby was born but he wasn't breathing and I was just freaking out. There was no doctor with me — just the nurses — and I was panicking. They were putting tubes down his throat, it was horrible, and all I could say was, 'Please, God, let this baby survive.' And they got him breathing and gave him over to me. I just couldn't believe it. For the first time in my life I had someone that was going to love me and need me. I can honestly say it was the happiest moment of my life.

After I had Tye it was like the doctors didn't give a shit. They didn't even stitch me up properly. Later on in life I had to have surgery to fix what they hadn't done. But at the time I didn't know and didn't give a shit because I had this precious little baby. I loved him so much but I was shitting myself because I didn't know what I was supposed to do. And being a tomboy all my life, I didn't want to breastfeed.

I picked the name Tye and I remember my brother Mick really hated it because he said it sounded like an Asian name. He was pretty racist. I just said, 'This baby's mine and I'm going to name him what I want.' And I wanted to put something of my dad in his name, so I named him Tye Lawrence because even though Dad's name was Emanuel on his birth certificate, he was only ever called Lawrence or Laurie. I remember I was in hospital on New Year's Eve and I paced the floor because Tye had wind. I loved that, to know he needed me and I could help comfort him.

Mum was actually really good at this time, trying to help and getting involved. She and Josephine would come every night and bring me food, and Sharon used to come and bring me fresh clothes each day and wash all the dirty ones. I was in hospital for two months because of the medical issues with the pregnancy but I was allowed to go out a few times for short periods so I went back to Mum's house and she even said to me, 'If you don't find anywhere to live you can bring the baby home here.' I was so excited.

I was still a ward of the state and David Mackenzie helped me get a place in Tootgarook near where my mum lived so she could help me with the baby. Every cent I got I wanted to buy new things for my baby, although David kept bringing me second-hand stuff. Josephine and Mum came and picked me up from hospital and took me home to Tootgarook but all the happy family stuff didn't last long. Three days later Mum turned on me and said she wanted everything back that she had bought for my baby and that she was ringing the welfare to take Tye off me.

I've no idea why she flipped. My sister Sharon was coming to the house and I think there was a bit of jealousy there. My mum would just snap, whether it was a little thing or a big thing, she'd make a big deal out of it. Later on when we had birthday parties for the kids we never invited her because she used to sit there and give people filthy looks and cause a drama, or backstab them. She was just nasty from bottom to top.

Mum threatened she was going to ring Human Services. At that time I didn't know that Human Services couldn't just come and take your baby off you, so I was stressed out. I was still a ward of the state so technically they had control of me until I was eighteen. I thought they'd come and take my son and put me back in Winlaton, so I packed up everything and moved to a place in Frankston and just hid from everyone. I rented a flat through a real estate agent and survived on the single parent's pension.

CHAPTER 4

CARLTON AND THE MORANS

My life changed in two important ways. Firstly, after living basically all of my life in Frankston or Seaford — when I wasn't in Winlaton or Allambie or somewhere — I moved into a Housing Commission flat in Neill Street, Carlton. It was there that I met the people who would change my life — and end some other people's lives. One of those people was Dean Stephens — he was fantastic for me. At first.

I used to go to my sister's friend's house to hang out and so did Dean, so that was where we met. I was there with Tye because I'd take him with me everywhere I went. He would have been about eight months old then but it didn't matter — if I went out he went out. Dean knew right from the start I had Tye and he was really cool about it. Dean was a tough guy and I loved that about him. I don't mind saying that I was attracted to guys who were pretty tough and Dean used to do boxing and probably scared a lot of people, but I was instantly attracted to him. He loved Tye to death and that also attracted me. The fact that he loved Tye showed he was a soft guy at heart and I really liked the fact that this tough guy was so gentle with my son. The way he was with Tye really meant a lot to me and we met his family and they idolised Tye as well. We were like a little family right from the start.

Dean hated the idea of us living in a Housing Commission flat. He wanted us out of there and in our own place as soon as possible, so after about six months of saving we were able to get a flat in Sunshine. Dean worked at the abattoir, like his dad, and he was always a hard worker but the money he earned didn't come as easy as it did for Sharon and me one night. Shaz and I used to go to Crown Casino once a week — this was way back when it was that bloody awful place at the old World Trade Centre — to spend time together and have something to eat and a few drinks and put some money on the roulette wheel. We'd take $150 with us and what we didn't eat or drink we put on numbers on the table. This one night we won $20,000 — remember this was like almost twenty years ago so twenty grand was a shitload of money. I couldn't believe it. Dean and I had already got to the top of the list for a Ministry of Housing loan so we used the money we won at the casino and bought a house in West Footscray.

It wasn't all happy families and picket fences though. You can't just walk away from a life of trouble on the streets and expect things to be perfect. It was certainly better than it had been, but I wasn't able to cut myself off from life in

Frankston so easily. Before I moved from Frankston I got in a bit of trouble with the police. Like I said, I survived by buying small blocks of hash and cutting it up and selling it in bits to mates for a small profit. There were a few other drugs I dealt too, but only small amounts and only to survive.

One night the jacks raided my house looking for amphetamines. They kicked in the door, which Tye was behind, and it smashed him in the face, splitting open his lip and nose. I was going crazy because they wouldn't let me hold him — his face was bleeding from everywhere and he was screaming because he was scared and in pain and wanted his mum, and I was screaming and going off my head because they wouldn't let me near him. I was really getting worked up because no-one touches my kids, jacks or no jacks, and I was going to hurt someone badly. They finally let me have him and I was able to calm him down and that calmed me down. They found some amphetamines in the house and I got charged over it and locked up.

My brother Mick came to my place after the police raid and took Tye for me. For some reason he took him around to Mum's place for her to look after him. Why he thought she'd be a good person to leave a kid with after the way she looked after us, I have no idea. Sharon went over to Mum's house the next night to check on him and there was Tye asleep on the couch with a sopping wet nappy because my mum hadn't even bothered to change him. So Shaz picked him up and started yelling at Mum and went crazy and took him with her. While I was in Fairlea Women's Prison, they used to let me have Tye every Sunday — Michelle and Shaz would drop him off in the morning and I'd have him all day. I eventually got bail, and it was after that I moved to the Commission flat in Carlton and met Dean.

I might have been out of jail on bail but a few of the girls inside still used to ring me up. It wasn't because we had become super great friends and they couldn't do without me — they wanted me to do something for them, obviously. They wanted me to collect a parcel and take it to the prison and throw it over the wall. Of course I knew it was drugs — if it was legit someone could have walked through the gates with it, not thrown it over the fence tied to a rock.

I was twenty at the time and I knew that even though I was out on bail, I would be going back to jail and if I didn't do what they wanted there would be dramas and punch-ups when I went back inside. Jail's a small place, so you can't hide. No-one tried to stand over me or beat me up before I got bail but it would be different if I went back in after not doing what they wanted. I remember before I got bail there was this bitch who used to think she ran the prison and she came into my room once trying to speak down to me and pushing me around, so I smashed her in the face with the stereo. I thought, 'Fuck this, I might be young and small but I'm going to stand up for myself and not take any shit.' After that nobody said a thing to me, but there would have been a lot of punch-ups and shit when I went back in if I didn't do what they said when I was out. That is how jail works.

In the end I figured it was easier to just do it, so I picked the rock up like I was told to do on the phone and took it to the prison where we were to throw it over the wall. Unfortunately security had been listening in to the phone call so they were already in the car park when we got there. I was waiting in the car when a friend I'll only refer to as Jim threw the rock over the wall. As soon as he threw it these prison guards appeared out of nowhere. Apparently the guards inside grabbed the rock as soon as it landed and the ones outside the wall came running at us.

I floored it and we drove off. Unfortunately one of the guards got in the way as I was trying to get out of the car park and I ran him over. Obviously they got my registration number — pretty dumb to use my own car, I know, but we didn't think it was a risky thing to throw a rock over a wall — and about a week later the police raided the flat to get me. I tried to hide behind the bed so they wouldn't see me, but Tye woke up and they heard him cry so I had to open the door.

Dean and I had broken up for a while but I rang him to come and get Tye when they locked me up in Northcote cells. I was on remand for seventeen days before I went to court and got bail on a $5,000 surety, which Dean had to raise by borrowing money from a friend of his dad's. The whole time I was in there Dean looked after Tye and dropped me off clothes every day, but the police only gave me the clean clothes every four or five days. I got bail but I knew when I went back to court I wasn't likely to be allowed to go home. I was right. I got eighteen months' jail for recklessly causing serious injury for running the bloke over in the carpark, but with good behaviour as well as bits and pieces I had already spent on remand I had only seven months to serve.

I cried for Tye every day in jail, I missed him so badly. I always doted on Tye and gave him everything I could. I would go without food and clothes and stuff just so I could put him in the best clothes because my mum never did that for us and I wasn't going to make the mistakes my mum made. People used to say, 'My God, look at the way you dress that child — look at everything he has.' The first Christmas, I remember going to Toyworld and lay-bying three dockets half a metre long. I bought him everything.

Dean came to visit me every day when I was in Fairlea and then when I was transferred to Tarrengower, a minimum-security women's prison. He was fantastic — he'd have Tye bathed, in his pyjamas and in bed every night at a set time. He was the best father you could ever imagine and he loved that kid to death. Even though I was inside and not with Tye, at least I knew I could trust Dean to look after my baby better than anyone.

By the time I got out of jail Tye had started at kinder and Dean had thought it was better not to tell the other parents that I was in jail, which was probably wise. But that meant they just thought I was some nasty bitch, so when I first started going there they used to give me these filthy looks and never included me in their little mothers' clubs. I looked about sixteen when Tye was in kinder even though I was twenty-one or two, but to the rest of the mums I was this horrible slutty teenage mum who'd abandoned her kid and husband. I didn't know if that was what they thought but as a woman you get all this guilt about your kids and being there for them and what other people think about how you treat your kids. So they'd look at me and I'd think, 'Oh fuck, they think I'm a terrible mother and a shocking wife,' and I couldn't tell them I'd been in jail — it might have made it worse — so I just went along with it.

When I was in jail Dean and I had agreed that we wanted to have a baby as soon as I got out. Within a month of getting out of jail I was pregnant with Danielle — maybe I inherited something from Mum, because she obviously never had trouble getting pregnant and here I was a month out of jail and already pregnant. Danielle was due on 18 April and was born ten days late on the 28th. She was another dream come true.

I was so excited when Danielle was born, but I have to say Danielle was the ugliest baby. I tell her, 'Dan, you were so ugly, but you turned into a beautiful girl.' She was the ugly duckling, but she is a beautiful swan now. When I first fell pregnant with Dan I stopped smoking. Once she was born we moved into the bungalow at the back of Dean's parents before getting a house at Footscray, which we renovated. Once that was done, we moved in and set up a beautiful little nursery for Dan. We didn't want to stop there though, we immediately had plans for more babies.

Dean was already kind of abusive to me but nothing like he became later on. On the one hand we were setting up a house and having babies and working hard to make a life, but on the other he used to lash out and hit me. Even back then right at the start he'd give me a backhander or a punch.

He wasn't dragging me around the house by the hair and punching my face. He wasn't coming home drunk, ripping me out of bed and beating me so badly that I thought he would kill me. That came later.

The thing was, right at the start when he hit me I didn't think it was strange or wrong. I was used to that kind of behaviour and in a stupid naive sort of way I expected it and thought it was part of the deal with men. I didn't know you could have a relationship with a man where you didn't get knocked about. In some ways I looked for it because I was sort of thinking that if Dean hit me it was almost a sign he cared for me. At the time we were trying to get pregnant again and it wasn't happening. Because it happened so easily the first time Dean blamed me that it didn't happen straight away again and it made him angry and more abusive. We didn't know at the time that I had endometriosis. The doctor thought that it was because I was breastfeeding Dan that I couldn't get pregnant. It is a common belief that breastfeeding acts like a form of contraception, so he figured that was what was happening and we never got it checked out at the time.

Eventually I did fall pregnant with Breanane and she was born on 10 January 1994. Sharon came with us to the hospital when I had Bree and she was in the labour ward with me. When the baby was born, we let Sharon name her and she decided on the name Breanane. She was a beautiful, healthy baby but I look back now and wonder how I looked after three kids who were all so little, because Danielle was just twenty months old when Bree was born. At the time I just didn't think anything of it.

Once the other kids came along I stopped any of the small-time drug dealing I was doing and really Dean was the main reason for that. As abusive as he was he was also my godsend in a lot of ways because he kept me out of trouble for a long time and kept me normal. But everything comes at a price. We never went without and he provided a roof over our heads and loved the kids. He was never abusive to the kids. He'd smack them, which I didn't believe in, but it was just regular parent disciplining and he wasn't being abusive or anything.

Dean thought Tye was spoilt so he would take things off him. And he was probably right, I did spoil Tye — he had a Ferrari bed, and a TV and a video in his bedroom and every toy you could ever imagine, because I wanted him to have all the toys around him that I never had around me, so if people want to blame me for that and say I spoilt him, well too bad. I'd rather he be spoilt for having things than to having nothing like I did. I just wanted him to have everything. But Dean said wanting to make up for what my mum didn't give me was one thing but spoiling the kid rotten was another, and he'd take things off him.

It was for the same reason, really, that I always had a dream to go to Disneyland and to take my kids there. To me it was like the ultimate kids' paradise and I wanted to give my kids paradise. I wanted to make sure I gave my kids the thing that every kid dreams of. I also wanted to see it myself because, I don't know, maybe I thought that if I went there it would be like giving my own childhood something it never had. So we went. Bree was just five or six months old and Dan was just two, so they don't remember it, but Tye was seven and he still talks about it. I remember walking up to the entrance of Disneyland and breaking down in tears. It was a dream come true.

Dean paid for our airfares, even though he didn't want to come himself and stayed home. Sharon came along and she paid her way. I kept thinking as we got on the plane to America and when we were walking around Disneyland that it was a far cry from sleeping in the trains at Frankston station. We were there for fourteen days, staying at the Sheraton in Anaheim. Dean gave us $5000 spending money but we actually came home with some of the money, so we didn't go crazy. At the time it was good to be away from Dean and his shit because at home things were getting worse.

In the end I left Dean because I just had enough of the violence after eight years. He would come home drunk, abuse me, scream and rant and carry on. I put up with it for a long time but it was getting out of control. One hot night when we were at home Dean slept on a mattress out near the front door. First thing in the morning the jacks raided our house looking for drugs. Dean had picked up some hash from Mark Moran who, it turned out, was working with the police. These so-called friends of Dean's, Mark and Jason Moran, used to meet the police each week to pay them money and give them information, and in return they were given a 'green light' to do what they pleased with drug dealing and shit. Anyway, Dean had picked up some hash from them and the Morans obviously told the police Dean had it because the Special Operations Group came bursting through our door barging over Dean lying on the floor in the doorway.

They searched the house and didn't find anything, then they went out to look in Dean's car and came back inside carrying a bag. They brought the bag in to me and said, 'Whose bag's this?' I said, 'It's Dean's mum's laundry bag', because I didn't know there was anything in there. Dean had obviously put the drugs in the bag and put that in the boot of his car without telling me. It contained a couple of kilos of hash, which is not a small amount.

Until then I didn't know Dean had anything to do with drugs or anything like that, so when the SOG came through the door that morning I didn't know what the fuck they were there for. It was only later we found out from someone else that Mark had told the police he gave Dean some speed to hold for him, but Mark had kept the speed and given Dean hash and lagged him in to the jacks, so when the jacks raided they were walking around yelling at us all the time, 'Where's the amphetamines?' I said, 'What the fuck are you talking about? I don't have drugs here.' I was going crazy.

Danielle was only about seven months old at the time and she was in the bed with me when the jacks came in and went to jump on the bed. They started giving me shit and one policewoman said, 'Give me the baby.' I said, 'Like fuck you're touching my baby,' and started going schizo. There was a copper there who had been a uniformed jack in Frankston when I used to get in trouble and he came in and said, 'Don't touch her baby.' He knew I would attack them if they did, especially after the incident with Tye when he got hit in the face during that earlier police raid. The thing was, at that stage I honestly didn't know why they were at our house or what they were on about. I just thought they were being arseholes raiding our place so I was abusive to them. Things calmed down after they said I could hold on to Danielle. They took Dean away and charged him over the drugs.

Before that day I didn't know Dean had anything to do with drugs at all. He was the one who stopped me doing any dealing when we got together, so I didn't think he would be into that sort of thing. And I honestly don't think he was that much, I think he was just helping out the Morans. The Morans were into things on a different level to everyone else, they were like these big tough gangsters at the time and we were just normal people trying to get by.

Dean got bail but he ended up having to serve six months' jail over the drugs. The very first day he got out of Dhurringile he went around to see the Morans and — can you believe this? — Jason and Mark asked him where their money was. The drugs the jacks had confiscated were theirs so they figured Dean owed them. When the jacks raided our house one copper said to me in passing, 'You know who gave us this information, don't you? Think of the last person you saw last night.' We'd seen Mark Moran the night before. So when the Morans asked Dean for money for the drugs I thought they were kidding. We were trying to save money for our wedding at the time but Dean had to

51

pay them the money — $15,000 — for the drugs he'd 'lost'. Dean only got arrested because of the Morans lagging him in and in return they got the green light to sell their drugs somewhere else. That was what the Morans were like. Silly Dean has never worked that out.

If you know anything about me already, it won't surprise you to know that I never liked the Morans. Even before I got involved with Carl and their feud started, I hated them. People talk about love at first sight, well this was the opposite of that — I fucking hated the pair of them from the first time I saw them. They acted like they were the centre of the universe and everyone else had to bow down to them and fall into line around them. And Dean was more than happy to fall into line, but I wasn't.

Dean always thought they were his good mates, even after they lagged him to the jacks and made him pay up as soon as he got out of jail for the drugs the jacks took. So I had to get along with them even though I never liked them. I hated the way they always thought they were better than us. Dean was supposed to be their mate but they talked down to him and treated him like shit and he kept coming back. He was like one of those stupid dogs on the cartoons that tags along after the big bulldog and keeps bouncing back when he gets a slap.

Dean had known them since he was a kid and they had all grown up together. Dean and Mark played footy together for Kensington and Jason used to go along and watch. Jason was banned from playing because he used to go on the field and king-hit blokes behind play, which is typical of the coward he was. I don't think he was much good anyway. I always thought Mark was a poofy sort of bloke because he always carried on in a sort of gay way. He was always very worried about how he looked and being really fit and showing off his body and that, like gay guys do. Mark always acted very superior, as though he was too good to be hanging out with the likes of us. He always stood back and never really said 'hi' or anything. He was always the type of bloke who expected you to go up and say hello to him. It's pathetic, but that's how Mark was.

To me the Morans were like big gangsters because Dean had told me that Jason always carried a gun. Even as a fourteen-year-old riding around on a BMX bike Jason would have a gun and carry wads of cash in his pockets. He was standing over people basically from a very young age. I knew they were drug dealers, because everyone talked about them as drug dealers, I just didn't know how big they were. Dean was just a worker, he worked at the abattoirs, and as far as I knew — at least before our house was raided and he got arrested — didn't get into all this shit. I'd never been exposed to that level of criminal activity before because the people I knew who got involved in crime were just homeless kids hanging out on the street. It was all just regular low-level, street crime shit, they weren't serious drug dealers on this big level paying off jacks and trading in big amounts of gear. Maybe that was one of the reasons the Morans thought they could talk down to us, because they considered me just street scum.

Part of that superior attitude seemed to rub off on their

wives and girlfriends, who used to hang out together and watch the footy. I never really got on with them because I wasn't a fancy chick and didn't spend all my money on clothes and hair and make-up. I used to spend whatever money I had on my kids, not on me, but they were really concerned with how they looked and what they were dressed in and making sure they had expensive gear on. It always had to be Versace or some big designer label, and I would be wearing daggy old trackies or something.

The dumb thing was that while they were carrying on talking down to me, Jason was coming around to our place with all the girlfriends he had behind his main girlfriend Trisha's back. He got married to Trisha but back then when he was going out with her he would still come around to our place with these different girls.

When I had Breanane I set up a beautiful nursery for her, and Antonella, Mark Moran's wife, came to have a stickybeak so she could copy the look of the nursery. Then they set up their nursery the same and showed it off like it was their idea.

Dean made me take Breanane to footy training one night so he could show her off to all the boys. It was a really hot day, but we went anyway, because Dean wanted us to, but when we got there Mark just completely ignored us and didn't talk to us. I don't know what we had done to upset him. To Dean, the Morans were his best friends from growing up, but to them he was just an associate. When Dean was in jail I was living off Centrelink benefits and Dean's parents were helping me out, but it wasn't enough and we were struggling to survive. I called Jason to see if he could give me some money so we could eat but he said he didn't do anything wrong and he had no money for us. That was the sort of bloke Jason Moran was. I never forgot it.

CHAPTER 5

BACK FROM THE EDGE

While Dean was in jail friends of ours had a christening for their baby and I went along late in the day. My sister Sharon's ex-husband, Ernie, was there and I was talking to him for a while and I gave him a kiss. Well, all the Moran women saw it and went running around talking about it like it was some big scandal. Word obviously got back to Dean about me kissing Ernie and how it was some full-on pash and we must have been rooting around behind his back. It was such shit. Yes, I kissed him, but it was a normal harmless kiss because he was my brother-in-law, for God's sake. There was nothing sexual about it, it was just a kiss. But that kiss cost me more pain than you would ever imagine.

I never fitted in with these Moran women. They were all so bitchy and it wasn't just the clothes and the make-up and that. I never fitted in because I'm outspoken — I say what I think and don't arse-lick and talk bullshit just because I think it's what someone wants to hear. I always thought that was what they were like. So this story of the kiss wasn't true, but it didn't matter, they all just liked to create dramas.

I don't think Dean really believed it either but it played on his mind, and that was the problem. When he was sober and thought about it he knew it was bullshit but then he'd go out and get drunk and come home and he would start on me. At that time he didn't need much of an excuse to start on me. A kiss was enough. I think because it was the Morans who told him about it, he felt he had to look like some big man in front of them. All I know is I would be asleep in bed at night then all of a sudden I would be dragged out of bed by my hair and hauled halfway across the floor with Dean screaming and abusing me and kicking the shit out of me. He'd be accusing me of rooting around behind his back and all sorts of crazy shit. He must have bashed me up fifty times for that kiss. I still can't believe how much shit I got in, how many bruises I copped and how much blood I spilt over one innocent kiss with my sister's ex-husband. The dumb thing was, I told Sharon about it and she was like 'as if …' If anyone was going to be upset or offended by it it would have been her, but she knew full well it would have been innocent because she knew me. But that didn't stop Dean.

The beatings were getting worse but Dean almost had me brainwashed by then. I felt trapped. As he was bashing me he kept saying, 'Who'd want you with three kids? Where are you going to go?' One time we went to McDonald's for a kids' party and he was kicking me under the table for some reason. I don't know why, I must have got him the wrong burger — maybe he wanted a Happy Meal, the big fucking child. Anyway Shaz saw him kicking me and said, 'What the fuck are you doing?' She couldn't believe what she was seeing so she followed us back to our place after the party because she was scared Dean would hit me. Dean and Shaz had a big fight and she ended up storming off and Dean just bashed my head in that night, because Sharon had stuck up for me.

Another time we were stopped at the traffic lights just before the North Melbourne Football Club in Arden Street and Dean was laying into me in the car. There was a police vehicle two cars back and the people in the car next to us could see what was happening so they quickly reversed and got the police, who came running up and ripped Dean out of the car. He was arguing with them and trying to run away. The police came and checked on me and told me to just leave and they would deal with it. At the time I was still living with Dean so I had to go back home. The jacks then stupidly gave Dean a warning and didn't charge him, so he came straight home and I copped another beating. The jacks are such geniuses!

Eventually when Breanane was four and Dan was five I got legal advice about what I could do to try and stop the violence and I decided to kick him out. Amazingly, he left. But that didn't stop the trouble because he didn't stay away for long. Soon enough he began stalking me. I rang the police about him a few times and they'd hang around and tell him to leave, but then I wouldn't follow through on it. I never pressed charges. I know now I should have but I never did. That is the problem with being attracted to tough guys — if it doesn't work out and they turn nasty like Dean did, then all you are left with is a tough guy who scares the shit out of you.

Dean used to ring up and threaten me and then I would sit up all night looking out the window terrified, too scared to go to bed in case he snuck in and attacked me. At the time I genuinely thought he might just come and kill me or, worse, hurt the kids. Like I said, Dean had never hurt the kids before and I had no real reason to think he might start now, but when someone is going off like Dean was you just don't know what they are capable of.

One night I was so exhausted from sitting up and watching out the window that I fell asleep on the floor in front of the heater in the lounge room. When I woke up Dean was dragging me around the lounge room by the hair and smashing me in the face and head with a gun. He dragged me out of the house and across the front yard by the hair and shoved me in the car. I remember seeing the front door was wide open and the kids were still inside, hopefully asleep, but Dean didn't give them a second thought — he just put me in the car and drove off. I was scared for my life but I was more scared that we were driving away leaving my babies in the house with the front door wide open. I remember screaming in the middle of it all, 'Just take me home, the kids are still in there, *please*.'

But Dean wasn't in a mood to listen because it was like he had snapped and this was going to be it, so the kids were the least of his worries. He drove me to a paddock at the back of Braybrook — there's a new housing estate there now but at the time it was vacant land — and there was this sort of cliff in a paddock. Dean drove right up to the edge of the cliff and I thought he was going to drive over. He stopped and he was screaming, 'I'm going to kill you, you dog.' He put the gun to my head and I thought he was going to pull the trigger but at the time I didn't care. I honestly thought, 'Please, just pull the trigger and stop the pain.' I was so badly beaten.

He put the gun to my head and held it there, looking at me with these crazy eyes. You could see it going through his head whether to pull the trigger or not, it was written all over his face. I don't know why he didn't, but he didn't. He turned the car around and drove off, but all the way he just kept hitting me in the head and face with the gun and slamming my head into the dashboard and the window of the car. He hit me the whole way from the back of Braybrook to Footscray. I could feel my head was blown up like the elephant man. I couldn't see out of my eyes anymore because they had puffed up like a boxer after a title fight and my nose was so badly damaged I could barely breathe. We arrived at the house and he dragged me out of the car by the hair and back inside and started kicking me around the lounge room again.

What happened next is a bit of a blur but for some reason my sister rang. I don't know if one of the kids rang her or something, but she rang and the phone got answered and she could hear me screaming in the background before the phone got hung up. She knew immediately it was Dean so she rang him straight back on his mobile and said, 'Leave her the fuck alone. I am calling the police.' Dean got up and just ran out.

Sharon walked in and saw me and had to turn around and run out of the house to vomit. The Footscray police couldn't believe the injuries. They took me to hospital and I was kept there for two weeks. The jacks took photos of my injuries and they were just shocking. My face was fucked — my jaw was broken, my nose smashed all over the place, my cheeks were fractured, my skull was fractured, there was swelling and bruising and it looked awful. Sharon had to feed me through a straw for six weeks. She eventually brought my kids in to see me in hospital because they were getting so upset not knowing what had happened to me, but they were so hysterical after they came in and saw me that it took her hours to calm them down. She couldn't bring them back in again.

That was the last straw with Dean. He'd beaten me before, but never this badly. In my mind the relationship was over. The beatings had been getting steadily worse and I remember I used to stand in the shower and cry to myself saying, 'God, please just let him die. Please just let it all stop.' He always used to threaten me, saying that if I ever left him he would get me and I wouldn't even see it coming. He'd say shit like he'd get me while I'd be hanging the clothes on the line out the back. And he was right. The night he took me in the car and beat me I didn't see it coming — I was asleep. But that was it, after that I knew something had changed. I wasn't afraid of his words anymore and by then I didn't care if he did kill me — at least I would be free of him. The only reason I wanted to survive was for the kids. And maybe knowing he had taken me to the cliff and didn't pull the trigger, I sort of figured he would never actually do it anyway.

Dean was charged over the assault — I think with causing grievous bodily harm — but by the time it got to court Shaz had convinced me to drop it. She said if I pressed it he would go to jail but when he came out he would come back and get me again, or he would get the Morans to get me as payback, and that I was better just getting away from him. Stupidly I felt bad pressing charges anyway because he was the father of two of my kids and I didn't think it would look good for them to see their mum in court with their dad trying to have him put in jail. So when it got to court I decided not to give evidence against him and the charges were dropped.

Dean got the message that the price for dropping the charges was that I never wanted anything more to do with him and he had to leave me alone. Still, now I regret that I was weak at the time and even though I got myself out of an abusive and violent relationship, I wish he had been made to pay for what he did to me. I wish now I had gone to court and pressed charges and sent him to jail because I know from relationships he has had since that he has done it again and he hasn't got the message at all. By not going to court he felt he had got away with it with me and he would get away with it every time, and he still didn't realise it is fucking wrong to beat your wife.

Sharon used to come and look after me every day but she didn't tell my brothers what had happened, because she knew they'd have killed Dean. Later on when Carl and I were together I told him what Dean had done to me and he wanted to kill him — and when Carl says something like that he means it more than most people do. I said to leave him alone because in the end he was Danielle's and Breanane's father. Carl hated his guts. One night Carl and I were sitting at Crown Casino and Dean snuck up and king-hit Carl from behind. Another time at the boxing he got Carl again when he couldn't see him.

At the time even Dean knew the beating he gave me was the final straw. I suppose he expected it to be the final straw when he did it. He knew we'd never be together again the night he drove me to the cliff and put the gun to my head, the reason being that he expected me to be dead, but he didn't go through with it. Whether it was because he couldn't do it or he came to his senses, he also knew when he woke up the next day that things could never be the same again. He said to me, 'You move out of the house, because you're going through a hard time, and I'll have the kids here until you get settled.' Part of me thought it was a good idea so I found a place but then I didn't end up taking it and stayed in the house. Finally Dean came and kicked me and the kids out on the street with no clothes, nothing.

Tye has seen psychiatrists since Dean and I broke up and has told them he used to wake up every morning wondering if I was going to be alive. He said his biggest fear was waking up one morning and finding me dead on the bathroom floor because his dad had bashed my head on something. He still says it now: 'Mum, I was scared he was going to kill you. Every night I would go to sleep and I would get up the next day and your face would be all swollen. I used to wake up each day wondering if you were still alive or if he had killed you.'

When Dean kicked us out I had nothing at all and it was Carl Williams who helped me find a place to live in North Melbourne. Carl and I were friends at the time and nothing more. There was nothing sexual between us despite what Dean reckoned and was telling people. I've got no reason to bullshit about it now; we were just friends. We found a place but that roof over our heads was all we had. At the time we slept on the floor until I got enough money to buy bunks. I used to have to buy bags of ice and fill up the sink just to keep the milk cold for the kids' bottles and stuff like that, because we didn't have a fridge.

One night I went back to Dean's place when I knew he wasn't home so that I could get some things of ours. I looked in his cupboard and there was a bullet-proof vest and $6,000 in cash. I thought, 'Fuck you, mate,' and I took the vest and the cash. The next thing I get a phone call from Dean screaming at me: 'You fuckin' dog, that vest is Jason Moran's, he's going to knock you — give me back my money, you fucking bitch blah blah blah …' A friend of theirs from Kensington, this guy they all hung around with, rang me and said, 'Look, Roberta, he won't do anything to you. I'll just come and pick up the money and the vest and there won't be any trouble.' I said, 'Fuck you, you're not getting jackshit off me.' Dean had already stolen my Louis Vuitton handbag and a Rolex watch he had bought me from a wholesale jeweller friend in Hong Kong.

The problem for Dean was yet again being seen to be shamed in front of the Morans. If it was just the cash I might almost have got away with it, but taking the vest meant the Morans knew about it and Dean could not be embarrassed by his wife, or ex-wife, so he had to get it back. When Dean arrived at my place one night to get the vest and the cash he booted in the front door. I rang the police because I was scared he might actually kill me, and the kids were screaming and going hysterical. In the end I just thought it was better to get him out of the house and not risk him doing something to the kids, so I said, 'Here take your bullet-proof vest and your money and fuck off.'

But I wasn't finished with Dean. I figured that I couldn't let him push me around — I had to let him know I was even crazier than him and prepared to go further than him, so I went to his house this one night and crept inside while he was asleep. I went into his bedroom and he was snoring away. There was a gun on the bedside table so I thought, 'Fuck you, you've had a gun at my head, now it's time for you to find out what that's like. I'm going to scare the shit out of you.'

I picked up the gun and pointed it at him and started singing this song, like a crazy person would. I can't remember what song it was now but it was something really calm and spooky. I wanted to play mind games with him, but fear overtook me. I sang a bit of the song and said quietly to him, 'I could fucking kill you right now.' And then I turned and got out of the place. It had been worth it just to see the fear in his eyes. He just lay there and didn't do anything — he was too shocked. I think I scared the shit out of him and convinced him not to fuck with me because he became distant from me after that — he even stopped seeing his kids for some years.

I had a bit of a taste of giving it back to him and I liked it, so when he got with his new girl I decided to fuck with him some more. I went to his house and stole his phone bill from the mailbox and saw this number that he was ringing all the time. I then got a friend of Sharon's who worked at Telstra at the time to tell me the address from the phone number.

I went to the address I'd been given to scare his new girlfriend and I started calling out to her to come outside but Dean came flying out the front door and got hold of me and bashed me up in the street. This fucking thing was watching from a window, yelling at him to hit me again. I was thinking, 'You fucking idiot, can't you see now why I'm here doing this — because this is the sort of bloke he is, he just beats up on women. Surely you can see that Dean is going to do this to you one day too, if he hasn't already.'

My hand got pretty badly cut that night and I lost a bit of blood. I had to go in and get it stitched up and afterwards I went around to meet Carl at his apartment in North Fitzroy. We were sitting on the couch talking and we started mucking around like teenage kids, kissing. That was it, Carl and I were together. And that was, without doubt, the biggest change in my life.

CHAPTER 6

CARLOS

I was sitting on the couch reading the newspaper at Sharon's flat in Navigator Street, Maribyrnong, when this big fat bloke swaggered in. Sharon said to me, 'This is Carl,' and I just looked up at him and said, 'How you goin'?' He looked back at me with that cheeky grin on his face and just smiled and nodded. It was the first time I had laid eyes on Carl Williams. It was about 1994 and Bree was just a few months old, so I was still with Dean. I remember thinking he was nice, but he was too quiet for my liking. I'm loud and out there and he was real quiet. I remember looking at him that day and he was just a big fatty boombah, but he was good looking and he was always a really cool dresser. He used to wear Ralph Lauren tops and shorts — he always bought Ralph Lauren.

I was looking after the kids and was always around at Shaz's place, or she was at my place, and Carl used to call in all the time so we pretty quickly got to know one another.

Carl and Sharon were good friends and for a long time I wanted her to get with Carl because I liked him so much and I thought they'd be well suited. I wanted him as a brother-in-law, not a husband. They had a bit of a thing together and went out for a little while, but they broke up. I remember I was really disappointed when they did because I thought they would be good together.

Carl was always really kind. When I got to know him I used to ring him because he was never working and I had the kids and never had any money and he would be happy to hang out. We would go to the shops and he'd just give me $500 here and there to go shopping. It was behind Dean's back, because Dean was tight with money — we never went without but we didn't overindulge either. But that was the *only* thing Carl and I did behind Dean's back.

Dean and Carl were always friends but they were never really close. The way Dean talks about it now, though, you would think him and Carl were bosom buddies. He tells people, 'My best friend got with my wife.' He knows that's bullshit, but it was the same bullshit story they used in *Underbelly* where they made out I got together with Carl when I was still with Dean and rang Dean out of the blue and told him I was with Carl because he was better in bed. I suppose they had to make the show more interesting by making stuff up.

Dean was not happy about us being together, I am not denying that, but he and I were well and truly finished before Carl and I got together. It didn't stop him being shitty though. Once when I was driving through Kensington,

Dean came up and ripped my car door open and started attacking me. I wasn't even with Carl then, but Dean reckoned I was and he was attacking me for it.

At the time Carl and I were good friends and I knew there was something there between us but I didn't know if I wanted to be with him or not. We had kissed by that stage but we hadn't slept together and I went away to Queensland for a couple of days to clear my head and decide what I wanted to do — did I want to be with Carl or what? Dean actually looked after the kids while I went. The next thing I know there's a knock on my hotel room door and I open it up and Carl's standing there. He had this little backpack on and he looked really cute. We spent two days together at the Marriott in Surfers and it was then that we decided we wanted to be together.

On *Underbelly* Carl called me Bobby. That was bullshit too, he never once called me Bobby. He always called me Bert, like nearly everyone did. Only Laurie and Mick called me Billy, but no-one called me Bobby. He'd call me Bert and I would call him Carlos, like Carlos the Jackal. It was just a joke between us because they chased Carlos the Jackal for years without catching him. Well, they did in the end, I suppose, and they also got Carl. I called him Carlos, but later on Carl used to call himself the Premier, because he said he ran the state. Just being an idiot and mucking around he would say, 'This is my state, I will run it how I want. I am the fucking Premier.'

Underbelly also tried to make Carl and me out to be something we were not. They showed me as the pushy one standing behind him and making all the decisions, which was complete crap. Anyone who knows Carl would know he wasn't like that. He was his own person, Carlos, and you could never make him do anything he didn't really want to do. I basically tried to keep out of the business side of things, the drug dealing and that.

The show also had Carl always eating chicken and chips and said how it was his favourite food and he never ate anything else. Yeah, Carl and I did love Kentucky Fried Chicken but not to the degree claimed in that ridiculous show. It wasn't even Carl's favourite food. His favourite was always Chinese. You only had to look at him to know he was a big eater — he loved eating out and he loved drinking. When he drank it was either ouzo or Johnnie Walker Blue straight. Ouzo was his main drink, though. It was nothing for him to get up at seven in the morning and take a swig of ouzo.

Carl didn't live life like normal people who would get up and do chores or help with kids and go off to work. He felt like life was a long party and it was there to enjoy. He didn't give a fuck about what other people did or thought. For him a normal day was to get up and drink and take drugs and cruise the streets. He'd go out and organise his drug deals and eat and drink and hang out with his scummy mates. He should not have been married, because he didn't want the married life. He wanted to be single and living the criminal life. That was him — he was a partying person.

Carl never ever stayed at home. Every morning he'd wake up, have a shower, have his breakfast and be off. Even if he had nothing to do he would just get out and leave the house. His dad or someone would pick him up and off they'd go. One time I was as sick as a dog, lying on the couch and barely able to lift my head to get up. I had our daughter Dhakota at home with me and she was still really little at the time but I just couldn't get up to deal with her. It was footy grand final week and Carl was out partying. I kept ringing him to come home and help me look after Dhakota and he kept saying, 'Yeah, I'll be home soon.' Finally he did walk through the door. It was three days later.

Brisbane was in the grand final that year and Carl was partying hard. He loved the Brisbane Lions because he had always been a Fitzroy fan, and unlike a lot of other people, he kept following them when they went to Brisbane. I think partly that was because he was mates with some of the players and he just kept following them for that. He would go to the footy a bit. Not every week, but he would go. One grand final eve some of the Brisbane Lions were in a hotel just off St Kilda Road and Carl organised for me to take Dhakota down to get some photos with the boys.

When Carl was flying high and shouting drinks and handing out the cocaine and ecstasy in the nightclubs, they were in his arse. Whenever we would go to a club or somewhere — which was very rare for me — they would be there hanging out of Carl's arse. Some footballers wanted to be mates with Carl, hanging out with him to get his drugs and stuff.

I don't know how much money he used to punt, but Carl loved the horses too. People tell me he was a big punter and Carl would say he punted a fair bit but I don't know how much he would bet. He would often go to the track or hang out in the TAB all day. One time when I was pregnant with Dhakota I had to sit in the car while he quickly ran into the TAB. When he got back into the car we began to listen to the race on the radio and he realised that he had bet on the wrong horse. He had mistakenly written down the wrong number — I think he put down a one instead of an 11 or something — and he was going off his head about it while the race was on and was still carrying on afterwards, and he blamed me for making him rush. Then he realised the horse he had tipped by mistake had actually come in and he won $11,500. He gave me the winnings and told me to spend it on the baby because he knew his bet had lost and he only won because of me. Carl hated leaving me alone in the car while I was pregnant, so rushing to get out of the TAB and making a mistake on the bet, worked out for me.

The track, the TAB and hanging out with his scumbag mates, that was what Carl did with his time. He wasn't the type to mow a lawn or wash a car or do anything at all around the house. He was fat, but never cooked a meal, let alone washed a dish. He would do nothing other than make himself look good for going out and worry about the clothes he was going to wear. He never hung out at home to watch TV and we only ever went to the movies together once. It was in Frankston and my sister came along too. I'm too hypo to sit still in movies so I just talked and talked through the film and Carl and Shaz actually climbed over the seats to get away from me. That was the last film we went to see together.

For all the murders Carl and our mate Andrew Veniamin were connected to or committed, there were never really guns around my house. I mean, they were there at times, and of course Carl had a gun, but he never used to have it at home much. I knew he was drug dealing and involved in some of the things that were going on but it didn't happen under my roof in my house. It didn't happen in front of me so in some sense it was like it wasn't reality. I knew it was happening but it was not right in my face so it was not something I'd think about.

Life at that time spiralled out of control really quickly and it was like it wasn't real. We suddenly had heaps of money and it was like it was play money — we'd just throw it around like it wasn't real. Like I said, Carl liked to eat so whenever we had Chinese, we would get takeaway from the Flower Drum, which was the most expensive and most famous Chinese restaurant in Australia. Whenever we went out to eat to celebrate a birthday or anything, we went to the Flower Drum or Shark Fin House. I mean, we tried all of the best restaurants in Melbourne — all the best ones down at Crown and everywhere — but we always liked Chinese the best and liked the Flower Drum.

The people we went out with, I have realised since, were all doing business together. They were all in the drug trade. If it was one of their birthdays or one of their kids' birthdays we would all go out and eat together, and it was always lobster and the most expensive stuff. If they drank wine it was always the most expensive wine or the best malt scotch.

It was like that with everything: if you wanted takeaway Chinese you got the Flower Drum, if you saw a car you wanted you went and bought it. That happened once when I saw this beautiful Holden Statesman in the street and I said to Carl how much I liked it and that I would love one. So one day I'm at home and I open the door and there's Carl and Andrew and Snalfy (a friend of ours who I can't identify for legal reasons and will refer to only as Snalfy) all standing there giggling and excited, and there was this brand-new beautiful Statesman out the front. Then, like a complete bitch, I looked at Carl and said, 'What the fuck is that? I don't want that heap of shit.' And I turned around and walked inside like a bitch and that was the end of that. They were horrified. I was acting like that bitch Kim in *Kath and Kim*. It was a case of whatever I could have I didn't want once I had it. He gave the car to his dad who, needless to say, appreciated it a bit more than I did.

In 2000 we all went up to the Sydney Olympics when I was a few months' pregnant with Dhakota, Carl's only child, and we had a huge time. The kids all came, and my brother Robert and his girlfriend Sally were there and Carl hired this beautiful big boat for us all to go out on Sydney Harbour to watch the fireworks for the closing ceremony. The problem was we couldn't get a taxi to get down to the water to catch the boat. In the end you wouldn't believe it — the police gave us a lift. They'd have been sick if they knew who they'd given a lift to. And that wasn't the end of it. When we finished the boat trip and wanted to go back to the hotel we couldn't get a taxi again and Carl ended up stopping a bus to try and get us a lift. It turned out it was a police bus and they gave us a lift. That was the sort of police force we needed in Victoria — there to serve.

We went to all of the events. I don't know where Carl got the tickets but we were able to get in to see Cathy Freeman run and we loved the pole vaulting. We just had the best time. One night when we were watching in the stands we saw this woman wearing an enormous diamond ring on her finger. It must have been five carats at least and it was absolutely beautiful. Carl saw it and immediately wanted it for me. He went up to the lady and said he wanted to buy it from her but, of course she said it wasn't for sale. He said, 'Name your price, any price. I want it.' She just looked at him like he was crazy and said no. She wouldn't budge. Obviously if she could afford a ring like that she wasn't hard up for money, so she wasn't parting with it, but Carl didn't like it — he wasn't used to people saying no to him and not being able to buy whatever he wanted

Despite that Carl was actually a bit of a tight-arse. Well at least with me he was. He knew that whatever he gave me I would spend so he used to hold back on giving me money and never tell me what he was earning. He used to tell other people, 'Whatever you do don't give Roberta money because she just blows it.' And he was right. I didn't appreciate money at that time because it came so easy. Now things are different. Now I'm mortified at the way we used to splash money around because these days I have to work hard for what I get. Back then it was like a whirlwind. And Carl just wanted to make my dreams come true.

I had dreamt of going overseas, so I went. I took Sharon and the kids and we went to Paris and Carl paid. We went to Paris Disneyland for Tye's eleventh birthday and when we arrived we got lost and couldn't find our hotel. Someone directed us to this other hotel and it was a scummy hole, like one of those cheap Formula One motels you see, only it was scummier and even dearer. It cost me $450 a night for us and it was the shittest room I had ever stayed in, but we had no choice — we were in Paris with the kids without accommodation and we didn't know where the fuck we were or where our proper hotel was, so we had to take what we could.

The next day we went wandering around and we found out you could buy firecrackers and penny bangers, so Tye got some and he was walking along the street throwing them around, scaring the shit out of me and everyone else. When we got back to our hotel room he started throwing them out of the window. I said to him, 'Tye, the fucking jacks will come.' Then all of a sudden the jacks did come and I told him, 'You fucking idiot — I'm going to end up in jail in another country because of you.' We just played dumb, but Tye stopped throwing the firecrackers.

The money quickly ran out on that trip. I think Carl gave us twenty grand or something, which was a fair bit, but we went through it like water. I just bought the kids anything they wanted and we wasted it on clothes and restaurants and hotels and just anything. I rang him and said all of our money had gone and I needed some more money on my credit card. He put $5,000 a day in for the first few days just to be smart, because he knew I'd check how much had been transferred and that five grand wouldn't go anywhere. When we came back we had so much stuff that Sharon and I paid excess baggage from London, and it cost as much as all of our airfares.

I tortured Tye for the way he treated me in Paris with the firecrackers by getting to London and going and staying with a friend of ours who lived in this shithole called Hull. It was miles out of London and was an absolute dive and the kids hated it. But we stayed with this friend of ours who had been deported from Australia to England for drug dealing. Every morning as soon as I saw the Macca's sign come on I would wake the kids up and make them walk with me to get breakfast. The kids couldn't deal with it — they hated it.

At the time we flew business class wherever we went. For ages my kids never even knew economy class existed because they travelled business class everywhere as well. One time we went to Queensland and the only tickets I could buy were in economy so naturally I bought them. When we hopped on the plane the kids started looking around for their seats in business class and of course there were no seats for them. And they looked at the flight attendants like there had been a big mistake but the hostess looked at them and said, 'No, you guys are down here,' and she took them through to economy. Well, you should have seen their faces. At first they thought it was a joke and they didn't believe it, then they cracked the shits like spoilt little brats and kicked and screamed all the way. They were mortified. I think that in the past when they saw people walk through the curtains to the back of the plane they just thought all the seats were the same.

Shaz and I went to Hong Kong on a shopping trip later. We decided to go overseas to buy all the right stuff for the baby. We ended up with so much stuff I had five full suitcases that they wouldn't take on the plane. I had to send them home separately and they got lost on the way. The suitcases were full of Gucci perfume, Ralph Lauren baby clothes for Dhakota and all this other expensive stuff, because we went a bit crazy over there. But we lost the lot and it wasn't insured or anything.

At this time the real crazy shit of people dying wasn't happening and Carl was just making shitloads of money. We were having a baby, making a fortune — life was good. I didn't know how much Carl was making then but it was a lot — hundreds of thousands a week out of speed — but he never told me how much because he knew the more I had the more I would want and the more I would spend. I had never had money and I got greedy, so no matter how much I had or what it was I got, I always wanted more or a different type of thing. Everyone who knows me knows I spend money like crazy.

Back then Carl and I used to go to Bali all the time, just at the drop of a hat. We'd decide to get away to relax in the sun and we'd just book tickets for the next day and hop on a plane and fly business class. We'd stay at the best hotels there and have a great time. Once we shouted a trip for his best mate Andy Krakouer, who was the brother of the two blokes who played for North Melbourne, and one of Andy's nephews, but not the one who also played football for Richmond and has been to jail in Perth.

Carl and I had a punch-up in the street in Bali on one trip. It was funny as. I wanted to get these suitcases for my daughters and I had traipsed Carl all around Bali in the heat looking for them. He'd had enough and said, 'Fuck this, let's go back to the hotel and swim. We'll find the suitcases another day.' But I wanted to find them straight away and he got shittier and shittier and began getting nasty, so I whacked him. Then he whacked me back and we started boxing in the street. I ended up running away from him and tried to run into a shop but they closed their doors on me and wouldn't let me in. They didn't want this crazy woman in their shop.

I turned around to look for Carl and we both started laughing. I said to Carl, 'Do you know how funny it was seeing you running up the street, you big fat thing?' It was hot and sweaty and Carl had gone pink in the face and his guts were hanging out, so I was pissing myself. And Carl said, 'Do you know how funny it was seeing you run away screaming and everyone closing their doors on you?' We just started pissing ourselves in the street and all the Balinese were looking at us like we were crazy. Life was like that with Carl. It was a rollercoaster and he made you laugh and cry, but it was never dull.

CHAPTER 7

PUT ONE IN HIS HEAD

Everything changed the day the Morans shot Carl in a little park in a suburban street in Gladstone Park. It was the start of the real feud with the Morans and was the moment that led to a lot of other people being killed. It is true that a lot of the killings and madness that happened in the years afterwards can basically be traced back to that day — the day Jason made the biggest mistake of his life when he shot Carl and didn't kill him.

Carl learned a big lesson that day. He learned what dogs the Morans really were but he also learned never to leave a job half done. Luckily for us the Morans were stupid because they let Carl live, and he knew he would never make the same mistake they did. *Underbelly* made Carl out to be the dumb one and the Morans the cunning ones, but think of this — they are dead and he is alive. Who is the dumb one?

Who knows why they shot him? I've asked Carl about it and he has his own thoughts and I've heard lots of other reasons why. There was some talk about, and Carl believed it, that Dean had paid the Morans to get him because Carl and I were together. But when Carl explained the story it became clearer that it was more about money the Morans owed Carl than it was revenge for Dean.

According to *Underbelly* Carl owed the Morans money when it was actually the other way around. They said Carl was undercutting the Morans on pills he was selling, and they got that half right. Carl *was* selling pills cheaper than the Morans but that was because they were selling pills made up of all speed and people wouldn't have paid $20 for pills from Carl, which had only 0.3 grams of speed. But that wasn't what the shooting was about. Carl didn't undercut them or owe them money, they owed him money.

The TV show said Carl was using the Morans' pill press when he shouldn't have been and that Carl gave the Morans pills that didn't have enough binder in them. They said those pills crumbled and were shit, so the Morans reckoned Carl owed them $400,000. That is all bullshit.

I have spoken to Carl in detail about all of this. He is in jail and isn't getting out so I have no reason to doubt what he has told me. And, well frankly, the Morans aren't around to argue about it anyway.

Not many people get shot and live to tell the story, but Carl did. It all happened on 13 October 1999, Carl's 29th birthday. It was, no doubt, a birthday he'll never forget.

Just before this day when all the drama happened, Carl got a call from Shane Moran, who was the brother of an ex-girlfriend, Priscilla. It is all a bit involved and confusing because everyone seems to have the same surname, but Priscilla was the daughter of a well-known criminal in Australia called Kiwi Joe Moran. Kiwi Joe was no relation to Jason, Mark, Lewis and Judy and the notorious Moran family. At the time Carl got the call from Shane his dad, Kiwi Joe, was in prison and Shane was living in Mark Moran's house. Shane told Carl that Mark Moran wanted him to call him. This might sound a bit suss now, given everything that happened afterwards, but at the time there was nothing unusual about Carl being asked to call Mark Moran. I mean, you might think if it was not suss why wouldn't Mark Moran just call Carl himself, which is a fair point, but even though it wasn't completely suss, Mark still obviously knew there was a bit of an issue there with Carl and therefore got Shane to be the go-between.

Mark and Carl had been friends, or associates, for a long time and had both made a lot of money for each other over the years. Before Carl went to prison in 1995 he introduced Mark to these other drug dealers so that when Carl was in jail Mark would continue working with the dealers and Carl and Mark would split 50-50 any money that they made while Carl was inside. It was supposed to be a win-win for both of them because Carl kept earning while in jail and Mark earned money from people he never knew before.

For a while because of that Carl said that him and Mark were actually pretty close friends. When Carl got out of jail in 1996 he went to see Mark to find out how much they had made while he was inside. Mark said they had earned $1 million to $2 million in just that six-month period. Carl was stoked, as you could imagine. With his half share he was obviously looking at half a million to a million bucks. Carl hadn't even dreamed they would earn so much and was pretty keen to get his hands on the cash as soon as possible. However, Mark said he had invested the profits in another big deal but he would give Carl something to tide him over in the meantime.

They didn't go into the details of what the big investment was, which might sound a bit slack or dodgy, but it was obviously another big drug deal so you didn't sort of ask too many questions about it as long as you got your money. And that became the problem — where was Carl's money? Mark gave Carl a measly $4,000 and whenever Carl asked for more it made him feel like a beggar and that Mark was doing him a favour dropping a few crumbs off the table. Which is all bullshit because you aren't asking for favours when you're asking for money you're owed. Mark kept putting Carl off about when this investment was going to come in and therefore when Carl could get his cut of the money he was owed, but after a few months it became quite clear he wasn't going to get any money. The penny dropped for Carl that the Morans had used him, or to put it bluntly, robbed him. After all, they'd only short-changed him of $996,000, worst-case scenario.

That was what the Morans were like — they would burn anyone to make money. Carl isn't the only one who thought that way about the Morans, there was a hell of a lot of other people out there who felt the same way. The funny thing was the Morans thought they were hard pricks and portrayed themselves as gangsters. They looked down on everyone else and thought they were superior and that really pissed Carl off as well.

Anyway, Carl finally rang Mark after Shane had asked him to. He called him from a local telephone box and they agreed to meet in the car park of the Gladstone Park Shopping Centre. They both knew exactly where in the car park to meet because they had met there quite a few times before. At this particular time Mark owed Carl more money from a separate drug deal — about $60,000 for drug chemicals that he'd recently got for him. It is a bit fucked, I know, that Carl was still doing business with Mark Moran when he owed him so much money but he decided it was the best way to get them back and get some money out of them. Carl charged Mark $60,000 for the drug chemicals that had only cost him about $5,000. Basically Carl figured he had been robbed by Mark so anything he now wanted to get from him he was going to get charged a ridiculous price for. It was Carl's turn to get back some of his money. The fact was Carl didn't really care if Mark bought the chemicals from him or not as he didn't really want anything to do with him any more, but if he was prepared to pay a stupid price then he was prepared to deal with him.

So Carl went to meet Mark Moran in the shopping centre car park. Carl was driving a hire car this day, a white late model Camry. He saw Mark already parked there in his white Holden Commodore ute — the same one he was eventually blasted to death in outside his house in Combonere Street, Essendon. When he looked closer Carl said he saw something that made him a bit uncomfortable — Jason Moran was there as well. It was no secret to anyone at the time, least of all Mark, that Jason and Carl didn't get along. Anyway, Carl parked his car near theirs and they all got out and said hello and shook hands and walked away from the cars, because they were all well aware that if the cars were bugged by the police, the listening devices could still hear what was being said if it was in close proximity to the cars.

Mark asked Carl if he could get him some chemicals to make ecstasy tablets and Carl told him the price and reminded him of an outstanding debt for other chemicals he had recently given him. Mark cracked the shits over the price for the new chemicals and said to Carl he knew he was getting it much cheaper than that. Carl just said, tough shit, that was his good luck and what would the Morans do in his position? Carl said Mark's face just changed and he was filthy on him.

Apparently a few cars came past that they thought were suspicious and could have been police surveillance so they decided to go somewhere else and they all hopped into Carl's car and drove a short distance away. They wound through the streets a bit to make sure they weren't being followed and ended up at a small park and all got out and walked in there. Mark started telling Carl that he had heard a rumour that Lee Torney (who is now dead), Mr Z and Carl were all planning to do a run through of their houses and steal all their money and drugs. Carl just said he shouldn't believe rumours and that it was all bullshit. He told him Lee Torney had been in prison for at least six months, and was still there.

Then out of the blue Mark apparently pulled out some sort of piece of wood or something and swung around and whacked Carl in the head with it. It must have been some sort of wooden baton or something that Mark had hidden in his jacket. Anyway, Carl said the baton broke because he hit him so hard with it but that even though he was dazed and dizzy he just ran at Mark and sort of tackled him to the ground and they were wrestling.

Carl said the next thing he knew he heard a gunshot and looked up to see Jason Moran pointing the gun at him. Jason had fired a few shots but fortunately none had hit Carl. Not yet. Mark was apparently yelling at Jason to put one in Carl's head. Carl said it was obvious Jason was shitting himself and the whole time Mark was screaming at him to just shoot him in the head and kill him.

Carl was fucked. He was totally at their mercy because he had gone into the park wearing a bum bag that had his keys and money in it and a fully loaded Glock semi-automatic pistol, but the bum bag had come off him in the wrestle with Mark and now Jason had picked it up. Carl had no way of defending himself.

Carl remembers looking at Jason pointing the gun at him and he almost laughs about it because he reckons Jason's hand was shaking that much it was like he had Parkinson's disease. He reckons if Jason had a steady hand and any balls he would have just shot Carl in the head then and there, but when it came down to it he fucked up. Jason held the gun to Carl's stomach and shot him. Carl reckons he didn't feel a thing because the adrenalin was probably pumping so fast. He got up and the two of the Morans were yelling out not to fuck with them and bragging about how many people they had shot. They were boasting about shooting Alphonse Gangitano and carrying on about getting away with that and having all these jacks in their pocket. They kept saying they ran the fucking state. Mark then said to tell Mr Z they were going to get him, and that he wasn't going to be as lucky as Carl, because they were going to kill him and Torney.

Carl reckons he just shut up and didn't say another word because they had two guns and he had a hole in his gut. He reckons he just kept thinking how much the Morans would live to regret it if he survived. The three of them all went back and got in Carl's car again with Carl in the back seat. Jason had taken the Glock out of Carl's bum bag and was pointing it at him while they drove back to the shopping centre to Mark's ute. When they got out of the car Jason told him to get the bullet out of his gut and give it back to them. Carl was going to give them a bullet back all right, but not the one sitting in his fat guts — he'd get a brand new one especially for each of them.

They left and Carl got in the driver's seat and drove off. He said he looked down and could see a hole in his stomach, but no blood or anything. He could see the powder burn on his top from the gun being fired into him at point-blank range. He drove home to his mum and dad's house in Broadmeadows and when he arrived he must have still looked stunned from being shot because Barb said she said to him straight away, 'What's wrong? You look sick.' But Carl said he was fine and went to his room and called out to George to come and see him. He told him what had happened and George was wild, as any father would be.

Carl said he didn't feel any pain and wondered if it would be alright to just leave the bullet in there or should he go to see a doctor. The problem with seeing a doctor would be that the doctor would have to report it to the police. You can't just walk into a surgery with a bullet hole and expect that they say nothing to the jacks. Carl didn't think it was a good idea for the police to be involved because he always thought they were working with the Morans and Mark and Jason had just said as much when they shot him.

Barb then decided it would be best if she went to the family doctor and asked a hypothetical question of what would happen if she was shot in the stomach and the bullet was left there without seeking medical attention. The doctor said you could have serious internal bleeding and possibly die. When she heard this, Barb, understandably, shit herself. So Carl had no choice but to go see a doctor. He first went to this doctor who was a bit shady and he said he couldn't do anything as Carl had to go to the hospital for an x-ray and to remove the bullet, because there were far too many vital organs around for the doctor to do it himself.

So Carl went to the John Fawkner Hospital in Moreland Road, Brunswick and made up some bullshit story that he had been walking home from the shopping centre in Broadmeadows when he was suddenly hit over the head and knocked unconscious and woke up with a hole in his belly that looked like a gunshot. It was so obviously bullshit, but he had to say something. They took x-rays and said that the bullet was still inside him, which was pretty fucking obvious because there was no hole on the other side where the bullet had come out, so where else was it? He was told he would have to have surgery to remove it. The police turned up soon after and Carl told them the same crap about being mugged. They basically said straight away to stop bullshitting because they already knew what had happened and where it had happened and they described the incident. They said they knew all of that because the Morans had been bragging about it and they had picked it up on a listening device, but if Carl wasn't going to help them they weren't going to do anything about it. They left after that and it was the last time Carl heard or saw the police about it. Carl reckoned that if he wasn't 100 per cent certain the police were in the Morans' pocket before that, he was absolutely convinced they were after they left the hospital.

CHAPTER 8

THERE'S BEEN A BIT OF DRAMA

I was at the hairdresser's when Carl rang. I was getting ready for us all to go to Amarettos on Victoria Street that night for a birthday dinner for Carl. I could tell straight away from his voice that there was something wrong but when I asked him he brushed it off and said he'd ring me back later. When he rang back I could tell something still wasn't right and this time I wasn't going to be brushed off, so I pressed him and he said, 'Something's happened, there's been a bit of a drama.' And he went on to say he'd been shot in the gut and what should he do.

'Well you fucking go to hospital, what else do you do when you've been shot? We've got private health insurance, I'll meet you at the John Fawkner Hospital.' Meanwhile his mum, Barb, had been to a doctor to ask him if, hypothetically speaking, she was shot in the stomach, would he operate on her. No surprises for guessing the doctor told her she was crazy (very clever doctor, that one). He said that vital organs might have been hit and whoever had been shot could be bleeding to death internally so they had to get to a hospital urgently. But they didn't go. At least not straight away. Carl's dad knew a bodgy doctor so he took him there to see if he could fix him up without the jacks having to be called and questions being asked. But even that doctor took one look at Carl and refused to do anything. So we arranged to go to the John Fawkner and I rang his mate Andy Krakouer to tell him and he came over and helped to get Carl to hospital.

We got to the John Fawkner and I still had no idea what the fuck had really happened to Carl. All I knew was he had this wound in his gut and it was pretty serious. Carl told the doctors and nurses that he was walking to the Broadmeadows shopping centre through the Commission flats when he got knocked unconscious from a hit to the head and when he woke up he was bleeding from the stomach. They could tell straight away from the burns and the wound itself that it was a gunshot injury so whether they believed Carl or not — and even I have got to say, who would believe that story? — they called the police. The scans they did on his gut confirmed he had been shot. I was freaking out at this stage because no-one had had a chance yet to talk quietly to me to explain what the fuck was going on, who had shot him or why or anything.

The police arrived and split us up to question us about what we knew of his injury. It was easy for me to tell them what I knew — fuck-all. At that stage the jacks thought

Dean had done it, so I also started to think it might have been Dean, because I remembered that I'd seen Dean with guns many times. The police left and Carl was getting ready to go in to be operated on when he said to me that he'd had a meeting with the Morans. At that stage he didn't say that they were the ones who'd shot him, but he didn't need to.

While Carl was in surgery the police waited outside the theatre to collect the bullet so it could be examined by forensics. When Carl finally got out he had a wound from under his breastbone down to his groin. I know it sounds funny now, but when we were allowed in to see him I didn't realise that part of the bed dropped down so I was trying to fix the bed for him to make him more comfortable and suddenly the whole thing collapsed with a huge bang and Carl went with it. He screamed in agony and he wanted to kill me. I stormed off in a shit and didn't return. I got upset because it was obvious I was only trying to make him more comfortable and made an honest mistake, so I said, 'Fuck you,' and left.

The next night my daughter Danielle was playing on the roof of my house with Tye — don't ask, I have no idea what they were doing up there — and Dan fell off the roof, hit her face somehow and knocked herself out. Tye jumped down and ran in and grabbed a towel and put it on her mouth. He just said to me, 'Mum, don't look at her, just get her to hospital.' So we arrived at the John Fawkner Hospital and they took her straight in and fixed her up.

The next thing I knew she'd rung Carl to tell him what happened. I don't know how she was even able to speak at the time, but she told Carl where she was and why and Carl said, 'That's where I am too.' Dan thought it was funny that Carl was already in the hospital — she wanted them both to get beds in the same room so the nurses could look after them together. Then, unbeknown to me, she rang her own dad, Dean, to tell him what had happened. She also said to him, 'Guess what? Carl is in the hospital too.' Big mistake. Suddenly the Morans knew Carl was there.

So the Morans send this guy in to talk to Carl and warn him about talking to the jacks — as if Carl needed to be told. The bloke's name was Lee. He'd been a friend of Carl's but then he started going out with Suzanne Kane, the sister of Jason Moran's wife Trisha, so the Morans, knowing Lee used to be Carl's friend, thought he would be able to get close to Carl without raising any suspicions.

Carl knew what Lee was doing. But the Morans weren't content just with Lee's quiet word. Carl then got a phone call from Jason Moran abusing and threatening him. Carl hung up and thought, 'They're going to come and finish the job in hospital.' The Morans obviously didn't think Carl would go to hospital to be treated for the gunshot wound, so they figured that if Carl was in hospital then the police would already know it was a shooting and that Carl would have lagged on them to the jacks. Even if they had some jacks in their pocket this was a bit different.

Unbeknown to the Morans, before the jacks even got to the hospital they had already heard them bragging about the shooting on a listening device, so the jacks already knew full well that the Morans had done it because the fucking stupid Morans had as good as told them.

After Lee left and Jason had called, Carl knew he had to get out of the hospital or there would be more than one life-threatening injury the hospital had to treat him for and this time he might not be so lucky. Carl's dad arranged for Carl's aunt to collect him and take him to her house in Doncaster for a few days. He didn't stay there long because he wanted to keep moving around, so he returned to his parents' house briefly, then went to his dad's friend's house and finally to a flat in Broadmeadows. He kept moving because even though he was recovering from the gunshot wound and needed to relax, he was more concerned that the longer he stayed in one place the more likely he was to be found by the Morans. Unfortunately the Morans already knew.

When Carl arrived at the flat in Broady Mark Moran was coincidentally waiting around the corner watching the place and saw him go in. The reason Mark was there was because it wasn't an ordinary flat — there was a pill press inside and they were making drugs. The Morans knew there was another pill press working somewhere and they were tipped off by someone that it was in this flat, so I think Mark was watching it to see who came and went and to be sure the press was in there. I think this is where *Underbelly* got confused and figured that the Morans shot Carl because they wanted to know about the pill press. The guy who had the Housing Commission flat with the press in it had a friend that he didn't know was also friends with the Morans. That guy found out about the press and he told the Morans, so they wanted to nick the press or stop it somehow.

Mark was working with the jacks so he rang them and tipped them off that the press was there. Next thing, the jacks are knocking on the door to execute a warrant for some fraud, but it was just their excuse to get in the place. When they got there Carl was asleep upstairs in all his clothes. George Williams, Carl's dad, was hiding somewhere in another room but the jacks found him pretty quickly.

I had barely spoken to Carl since I crashed his hospital bed, because after Danielle got injured Carl went into hiding and I never spoke to him. So suddenly Carl rang me out of the blue saying he was in prison. I already knew that, though, because it had been plastered all over the news. Carl wasn't that well known at the time but I saw all the news of this drug raid and knew which flat it was and I saw Carl on TV.

In the end Carl got off that charge because corrupt jacks had turned up at the scene. The first police who kicked in the door and found the pill press were from the Broadmeadows police, I think they were the CIU [Criminal Investigation Unit], but they were only there for the summons. Because drug dealing and manufacturing on this scale wasn't their jurisdiction they had to call in the drug squad. The drug squad turned up and one of the jacks who arrived on the scene was a Detective Sergeant Malcolm Rosenes; later they found out he was corrupt and he was kicked out of the police and jailed. Rosenes was involved in the drug trade to the hilt at this stage.

Carl has told me that back then he didn't know Rosenes or any of his corrupt colleagues. He said he had never had dealings with them and didn't know they were corrupt. The problem was, they mixed stuff, like mixing bowls, from the kitchen and everywhere else in the house in with all the drug equipment. The only fingerprints of Carl's they found on any of the drug gear in the flat were on a mixing bowl that came from the kitchen, not from the room where the drug manufacture was going on. Rosenes had taken the bowl from the kitchen and mixed some drugs in it in the lounge room.

Carl was no angel and I have done drug deals and done time in jail for them, but Carl was there to rest, not to use the pill press. I know it sounds like a strange place to rest with a pill press clapping along in the background but all I can say is what Carl told me and what the police forensics found, and that was that Carl hadn't been touching the drug stuff.

The other thing was, I know Carl and George would have been thinking that, yeah, there was a pill press there and it might be a bit noisy if you wanted to rest but if you were in Carl's predicament, trying to find a safe place to rest, then what safer place than in with a pill press? You have got to remember that whoever had the pill press wanted to keep the press hidden from the Morans more than anyone else, so it should have been a good place for someone to hang out if they were also trying to hide from the Morans. And if you have 20 kilos of speed in your house, it's normally kept pretty safe.

Giving up the pill press to the jacks meant the Morans got another free ticket from the jacks, got Carl out of the way and got rid of the competition. I don't know if Rosenes was working with the Morans when he tried to fit Carl up by making sure his fingerprints were on drug stuff in the flat or if he was just acting on his own to make sure Carl was locked up. It was Rosenes who took the bowl from the kitchen and transferred drugs into it and it was Rosenes who took it upon himself to test the pill press while they were in the flat because he said he wanted to see how many pills it pumped out in a minute. But he had no jurisdiction to do anything like that — that was for forensics to do, not some drug squad detective. Obviously Rosenes was doing his own research for whatever reason. The jacks knew that by grabbing Carl there with such a big haul he would be on remand in jail for a while. It was 25 November 1999 — six weeks after he was shot — that he was arrested and charged with the ecstasy haul.

Carl wasn't high profile then so he was just put into the Melbourne Assessment Prison like any other prisoner. Later on they gave him special treatment and it was much harder to get access to talk to him, but back then I was able to visit him and discuss what had happened. Even then he still wouldn't say anything to me about the Morans being involved in shooting him because he was paranoid about police listening in. I wasn't up with bugging at that stage but I knew you didn't ask questions. My sister Shaz's ex-partner

Graeme Jensen, who was shot and killed by the police years ago, always told me, 'You don't ask questions because you can't be blamed for lagging if you didn't know anything.' I always remembered that advice so I never pushed Carl to tell me too much. I knew he would tell me when the time was right. It was enough stress for me to know that he'd been shot.

The night Carl got out of prison on bail we stayed at the Royce Hotel right across the street from St Kilda Road police station. I suppose we saw the hotel when Carl was taken in and out of the station by the drug squad but we just liked the look of it and it was just a coincidence it was over the road from the jacks. Carl and I stayed up all that night partying.

The next morning Carl said to me, 'Let's go for a walk.' Carl wasn't big on exercise so whenever he said he wanted to go for a walk I knew he meant he wanted to go somewhere safe to talk. So we walked up the street and around the corner from the hotel into Domain Road, next to the posh Melbourne Grammar School, and up to the Botanic Gardens. Carl explained to me that the Morans wanted chemicals from him to make drugs and he wouldn't give them the chemicals. He'd discussed it with Mark at the meeting where he was shot and Carl had put the price up high because he'd asked Mark for chemicals once before and Mark had set an astronomical price that Carl knew was massively over the odds.

He still hadn't told me the Morans were the ones that shot him but it wasn't hard to work out. It wasn't until much later that I found out Carl was shot because of the money Mark Moran owed him. When Carl told me it was because the Morans wanted to buy chemicals from him, I was just blown away because until then I didn't know Carl was into heavy shit like that. That was way beyond anything I'd been into. I had done shitty little street stuff but this was like, whoa, this was massive. Before that moment I'd known Carl was a bit dodgy but I didn't know how dodgy. And I didn't suspect he was anywhere near on a level to be talking about dealing in chemicals.

The thing was, Carl didn't live extravagantly. He wouldn't go out and buy a $300,000 Mercedes Benz. He was the sort of bloke who just got around in his shorts or his tracky and did a bit of gear here and there. So I suppose he was nothing like the Morans and their girlfriends, because they were big on being all showy and splashing money around. It just blew me away to think Carl was involved at this level and it just scared the shit out of me. I thought, 'Hang on, he's been shot here and we're talking about dealing in chemicals for manufacture here, so that is millions of dollars' worth of drugs on the street — it's not just a bit of speed we're talking about here.' That *Underbelly* show makes out that we got all excited about it but really I was shitting myself.

If I think about it now I probably should have walked away from Carl and tried to get out of all the bullshit right then and there but it was like a whirlwind. There was so much going on: Carl had been shot, Dean was still hanging around in the background with threats and stuff, there was all this shit going on with the Morans and Carl, and I was scared they might come after me and the kids to get to Carl. So if I thought anything at all it was that it was safer at that point to stay close to Carl. Honestly, though, I didn't think much about it at all. I didn't have time to absorb what was going on, I just had to keep moving and doing what I needed to do. Because of my previous life, I was used to dealing with the moment, not the past or the future, and that was what I did then — it was just deal with what was happening right now and don't think about what might happen down the track. I remember saying to my brother Mick, 'They're just horrible people,' about the Morans and a lot of the people I was coming across.

Three days after Carl got bailed on 21 January 2000, Jason Moran was arrested over a pub brawl with Alphonse Gangitano. That was the brawl in the Sports Bar in King Street from December 1995. Carl didn't know Alphonse Gangitano — he'd never met him. I want to make that really clear because people think of this whole *Underbelly* thing and gangland murders and think there must have been something between Carl and Alphonse Gangitano as well, but he died before Carl ever had a chance to meet him, and I certainly didn't know him. But the thing was, Jason was in jail, then Carl was in jail, then Carl got bail three days before Jason went to jail, so really one or other of them was in prison the whole time, so they couldn't do anything to one another.

Carl isn't one to make big statements about things, so he wasn't going around swearing and carrying on about what he was going to do to the Morans or anything. He wasn't like that. He'd just do it with no big-noting. I never asked him about it, or asked him what he was going to do about it. They wanted chemicals from him and they had shot him in the guts and I just couldn't believe somebody would do that — it was so far beyond what I'd experienced I wasn't going to tell Carl how to deal with it. The only thing Carl said was that he wasn't going to deal with them anymore; he was more or less saying, 'Fuck them, they're not getting anything off me. I'm not selling them shit.' And they owed him so much.

The only thing I remember thinking was why would they think he would want to give them gear when they owed him money already? It was fucking madness. I don't think I ever said this outright to Carl because it wasn't my business to be telling him what to do, but I remember thinking: 'They owe you heaps and they want to buy more from you — why ever would you even have thought about selling them chemicals?' In a lot of ways people do some weird shit in the drug trade and have to deal with some crazy people, but even so this was bullshit. I kept wondering what would happen next and I started to get stressed — for the first time I began to get a bit wary of everything. I worried about where we went and who we saw and who we talked to and what Dean was going to do. It was all just building up and scaring me.

Dean was ringing me at the time saying, 'Tell that weak dog if he wants his bum bag, we've got it. Tell him to come and collect it from me.' So that was the first time Carl got wind of Dean's involvement and thought he might have been behind the Morans shooting him. It was where the hatred between Carl and Dean really started. Before that Carl didn't really care less about Dean other than wanting to bash him after he found out how bad he bashed me.

CHAPTER 9

LIKE FATHER LIKE SON

The police don't want to hear about what happened next. Even though they never tried him for it the jacks still reckon Carl killed Mark Moran. Carl didn't kill Mark Moran. Carl had a lot of reasons for wanting to kill Mark — a shot in the guts is a pretty good one for starters, and being owed a million bucks by the bloke isn't a bad reason either — but that doesn't mean he did it. There is no doubt Carl was happy when Mark was killed — we all were, fuck him, he had tried to kill us — and I was happy he was dead but that doesn't mean Carl did it. The real reason Mark Moran died was because of some drug chemicals that were stolen from him — and it had nothing to do with Carl.

The Morans had some chemicals for making speed stored in a warehouse or factory which burned down. Mark's killer had some involvement in burning the place down but before he set it alight he must have taken some of the chemicals out because they 'miraculously' survived the fire. They were the Morans' chemicals. Naturally, the Morans found out that their chemicals hadn't been burned in the fire and were still around because you can't keep something like that secret in the drug trade. Whenever chemicals are around everyone finds out because the people who have them try to sell them to others who can either cook them or sell them to someone who wants to cook them. And no-one buys chemicals without seeing the labels on the drums, otherwise they'd never know what they were buying. Stuff can smell like it should and look like it should, but it doesn't always cook up like it should. This is the sort of knowledge I have learned during my journey with Carl.

What that all meant was that as soon as the killer tried to do anything with the Morans' chemicals they'd find out about it. It also didn't take long for the killer to know that Mark had found out. I mean, it was pretty stupid or pretty brave of him to try and steal the Morans' drugs out of the fire and use them. I don't know if he was just blatantly dumb, ballsy or did things out of fear, but whether or not he took the drugs out of fear, he definitely killed Mark Moran out of fear. He knew Mark would kill him for stealing his drugs, which no doubt he would have. But the jacks don't want to hear this because they would look stupid.

Mark died like his dad before him. His real dad, Leslie Cole, that is. Everyone in the media and the police call him Mark Moran now, but his real name was Mark Cole. That was what we called him and that is what his daughter's surname is. The strange part is that Mark Cole's kids went to the same school as my kids, so we would see them all the time. His daughter is a beautiful little girl — it wasn't her fault her dad was a rat — and her surname is Cole. Leslie Cole had been shot outside his house in Sydney in 1982 and Mark was shot outside his house in Aberfeldie in June 2000.

I couldn't care less that Mark Moran was murdered. I'd had enough run-ins with him for me to be happy he was out of the way. On one occasion I was at the shopping centre and Mark saw me there and approached me as I was walking back to the car. I was on the phone to Carl, who was in prison at the time, and it was the last phone call he was allowed for the night. I said to Carl, 'Mark's coming over to the car — what do I do?' 'Run the cunt over,' Carl said. And I would have if I'd got the chance.

I was able to get into the car before Mark reached me, mouthing off and making threats, but I wasn't quick enough to start up the car and drive at him. He was standing next to my window yelling abuse at me spitting and frothing at the mouth. I just told him to get fucked and drove off while he kept screaming abuse at me in the car park, with everyone watching. Mark jumped in his car which, unfortunately, had been parked really close to mine, and he took off behind me. As I was pulling up at some traffic lights not far away, he swerved his car at mine as though to hit me, so I swerved to hit him. We both ended up stopped next to each other at the lights. He was with his goose of a friend Jesse Franco, and he got out of his car, came over to my car, reached in and ripped my keys out of the ignition, and threw them into the grass on the nature strip. I got out and went to get the keys and they just kept laughing and mouthing off as they drove away. I was mouthing off right back at them.

The thing was, Carl didn't know any of this because our phone call got cut off in all the activity. Carl was then locked up for the night and wasn't allowed to make any more phone calls, so he didn't know what was happening. The last he heard was me panicking because Mark Moran was coming over to the car screaming abuse at me. Carl stayed up all night freaking out, wondering if I had been killed by Mark Cole or whether I had run him over. He rang me first thing the next morning and I just said, 'No, everything's cool.'

Because our kids went to the same school I would often see Mark when I was dropping the girls off. He used to stop his car in the school driveway so I couldn't walk past. I'd get the girls out of the car to walk in and he'd block the way out. One day he got out of his car and came up to me and said, 'Tell that fuckin' dog that it's who gets who first.' He was making it pretty clear he was going to kill Carl. I went back and told Carl but he didn't really care at that stage — he was too busy making money. But you can understand that no, I was not upset when I found out Mark Moran was dead.

Carl was charged with Mark's murder but evidence given at his committal hearing proved that he couldn't have killed Mark. You can make up your own mind but this is what Carl was doing the night Mark was killed.

Dennis Reardon's son, Sean, had arrived in a taxi at our house in Taylors Lakes so that he could meet Dennis and

Carl and go together to a chemist in Melton to pick up his methadone. On the way they stopped at a service station to buy some stuff — petrol, drinks and smokes or something — and they all got out of the car at the servo before driving on to Melton. They got the methadone and drove home again.

On the way back Carl rang me and asked me to put his dinner on for him. He was on a slim-fast diet at the time, the big fatty boombah, and that meant all his food had to be weighed, so he wanted me to cut up his chicken and veggies and weigh them and get the meal ready. At the time I was not long out of hospital after having surgery so that we could try to have Dhakota, so I could hardly move around and I was shitty on Carl because he wanted me to cook his fucking dinner. I got it ready then went to bed, so I was not sure what time they got home. Carl had his dinner and watched a bit of TV and Rocco Arico came over at some stage during the night and hung out with Carl, having a few drinks.

Then, at 2 am, the police arrived in a riot van to raid our house. I don't know what they were expecting. There was no Purana task force at this stage, just the homicide squad. I was going crazy because the kids were asleep and I didn't want them to have to see all this commotion with jacks crawling all over the house and taking Carl away, so I kept saying to them, 'Do what you have to, but don't go near my kids. They're asleep, there's no need for them to see you all here.'

The jacks had Carl in one room and they were questioning him about the murder of Richard Mladenich who had been killed a month earlier. I was sitting in the lounge room when a jack came in and said, 'Do you realise that Mark Moran's been killed?' That was the first I knew of it. I was shocked. Like I said, I wasn't upset about it but I was surprised. I was sad for his daughter because she was a really nice girl and I thought it was sad for a little girl to grow up without her dad. I knew what that was like.

Richard Mladenich — Mad Richard — was shot and killed in a motel room in St Kilda. Some people said Richard was Mark's minder. He was a big bloke, and pretty crazy, and they said that Carl killed him because he was close to Mark. But that was bullshit — it was the other way around. Richard was a friend of ours, and him and Carl would hang out together every day. Not long before he died Carl and I took him shopping to the Nike factory and bought him a heap of clothes. He had had his troubles but was doing really well and getting his life back together. He used to ring me and say, 'Bert, I'm sitting on the beach meditating.'

I'd known Richard since I was a little kid because he was a friend of Sharon's and when we lived in Seaford he used to take a taxi to her house and jump it [run off without paying the fare] and hang out with us. Carl loved him. I remember the morning Carl found out he died — I think it was Mother's Day and Carl had given him money to buy his mum flowers. Carl was in the shower when Richard's girlfriend rang and she was crying so I handed the phone over to Carl and he just started crying his eyes out. He loved Richard.

I don't know who killed him. Sometimes I think it was Andrew. He'd have killed Carl at that point if he had the chance. We weren't close with Andrew then so it could have been Andrew — who knows? He was accused of killing enough other people so he might have done it. The night he was killed Richard was in a motel room hanging out with other drug users and they reckon that whoever did it just walked in, shot him and walked off really calmly. It sounded like someone who knew what they were doing, was pretty cold and had probably done it before. It sounded like Andrew.

I think Richard was murdered because the Morans felt he was a bit of strength for Carl. Richard was called Mad Richard for a reason — because he would do anything and if you put a gun in his hand he'd cause chaos. With him standing behind Carl the Morans were worried what might happen if Carl was killed. So much for people saying he was Mark's minder! We reckon he was killed because they thought he was loyal to Carl and if they did something to Carl they were scared of what Richard might do in retaliation. I reckon the Morans figured it was better to kill Richard first and then Carl would be more isolated and they wouldn't have to worry about some nutter with a gun coming after them for killing Carl. Carl loved Richard, they were genuine friends and for the first time in Richard's life he was getting on track, and that's what's really sad about his murder.

The point I am making is that I don't know why the jacks chose to think Carl killed Richard, let alone why they would choose that night to question Carl about it. That is, of course, if they were ever really serious about that being the reason for raiding our house. The jacks must have stupidly bought some bullshit line from the Morans that Carl had something to do with it. The chances are they wanted to raid us because of Mark's murder and they knew they had no reason to raid us for that so they invented this bullshit about Richard as their excuse.

Carl just lay there cool and calm on the bed as the police searched the room — Carl never stressed about anything. The only time I saw him stressed was when I was having Dhakota and the nurses told him she might die. It's the only time Carl panicked. Even when Dhakota was 'dead' in her cot once and I had to grab her out and revive her Carl just stood there — I don't know whether he froze, or what, but he didn't panic, he just didn't do anything. He stood by and watched as I revived her. So that night while the police were searching the place I eventually walked into the bedroom to see if Carl was OK and asked what was going on. He just looked at me and said, 'I'm cool, Bert.'

Eventually the jacks took Carl and left and Rocco left soon after like the weak little dog he was — he didn't even help me get a solicitor for Carl or anything. I rang a lawyer who was a friend of ours and he went down to the station and two hours later Carl was home. They didn't do gunshot residue tests on him or anything. Carl was still wearing the same clothes he had been wearing that night.

The police later went to the servo Carl and the boys had stopped at on the way to Melton and they checked the security camera and saw all the boys on the tape. They checked their clock against the clock on the security camera and they matched. Detective Senior Sergeant Ron Iddles of the homicide squad gave evidence at Carl's committal that 'under no circumstances' could Carl have been at Mark Cole's place at the time he was killed and then got to this service station in Melton in time to be seen on the camera.

Mr Z was the one who later gave evidence to say he had driven Carl to kill Mark and waited for him to shoot him then driven him to the end of the street after the killing. He said Carl had changed his clothes in the back seat and they disposed of the clothes. Then Mr Z said he dropped Carl back home at our place — and then Carl was supposed to have driven off and been seen at this servo. Even the police had to admit that Carl couldn't have done all that. It was bullshit.

So when the jacks checked the security camera at the service station they would have known two things — one that Carl was there at the time he said, and that it would have been impossible for him to have been at Mark Cole's to kill him *and* been at the service station. Secondly, the camera showed that when Carl was arrested by police he had put back on the same clothes he had been wearing the night before. You could see on the security camera what Carl was wearing and the video recording of the police interview also showed him wearing those same clothes. It is the bit of footage from the interview they show on TV all the time where he is yawning. Anyway, the point about them being the same clothes is that the jacks knew he was wearing the same clothes he'd worn the night before but no-one ever tested his clothes. If they thought he was involved in shooting Mark Cole you'd reckon they might have done that.

We rang the *Herald Sun* and tried to put a death notice in for Mark, just to take the piss. It was going to be from the dog squad and would say, 'Thanks for all your help, Mark, we'll really miss you — St Kilda Road Police Station.' But the newspaper wouldn't put it in. Pity.

CHAPTER 10

PIZZA WITH THE LOT

A few months after Mark died I went out to dinner with Breanane and a friend of mine and her daughter. We walked into the Moonee Ponds Pizza restaurant and sitting at a table there was Ricky Sequenzia and his family. Ricky and Paul Sequenzia were the brothers of Antonella, who was married to Mark Moran. Other than Carl, I was obviously about the last person he wanted to see. When Ricky saw me he slammed his knife and fork down on the table and just started mouthing off at me across the crowded restaurant.

I started giving it back to him but the next thing I knew two car loads of people pulled up out the front. I was thinking, 'Oh shit, there's gonna be some drama here.' In one of the cars was Paul Sequenzia and a guy called 'Eyes' — Michel Pastras, who was shot in Albion Street, Brunswick, a while after this — and some other blokes I didn't recognise.

I had said to my friend, 'We had better get out of here,' and as we were climbing into the car, Ricky and Paul were right in my face and mouthing off. I thought, 'I don't have to take this shit,' and I went to reach for the gun that I had in the car. But as I was reaching for it Breanane started to get a really bad asthma attack because of all the commotion. She hadn't seen me reach for the gun, thank God, because that would have set her off even worse, but with all the commotion she got scared because she thought they were going to bash us and that I would be killed. Then she started to vomit and I had to forget about the gun and the Sequenzias and deal with my daughter and get her out of there, so I quickly drove away.

About that same time I also saw Paul Sequenzia's girlfriend at the Highpoint shopping centre. She saw me at the same time and we both just started mouthing off at one another. We were in the drive-in for the Myer pick-up and she was yelling at me and I snapped and thought, fuck you. I said, 'Who the fuck are you, you slut? Who the fuck do you think you are?' and I went over and grabbed her by the throat and bashed her head in, the weak bitch. I stopped and said to my daughter to get my bag — I think Natasha, Paul's girlfriend, thought I was going to get a gun out and shoot her because they all panicked and security arrived. We just walked off and got in the car and left.

They all acted like they were so tough but they were just weak people. Another time years later I ran into Ricky Sequenzia again. I hadn't seen him since that day in the pizza shop. It was Tye's 21st birthday and we were preparing a hall for the party. Michelle and I had gone around the corner to Nandos for something to eat. Before we went in I saw Ricky in there and said to Michelle that we should go somewhere else or there'd be a drama. She said, 'Don't be silly, if he starts up just ignore him.' Well, we opened the door and he saw me and was into me straight away, mouthing off. I wasn't going to back down. He grabbed a Coke bottle like he was going to hit me with it and I just looked at him and said, 'Who the fuck are you? Your family are all dogs, that is why they're all six feet under.' Then I looked at his wife, who was mouthing off, and said, 'Shut your fucking mouth, you fucking slut, or I'll smash it in.' Ricky got upset and had another go and I said I'd fucking fix him too and he got all scared and left. They were always weak people.

The thing I always used to say to those women was that we all played the game but some people's husbands played it better than others. We were all the same, we were all drug dealers, we were all making money, but some people's husbands were better at it than others. Some people made more than others and some people stayed alive longer. That was how it was.

CHAPTER 11

TYING THE KNOT

Carl didn't get down on one knee to propose. He isn't that kind of guy. Carl isn't what anyone would call a romantic, he isn't into that kind of stuff. In fact he probably wasn't that into getting married, but he did it for me, so I suppose you could say that was romantic. Carl wasn't the marrying kind, but he knew that I'd always dreamed of being married when my babies were born. I was pregnant with Dhakota at the time and he knew I really wanted to be married before she was born.

Carl and I discussed having kids pretty much straight after we got together. He knew how much I loved kids and he said that he wanted me to be the mother of his kids because he thought I was a great mum. He knew that regardless of what happened to him his child would always have the love and attention it needed because he'd seen me with my own kids. And I always wanted more kids because

I loved having lots of my kids around me so I could shower them in kisses and cuddles. But because of the way the doctors treated me when I had Tye, and then with a few complications when I had my next kids, there were some problems there which the doctors said would stop me having more kids. I was told they could operate and fix the problem but we would still probably have to have our baby using IVF.

There was nothing to think about. I knew what I wanted so we started straight away with the IVF treatments and I went in for surgery. We had to try with the IVF virtually straight away after surgery — I was so sick, but luckily I fell pregnant really quickly with Dhakota. We'd bought a house in Hillside by this stage and we were busily buying towels and doonas and baby stuff. I had been overseas with my sister before the surgery. We went to Hong Kong, Singapore, London, France and America buying all this stuff for a baby that I hoped I would be able to have because I wasn't even pregnant at that time. Of course I knew the money Carl was making to pay for all this was from drugs, but it wasn't like we sat there and discussed it. I knew in my head where it was from but I didn't sort of say, 'What are you doing?' and, 'How much money are you making?' It's just not something you do.

So I was lying there in the bath one night and Carl walks into the bathroom and he passes me this box and says, 'Are you going to marry me? Here's your engagement ring.' It was beautiful, a one-and-a-half carat diamond with three little diamonds around it. I was over the moon, I was so excited. I just couldn't believe it because by then I wasn't sure if he would do it. I had a bit of an inkling because we'd discussed it but I didn't think he would actually come around to it. I was about three months' pregnant with Dhakota when we got engaged. I think it changed things for Carl because he knew I wanted both the mum's and dad's names to be on the baby's birth certificate and for it to say 'married'.

With Dean we had had all of our kids before we got married, so it was a big thing for me this time to be married before I had my baby. Carl wasn't interested in happy families and settling down like that, but he did it for me because he loved me and he knew that was what I wanted. He just wanted to make my dreams come true and to make me happy.

When the marriage celebrant came to speak to us, he explained that people chose all different types of services and told us about a few of those. I had been married before so I wanted something different and that was why we had the Celtic wedding ceremony, where you tie your hands together with this cloth and then the knotted cloth is placed in a bag symbolising that the marriage is sealed.

Obviously I am Maltese not Irish or anything, but we liked the symbolism and thought it was a really beautiful thing to do, so we sort of made our own wedding with the Celtic theme and I wrote my vows and we planned the ceremony together. Dhakota watches the video of the wedding all the time now.

The wedding service and the reception were at Lakeside Receptions, where we'd also planned to have Dhakota's christening. I was heavily pregnant with her at the time of our wedding in January 2001 — in fact, it turned out she was born just six weeks after the wedding. A lot of women would rather wait until after the birth when they are skinny again for their photos, but not me. I just wanted to be married before Dhakota was born, so I didn't care that I was pregnant.

My dress was a gold halter neck made by a really good designer, and it came out from under the breast and was nice and flowing. It cost Carl a fortune. Breanane was my flower girl, and my daughter Danielle, my sister Michelle, my niece Kerri-Anne and my brother Robert's ex-girlfriend Sally were the bridesmaids. Sharon was older — she was my bridesmaid when I married Dean. Andy Krakouer was Carl's best man and his groomsmen were my brother Robert, Snalfy and Dennis Reardon. I walked down the aisle with Tye — he gave me away — to the Shania Twain song, 'You're Still the One'. It suited us because everyone had tried to say we would never make it and we had made it. We danced to Lonestar's 'Amazed'. Carl wore a black suit with a long jacket and a gold brocade vest to match my dress.

My mum even attended the wedding, and after I had Dhakota we tried again to make friends. It didn't work.

Our wedding was a bit different to most other weddings aside from the fact that we had a Celtic service. For instance, most people don't have armed security on the door. Carl knew the Morans would figure it was the perfect time to attack him and that he would be vulnerable, so he had some armed blokes there. He never mentioned it to me because he knew I wouldn't be happy about having armed guards at my wedding, but you could tell they were there for a purpose because they weren't sitting down like other guests, they were doing a job. I didn't make a big deal of it because when I thought about it I realised it was probably wise and it would have been worse if I made a big drama and drew everyone's attention to it.

Carl didn't know how clever he was to have them there. We found out later that Victor Peirce was supposed to set us up. Victor was invited to the wedding but he rang at the last minute and said, 'I won't be coming, I've been out all night.' Then all of a sudden he walked in and he didn't look to me like he'd been out all night, he looked really on the ball. We discovered later that Victor was supposed to come inside and suss out exactly where everyone was seated so the Morans' hired killers could run through the place. Maybe Victor saw the armed blokes Carl had put on the door and realised they wouldn't have got far if they tried a run-through because for whatever reason they didn't do it.

Life for us was always going to be a bit different from most people's. We were living off drug dealing, which is not a normal family-type life, but I wanted kids and a family and a house and a nice big normal wedding before I had my baby and all these sorts of things that didn't fit with the drug-dealing lifestyle. It was probably why Carl struggled with being married. In some ways you could say Carl was leading a criminal life, but he also wanted a normal, peaceful life and what he did for money was just his job. He did grow up with a fairly normal family life and he just wanted the same thing for himself and his family. His mum worked her guts out the whole of her life, and so did his dad. His dad got into a bit of trouble here and there but nothing out of the ordinary.

A lot of people say to me that I don't sound like I'm divorced from Carl, and you know why? Because Carl always made sure that I was proud and carried myself with confidence no matter what happened, and I still love and respect him for that more than anything else. When I first left Dean and after all I'd been through with him I was shattered as a person and Carl helped me rebuild my confidence because he was always on at me to walk with my head high. I used to walk along with my head down looking at the ground and he would growl and say, 'Put your head up, what are you doing with your head down? Who are you looking at?' So I would put my head up and laugh.

I know I still love him now — I always loved him and always will. We didn't split up because we didn't love each other anymore. Well, maybe I shouldn't speak for Carl, because perhaps he stopped loving me, I don't know. I do know I never stopped loving him and even though I am over him and a lot of the shit he goes on with, I also know part of me will always love Carl. But he's not the sort of person to be with just one person for life so marriage was never going to work out for him. We should probably never have got married. I won't say we shouldn't have been together because we had Dhakota together and I would not give her up for the world, but we probably shouldn't have got married. I think I wanted something with Carl that I should have known we could never have. He was never really into marriage like I was, so he was never going to be able to stick at it and I should have realised that.

Just before the wedding he tried to walk away and call it off. At the time I said, 'No worries, if that's the way you feel, fine.' I mean, I was shattered, but I wasn't going to get angry with him for being honest with me and saying what he felt. I think when it came to it, though, Carl was being pushed around a bit by his mum, who was saying he shouldn't get married because she never really liked us together. And he was getting pushed around by me a bit because I did want to get married, and in the end he just said, 'Fuck it, everyone piss off and leave me alone, the wedding is off.'

I left him alone after that and a few days later he apologised and said he was just a bit emotional about getting married so he'd snapped, but he really did want to do it.

We didn't go on a honeymoon because I was so heavily pregnant and we needed to be in Melbourne near the hospital, so we only had four days on our own at Crown Casino. We just kicked back at the hotel — it wasn't as if we could go out and have a romantic night.

CHAPTER 12

CHRISTMAS BON BON

It was Christmas 2000 and I was seven months' pregnant with Dhakota but we had all of Carl's family over for Christmas lunch at our house in Hillside. I cooked everything and organised the table and everything, as you do, while they all sat around and drank. Nobody in Carl's family ever did anything — not just that day, but ever. They were drinkers so they'd just sit around and drink and smoke and expect somebody else to do the work. We had had lunch and everyone had eaten well and was sitting around drinking some more and smoking.

They eventually got up and left and Carl said to me that he had to go out as well, with his Croatian friend Vic and Tommy, Dhakota's godfather. They went to leave but because Tommy had a convertible coupe SLK Merc they couldn't all fit in so they came back inside and got my keys and borrowed my car. I had a 4WD Toyota Prado

Grande, which was the car I got after I carried on like an idiot about the Statesman and Carl gave it to his dad. So when they said they had to go out I just presumed they had some business to do somewhere, even though it was Christmas Day.

My brother Robert and his girlfriend, Sally, were still there with me and they helped me clean the house up. We had an enormous house at the time — sixty squares — and it was all white tiles and furniture. There was food and stuff everywhere so it was a big job to clean it up. After a while I started to get pissed off that Carl wasn't helping and I began to wonder where he was. The more I thought about it, the angrier I got. Who goes out on Christmas Day to do business? Who goes out on Christmas Day after having their entire family over for Christmas lunch and then leaves their wife, who has done all the cooking, to do all the cleaning as well?

So I rang Carl's phone to try and track him down and see what he was doing and ask when he would be back and whether he planned on helping out at all. He wasn't answering so I rang Vic's phone and this time there was an answer. Vic said they were all at Rocco Arico's family's house having a drink. I knew why they were there — Carl had been rooting Rocco's sister Grace. Carl used to sleep at their house occasionally and he'd tell me it was because he was protecting them — they were minor crooks and wannabe gangsters and people would give them a bit of grief.

I always had my suspicions that there was something going on between Carl and Grace. Not long before I had rung their house looking for Carl and Grace answered the phone saying, 'Yes, Carl, what do you want?' I knew something was going on and I said, 'It's not Carl, it's Roberta, and I want you to stop fucking my husband, you little whore.' She hung up.

The next day I rang their house to say to Grace's mother that her daughter was fucking my husband. I had sat at this family's dinner table with Carl and they had all been friendly and smiled at me, and the whole time they *must* have known that Carl was screwing Grace. But the mother was one of these Italian women who love the whole gangster scene, like *The Sopranos* or something. So this day when I called the house to talk to her another one of Rocco's sisters, Mela, answered the phone instead. She said to me, not really in a nasty way, that maybe I should have an abortion because if I was having these problems with Carl then maybe I shouldn't have a baby with him. She was just trying to get me out of the way for her sister and I was pissed off with her saying it because we had tried so hard to get pregnant with Dhakota.

With all of this going on I was really pissed off when I found out on Christmas Day that Carl was at Rocco's house. I was already angry that he had gone out and left me to clean all his shit up but to then find out he had gone off to see his little tart got me even more ropeable. So I drove over to their house in Albion Street, West Brunswick, in Tommy's Mercedes, ringing Carl's phone the whole time. He refused to answer.

When I got there I rang Vic's phone and told him I was

out the front and he came out and told me to drive around the back and swap the cars over. He said Carl was inside but he was more concerned to just tell me to take the car and go. I was saying to him, 'Where's Carl? What's going on in there?', but he didn't want to talk or give me an answer, he just said to drive around the back of the house and swap cars.

I went around the back and handed Tommy his car keys and was walking over to get into my car when Carl came out from inside the house. I saw him standing there with his gun in his hand, yelling at me to fuck off. Then he just lifted the gun and started shooting at me, firing off three or four shots — I can't remember exactly how many. Obviously none of them hit me or the car or — luckily — any of the neighbours or kids in the area who might have been out riding new bikes on Christmas Day. I don't know if he was trying to hit me but he was seriously angry with me and he wasn't mucking around. Obviously I had embarrassed him in front of his girlfriend and her family.

I remember feeling more horrified than scared. I just stood there staring at him in disbelief as he pointed his .38 at me and kept shooting. I mean, I was seven months pregnant so I couldn't run anywhere even if I'd wanted to. That shocked me the most, being seven months pregnant with his baby and he was shooting at me and his own unborn child. I suppose it was all about impressing Grace and her family: the big tough gangster pulling out his gun and shooting at anyone who embarrassed him. But to me all it showed was what a prick he was. And what a bad shot he was, because he missed four times.

Eventually he stopped shooting and I decided to get in the car and leave. I was a bit emotional and teary when I drove off. When I got to the front of the Aricos' house Grace's sister Mela was waiting and she walked up to the car to talk to me. I stopped and wound the window down and she poked her head in and said, 'They say you're a good fighter, well come on, get out and fight me.' I just looked at her in disbelief. If I was shocked already by Carl shooting at me then I was even more amazed that this dumb bitch would want to box on with me when I was heavily pregnant. I just thought, 'Are you serious?' In my head I thought I'll fight you all right, Mela, but not today, not on Christmas Day when I am seven months pregnant. It will be when I'm good and ready and on my terms. I don't forget shit like that so she'll get hers — she has a loud mouth and I'll shut it for her.

Anyway, after Carl shot at me I drove home and my brother Robert was still there with his girlfriend. I never used to like Robert when we were kids but then we sort of reconciled and we were close for a while before he later ripped us off over the house deal and building the units. When I got back home I told them where I had found Carl and Rob was ropeable. Robert was a loose cannon but he could really fight and he would have gone Carl if he had seen him that night. Carl can fight, but he would have come off second best that night and then things would have got out of hand, one thing would have led to another, and Carl would have shot him and I didn't want that so I talked Robert down a bit. I only told him where I had found Carl, I didn't mention anything about him shooting at me or Rob would have gone right off and that would have caused more dramas.

CHAPTER 13

LABOUR PAINS

I am probably my own worst enemy with men, because even though I was pissed off about it I still took Carl back. Not just over Grace but again soon after with the bitch he just refused to get rid of, Nicole Mottram.

I was sitting in the car one day waiting for Carl and Andy Krakouer while he went into his friend's office for something. I was sitting there bored when I noticed that Carl had left his phone in the car, so I picked it up and started reading the messages. I don't know what I was looking for but it didn't take me long to find what I didn't want to read: 'I love you Carl.' And it wasn't a message from me. Or his mum. It was some other bitch. I was gutted. I got out of the car and started yelling, 'You fucking dog, when you get out here I'm going to cut your fucking throat.' I was going crazy. His friend came out and tried to calm me down so I yelled at him, 'You shut your fucking mouth or

I'll give you one, too.' I was going ballistic, as you can imagine.

Carl and Andy eventually came out and got in the car and I drove off, but I was going crazy so I just stopped the car in the middle of the road and started attacking him. We were punching on in the middle of Lorimer Street, Port Melbourne. Carl was hitting me back. He always said that if somebody hits you, they deserve to be hit back, and I always thought that was fair enough. So we were going full on at each other in the street and these guys all came out of a factory and were watching us so I started yelling at them too. Andy got out of the car and calmed me down a bit and eventually we left. I was still so pissed off I kicked Carl out of the house and he went home to his mum. I was pregnant with Dhakota at the time and Carl texted me later on to say, 'Let's get over this, and get on with our life.'

I took him back after a while but I didn't let it go altogether. I had written down the phone number that was in Carl's phone and I found out who the bitch was. Her name was Nicole Mottram and her brother was a copper. It turns out her and Carl had been having an affair for years, a long time before I was even around. I started ringing her and abusing her and she got a restraining order issued against me.

I had no idea Carl was with her. Or at least I didn't want to believe Carl was still with her when I took him back. I just wanted my dream life back, I wanted Carl and I wanted my baby and I wanted us to be married and to have kids and make a family. So when he told me the affair was over I wanted to believe him, even if in my heart I never really did. But I was pregnant at the time and a bit emotional.

Dhakota was due on 28 February 2001, exactly the same day my son Tye had been due, but he ended up being premmie and she ended up being late. We set up her nursery and had everything made for it. It was a nice, safe, quiet place in the house where Carl and I would go every night. When the kids were asleep I'd sit in the rocking (feeding) chair and Carl would lie on the floor with his hands behind his head and we'd just talk about the baby and our plans for the future. We were convinced we were having a boy and we were going to call him Castor Troy from the name in the movie *Face Off* that we really liked. Then we thought we'd call him Castor Shane because of Carl's brother who'd passed away. We tried to think of a girl's name just in case it was a girl and I came up with Dhakota. We used to talk about it every night — Carl was over the moon about this kid.

We were booked in at the hospital to be induced on 10 March, so Carl and I went along at 7 am. They took me into the labour room and put the heart monitor on and it showed the contractions were really slow at first. Soon enough everyone started arriving at the hospital — heaps of family and friends turned up to be there for us, which was nice, but it became a fucking circus. There were people everywhere. One of Carl's friends came in during the labour and he kept leaving and coming back with different girls. First he came in with one girl, who massaged my feet, then he left to drop her off and arrived back with another one and she rubbed my back, then she left and the last one came in and she was rubbing my legs. They were all really nice and lovely, but it was funny — all these girlfriends.

They were all going to leave and go and have some dinner away from the hospital because not much was happening, but just as they were about to go the pain started to get worse and the contractions started full on, so Carl and I went back to the labour room for ages. I went and had a shower and Carl held me up when the pains got severe. Nearing the end of labour I wanted to go to the toilet, and Carl said, 'You can't, you'll have the baby in the toilet.' I was going, 'Carl, babies don't come out like that, mate.'

I don't make noise when I'm in labour — just breathing — and the lights were dim and it started to get tense. Carl left to have a break but then he was stressing more outside so he came back in. Then the nurse came in and examined me and said, 'Look, there's a few problems.' I have always had a lot of trouble in labour — they have to give me injections because my blood doesn't clot properly — and this nurse looked at us and said, 'Do you realise that your baby could die?' We didn't know any of this, and Carl just freaked out and yelled, 'Get the fucking doctor here, *now*.'

Carl wasn't that well known in Melbourne then, so they didn't look at him like, 'Oh my God this gangster is going off his head and is stressed about his baby,' they looked at him like he was a typical panicking father — which he was. Carl's mum had left the room at this point so my sister went out to grab her because Carl needed support. Here I was lying there in pain having contractions and being told my baby might die and my sister has to leave to get Carl's mum because Carl needs support! Carl was really freaking out — not aggressively, but he was panicking. The nurse told Carl the doctor was somewhere else and couldn't be there straight away and Carl nearly exploded at her, saying, 'Get him here — the midwife's not going to be much use — I want the doctor here for my baby, and I fucking want him here right now.'

I had to push and the doctor wasn't there at this stage and they were worried about me. We'd decided prior to going to hospital that we didn't want to know what sex the baby was — Carl would tell me when it was delivered. So it was getting right to the delivery moment and they told Carl to come down the other end and have a look and his eyes have just peeled back and his jaw has dropped and he's gone, 'Crikey ... fucking hell. Oh my God.' A couple of minutes before I had Dhakota Carl asked me, 'If it's a boy, can I call him Shane after my brother?' I said, 'Of course.' Shane and Carl were really close friends until Shane died of a heroin overdose.

Dhakota was born and Carl just looked at me with tears in his eyes saying, 'It's a girl. We have a little girl. I have a daughter.' Dhakota wasn't breathing. I was holding her, and saying: 'Carl, she's not breathing.' I couldn't pass the placenta immediately so they had to give me medication to do it, but in the middle of all this I was freaking and they weren't listening to me. I was screaming, 'She's not breathing,' but they picked her up from me and got her going and she was right.

She was born at 3.23 am. For some reason that number stuck in my head. After they bathed her, weighed her and dressed her, I had all the clothes ready for her and cloth nappies — I used cloth nappies on all my babies. I fed her, and she fed straight away.

I put a little cross on her and an 'eye' symbol to ward off the evil eye. We thought that because of the jealousy surrounding Carl's wealth, people might focus that jealousy on to Dhakota, so we had her blessed by the priest and then pinned the eye on her singlet until her christening, when it got put on a charm bracelet. But if the baby is not christened before they're one it stays on their singlet then on their clothes.

Carl's mum came in the room and she was holding her and rocking her. Because Carl hadn't had a lot to do with babies we didn't think he'd hold her until she was a few weeks old at least but he looked at his mum and said, 'Can I hold my daughter?' And we all started crying. I've got the first photo of him holding her, and he's crying his eyes out. I couldn't believe it. The nurse came in to check and said: 'Did she feed?' And Barb said, 'Does a duck like water?'

You know what it's like when you first have a baby — we were so excited, we couldn't sleep, so we rang everybody. They took us to our room, but I had so many flowers they had to move me to a bigger room, and Carl had to take the flowers home three times. It was like this room full of flowers. They came from everywhere, I couldn't believe it. I loved it at the time and thought how kind everyone was and how many friends we had, but looking back I think where are all these people now? Where are they?

We couldn't sleep because we were so excited and everyone was coming in with presents. Carl went shopping the next day, because he'd said, 'As soon as we have whatever it is and we know what sex it is, I'll go and buy everything.' One present he bought her was a red DKNY hat. Dhakota didn't know her dad bought her this hat and as she got older she would never wear hats but when she was about three and Carl was in prison she put this hat on one day and refused to take it off. She wore it to bed, to kinder, everywhere, even in the bath. Eventually about a year and a half later I said, 'No, not in the bath.' She only gave up wearing the hat recently and everyone was asking, 'This isn't Dhakota — where's the little girl with the red hat?'

Carl wanted her to have the best of everything. She had everything you could imagine. He loved this child like you wouldn't believe. When we got home, he'd have to watch her while I took the kids to school because I didn't want to put the baby in the car. Wogs don't usually take them out of the house for six weeks so Carl had to watch her. One morning he rang me frantically saying, 'The baby's crying.' He was ready to take her to his mum's, because he didn't know what to do and he was scared and panicking. I told him to relax and pick her up and pat her, and she calmed down.

Carl even changed her dirty nappies, which was something I never expected he would do. It didn't bother him. He just idolised this child. He used to hold her up — with her sitting in the palm of one hand and one time he said, 'Take a photo, I just can't believe how tiny her little bum is.' I've still got that photo.

Carl used to rub his nose on her face — he couldn't believe how soft her skin was. He's such a soft, gentle person. Unbeknown to me he was still fucking Nicole Mottram, though. I always kind of knew there was something going on with him and someone else. I suffered severe post-natal depression when I had Dhakota. I didn't know what it was at the time — I used to sit and cry really badly, and I felt something was going on with Carl which added to my emotions.

We had these dogs at the time Dhakota was born, they were Maltese cross shih-tzus called Milly and Mykee, and Carl loved those dogs. They had pups at the time I had Dhakota, so I was breastfeeding Dhakota and at the same time there was a problem with the dogs being able to feed. So every night after I fed Dhakota, Carl and I would sit up together bottle-feeding these four little pups. Unfortunately one of them didn't make it and later on when we ended up moving into an apartment block we had to get rid of them, because we couldn't have dogs in there.

When Dhakota was six weeks old, just before Carl was arrested, a whole heap of us — Carl, me, our kids, my sister Sharon, her daughter, Tommy, Dhakota's godfather, a few other people — all went to Yarrawonga. When we got to the motel it was late and I sort of half noticed as we arrived that there were these people throwing their things in a car and leaving. I didn't think anything of it at the time but Carl recently told me that Nicole had rung him and said, 'I'm at Yarrawonga and I can see Roberta standing out the front of the motel rocking a baby.' She was staying at the same motel and she had seen me. Carl hadn't even told her I was pregnant, so he had to say, 'I've got something to tell you — it's mine.'

Nicole left the motel and I suppose she and Carl had a few words about me having had a baby, but they still kept seeing one another. I suppose by that stage she knew she was the other woman and he was with me and she was happy for it to stay that way. I knew none of this at the time, though. I had no idea there were all these dramas going on for him in Yarrawonga, but maybe it helped fuel my suspicions because I was always worried something was happening.

One night I got a private detective to follow Carl. He rang me to say he was going to stay the night somewhere else for work or something and asked if I could get a toilet bag sorted and pack some clothes for him and he'd call in and get them. I did as he asked but I also rang this private detective and asked him to follow Carl, but the bloke reckoned he got there too late. He saw Carl drive off but he couldn't do a U-ey in time to follow him. But I think the police got to him and warned him off. I know they would have been listening in to our phone calls at that stage so they would have known what was happening and been able to intervene and warn this private detective off.

People don't understand that when Carl finally went to prison for the murders we weren't together anymore. I had broken up with him a long time earlier and I only went back to him to help him out because he needed me and because he was Dhakota's dad. I've seen comments in the *Herald Sun* from people and some woman wrote, 'Jeez, Roberta, Carl was in prison how long before you left him?' People don't know that I left him long before he went to prison.

For me, the emotional and physical ties were broken with Carl. I couldn't take the cheating. But like a lot of couples there were times when we got back together for a night or two, or even a little longer than that. But it was never the same, and never a full-on relationship again.

CHAPTER 14

HOME IS WHERE THE BULLETS ARE

Dhakota was only a few weeks old when I flaked out in bed upstairs one night after feeding her. Carl was still downstairs reading the racing guide. He'd been drinking and taking some coke and whatever but he suddenly came running up the stairs. 'Roberta, someone's shooting at the house,' he said as he burst into the room. He wasn't yelling or panicking, he just came in and said it like he wasn't sure.

I thought he was coked up and being a dick. 'You're off your fucking head, Carl,' I said, but I got up anyway and walked downstairs with him. We had big double doors with bulletproof glass panels in them at the bottom of the stairs. 'No-one's shooting at anyone,' I said and went back upstairs to bed.

A few minutes later Carl comes running upstairs again saying, 'Someone is fucking shooting at us, Roberta, I'm not shitting you.' Then I heard the gunshots and thought, 'Oh fuck, he's right.'

We had metal shutters on all the windows which were opened and closed electronically from the inside, and they were closed at the time so we were pretty safe inside the house. I suppose whoever was shooting at us was hoping that we would hear the shots and try to sneak out onto the upstairs balcony to see who it was or else come out the front door and they could shoot us. They were hiding behind the fence post and the huge gates at the front.

Sensing the plan was to lure him outside Carl stayed in and didn't even go near the door. It went quiet for quite a while and then they shot at the Mercedes Benz parked out the front of the house. I was shitting myself. I mean, sure we had shutters on the windows and bulletproof glass in the doors, but you don't know if that stuff is actually going to work and stop a bullet. And I wasn't going to risk it. I hid the baby in the big walk-in robes in our room because that was in the middle of the house and I thought it'd be the safest place for her. The other kids' bedrooms were at the end of the house so I got them out of bed and told them to crawl on their stomachs on the floor and I sat them in the robes against the wall. I thought if they started shooting at the windows, a bullet might ricochet and get one of them.

The kids didn't know what was going on. They didn't say anything. I'm sure they knew that something pretty serious was up because obviously we'd got them out of bed crawling across the floor to sit in a cupboard, and that didn't happen every day of the week. My first priority was to make sure the kids were safe so once I'd done that I went downstairs with Carl. And then the shooting just stopped. We still didn't go outside because we didn't know if they were still hiding and waiting for us like snipers or if they had left.

Believe it or not we settled down and were able to go to sleep. We got up in the morning and finally went outside because we figured they were not still going to be there to shoot at us in broad daylight when people can see and the jacks can come. When we got outside there were all these little holes in the door like buckshot or pellets had sprayed it. There was a shotgun shell outside and a plastic casing that had been full of little ball bearings. If it had hit someone, it would have done some damage but it was nothing like *Underbelly* made out. They had the house being all shot to pieces and bits of wood flying off everywhere, and the place looked like it was about to fall over. It wasn't like that at all, it was mainly just that the door had these little holes in it.

The jacks had heard us on the listening devices and turned up at our place the next day. They came up to the door and were nosing around and had these, like, half-smiles on their faces. 'Had a bit of a problem here last night?' one of them said. They saw the car had been shot and the front door had holes in it.

At that stage the jacks used to come around all the time to speak to Carl. We had a chair in the corner we used to call Stuart's chair because every time this copper, Stuart Bateson, walked in he'd just sit on this same fucking chair. I don't know why, but every time it was the same chair. At first it was this lady copper, Cindy Mullins, who came around but I felt like she realised there was corruption there among her colleagues or something and they were trying to fit Carl up for Mark Cole's murder, because for some reason she suddenly got moved to uniform in Geelong.

The police knew exactly what had happened the night before because they were listening in to everything we were doing at the time. They had our house and cars bugged and they had the Morans bugged. We found out later they overheard Jason Moran on their listening devices saying they were going to kill Carl at Dhakota's christening which was a month away. Andrew Veniamin was supposed to kill Carl there.

CHAPTER 15

ECSTASY

Like any parents of schoolkids, we had come to know some of the mums and dads of our kids' friends at school. Some of them you'd happily get thrown together with, others you wish you'd never met. Walter and Libby — parents of a friend of Breanane's — were in the latter category. They were just hopeless; they had nothing and were desperate. At the time they didn't even have enough money to buy nappies, so I was always giving them little bits of money here and there to help them get by. As with anyone in this sort of situation we were more than happy to do it, but when they pushed us to help them out for more, we should have known better than to get involved.

Walter and Libby wanted to deal some drugs to make a bit of money and Walter was trying to buy some gear. He had been mainly trading in cocaine with some guy, but when that bloke disappeared Walter was looking for a new supplier of pills. He had found these blokes who wanted to buy a fair bit of gear from him and he thought that if he could just supply them what they wanted he could turn a tidy profit and that'd help them get their head above water financially. The problem was, the buyers turned out to be undercover coppers.

This one particular night we were all supposed to be going out for dinner for my birthday when Walter rang on my mobile and Carl answered the phone. We didn't know it at the time but Walter's phone was 'off' (bugged by the police). So Walter was talking away to Carl about what time we were all supposed to meet for dinner that night and trivial stuff like that. They spoke for a long time and the police listening in to the phone call worked out — maybe because they traced the number Walter had rung — that it was Carl on the other end of the line. Obviously they thought, 'Hello, what's going on here? Carl must be the supplier.' The jacks just presumed the cocaine Walter had been getting had been coming from us even though it hadn't. We used to snort cocaine and I smoked a bit of hash when I was younger and took some speed, but we weren't dealing in cocaine.

After that phone call an undercover jack tried to set us all up by going to Walter and saying he wanted to buy 8,000 pills. Walter could never get his hands on that many pills so he came to us asking us to supply him with some. Carl was suss on it right from the start. He thought it was strange that the buyers didn't ask for a sample or anything, they just came in asking for 8,000 pills. We should have known to follow his instincts but it was me who talked Carl into it, telling him he was just being paranoid. Unbeknown to me by that stage all of our phones had been bugged — the house phone, the mobile, everything — so when Walter called one morning to see where Carl was because he was waiting for him to drop pills off to him or something, I answered the phone. I just said to him something like, 'Carl says it's all sorted.'

Carl picked up the pills for Walter and came home with them. He was still uncertain about it though, saying, 'I'm really suss on this — I don't reckon I should give him the pills.' Eventually he decided he would but he'd tell Walter to hold some back from the deal and just pass on half first, get the money, make sure the deal went OK, then do the second half later. Carl kept saying, 'I don't trust him. I reckon it's the jacks,' but I kept saying just do it. I suppose I was thinking that we wouldn't get burned because it was Walter who was dealing with these blokes, not us, and as long as Walter didn't give us up as his supplier then we'd be OK. I figured it was up to Walter to judge whether the blokes were legit or not because, after all, he was the one who had met them, not us. It was stupid, it was just pure greed on my behalf, and it cost us big time.

Walter finally picked the pills up and we were waiting on collecting the cash from him. I think it was $100,000, which was 10,000 pills at $10 each. It was the day before Dhakota was to be christened. We had booked out the Lakeside Reception Centre where we had had our wedding and it was going to be a really good party. Everyone was running around getting organised and I was planning to go and buy her a little porcelain doll or something as a special gift. But I was a bit worried about this money sitting around at Walter's house, so I decided it would be better if I collected it. The undercover jacks had given him the money in a shoebox and I just grabbed the money out of the box, put it in a plastic bag, shoved it in my pocket and walked out.

I went home to pick up Bree to take her to Watergardens shopping centre to get her nails done. Carl rang me when I was there and agreed to meet us there because he had to put the Tattslotto in. (We might have been making a little bit of money from dealing, but everyone wants to win Tatts, right?) The jacks were listening in and they presumed Carl was coming to get the money. Carl and I met up at the shopping centre and although we didn't know it, the undercover jacks were following us the whole time we walked around looking at things with money in a backpack I was carrying.

We went outside to the car so that Carl could take the money out of the backpack. When I looked up I could see Carl had all these red targets all over him. I automatically thought, 'He's off, here.' I didn't know who had the targets on him because I didn't hear anyone yell out 'police' and I couldn't see the word police on anyone. All I saw was these men hanging out of an unmarked van pointing guns at us. I thought the Morans had decided to get us and Carl would be dead so I was freaking out. I didn't even think it might be the jacks. I realised it pretty quickly, though, because within seconds they had ripped us out of the car, thrown us on the ground and put plastic strap handcuffs on us.

They put us in different police cars and drove us off in different directions. One of the drug squad coppers, Detective Sergeant Wayne Strawhorn, who was corrupt and was jailed, took Carl to a football oval and another lot of coppers took me to the train station. They took Breanane from the shopping centre and drove her to the oval as well. I don't know why they did that. Strawhorn said to Carl, 'I'm going to shoot you and leave you in that container over there.' Carl just said, 'If you were going to do it you would have done it so do what you fuckin' like, you goose.'

Meanwhile I was at the train station and they were trying to strip-search me in the car. I was saying, 'Get fucked, I had a baby six weeks ago, no-one is strip-searching me. You want to search me take me to the fucking jack shop, not in the back seat of a fucking car at the fucking train station, you dickheads.' The next thing I was being taken to Keilor Downs police station and I saw Breanane and someone else in a ute going in the other direction. That made me go ballistic because I was thinking if they tried to strip-search me at a train station, what were the police going to do with my little daughter in an unmarked ute?

In the meantime one of the jacks took pills from Walter's house and planted them in our cupboard at home so as to maintain a connection between the pills and the money. Unfortunately other jacks had already been to our house and taken photos in which there were no pills. We were pinched anyway and it didn't make any real difference to the case against us, we knew that then and I don't dispute it now, but the fact was these pills weren't in photos taken at our house and then they were, so someone other than us put them there while the coppers were there.

Dhakota was brought in to see me at the Altona North police station where they had eventually taken me, and the coppers kept saying, 'You'd better kiss her goodbye now, because this is the last time you're going to see her.' I was freaking out — I'd never been pinched for anything as serious as this before. The jacks asked where the pills came from and they were playing games with me so I thought I'd play games with them too. I said, 'Paul Sequenzia gave them to us.' I knew that when Mark Cole was alive he and Paul Sequenzia had been working with these dirty jacks so I was just saying it to be smart and let them know I knew they were in with the Morans.

'Don't be too cocky, Roberta. You're being a smartarse,' they said to me.

'Fuck you,' I said. 'Go ask Jason [Moran] where they came from.'

They took Carl back to our place and searched the house and while they were there someone stole my gold necklace from the bedside table. Carl got locked up and they took me to the cells at Melton police station. I was still breastfeeding Dhakota so they brought in a breast pump for me but I couldn't eat and I couldn't express any milk so I was freaking out.

Carl and I were both locked up and there was no way we were getting out for the christening, which only added to my stress. We didn't even get a chance to let people know what had happened and that we had put the christening off. We were told later that people still turned up at the reception centre expecting it to be on.

The police told us later that they'd overheard a conversation in the Morans' house that there was a plot for somebody to kill Carl at the christening. They had planned to kill Carl at our wedding and didn't go through with it, probably because of the security they found when they went in to check the place out. But because they had looked through the place at the wedding they would have known the set-up already so it would have been an easy thing to do a run through the christening and knock Carl. Andrew 'Benji' Veniamin was known around Melbourne as the guy you'd use to knock someone. He was apparently one of the people that was supposed to run through. Well not apparently, he *was* one of the people that was supposed to run through because he told us about it later on.

I suppose you could argue that the jacks did us a favour by arresting us because Carl would probably have been murdered at the christening if we weren't in jail. I probably would have been shot as well because I would have been right next to Carl, and Dhakota probably would have been killed too because Andrew had been told it didn't matter if Carl was holding his daughter, he should still put him off. We didn't know any of this at the time. I was just stressing about not being with Dhakota because I was breastfeeding her and she wasn't with me. Sharon went to court and got an order that she be allowed to bring Dhakota in to me every three hours for feeding.

I spent two nights in the cells and was taken to Melbourne Magistrates Court. While I was in the cells this Aboriginal girl was also in there and she came up to check out my tracksuit. 'Ooh,' she said to me, 'nice tracksuit and runners.' She was obviously trying to be a stand-over bitch — I had seen her type in prison before and I wasn't taking any of her shit.

Before she could do anything I had her against the wall by the throat and said, 'Get the fuck away from me before I fucking choke you to death, you fucking whore.' I was ropeable. I was stressing out over the baby and I didn't need some little fuckwit thinking they could stand over me. I had had enough and I wasn't going to tolerate some street kid trying to heavy me. She shit herself and backed off but I'd have smashed her head in there and then if she'd tried anything.

Eventually I got upstairs to court and was given bail and allowed to go home. Carl was still remanded so I was stressing out badly about what was going to happen next. I didn't have to wait long to find out because first thing the next morning the jacks turned up again with a warrant and they took all of our furniture and stuff. Suddenly we had nothing.

I wouldn't have been able to get in to visit Carl under normal circumstances. They'd have stopped me had I tried to get in under my own name — Carl and I had been married a few weeks earlier so my name was Williams now.

I couldn't have used my maiden name either because I had a criminal record under that one and they'd have tracked it straight away. But I had an old ID under another name from years earlier. A judge had recommended I get ID in my mother's maiden name when I took out a restraining order against Dean for bashing me. So I had changed my name by deed poll and I still had an ID from this period that I was able to use when I visited Carl during the fourteen months he was in prison.

Sometimes I think that being arrested like that was a way of God saying that Dhakota would never be with her dad. From six weeks old until she was sixteen months old Carl was in jail, so she never knew him, never bonded with him. For a couple of months he was in and out of jail, then he went to jail for murder when she was three.

CHAPTER 16

FAMILY FEUD

If everything changed for Carl after he got shot, it all changed for everyone else after Mark Cole was murdered. Mark had said to me that it was a matter of who got who first and, well, Mark was gone now but after that it was clear to everyone that it was all-out war — kill or be killed. Whether Carl did the murder or not didn't really matter at the time. All that mattered was that Jason thought he was behind it and wanted to kill Carl. And Carl knew it. Carl therefore also knew he had to kill Jason first. Even if, as I reckon, Carl didn't shoot Mark, I know he probably had something to do with it in some way, or knew who did it. At the least he probably knew someone was going to do it.

With Mark dead Jason wanted revenge, but he also knew he was isolated. The jacks apparently told him he was a target and that Carl would try to get him. They said he should get out of town before he ended up like Mark.

Obviously they also knew that Jason was intent on getting even for Mark because he had carried on at the funeral saying he would never forget and that he would get revenge. And he put a death notice in the paper that said: 'This is only the beginning, it will never be the end. REMEMBER, I WILL NEVER FORGET.'

Even though the Morans all probably wanted revenge like Jason did, they also knew Jason was a target and thought, like the jacks did, that he should get out of town because when he got out of jail on 5 September 2001, he immediately got on a plane and pissed off overseas. Jason would never have done that if it was just the jacks telling him he should go, he'd only ever have gone if his family was pushing him and telling him it was the best thing for him.

Jason went straight to London, even though at that stage Carl was in jail and couldn't have killed him even if he wanted to. Or at least he couldn't have pulled the trigger. Carl had been on remand since May on the drug trafficking charges over the 8,000 ecstasy pills. Jason was at least smart enough to know that Carl being in jail wouldn't necessarily make things any safer for him because being locked up in jail would be the perfect alibi for Carl if Jason was murdered. If I was Jason I'd have gone overseas too. Carl didn't kill Mark Cole, but he did want to kill Jason.

Jason was overseas for a while but unfortunately for him he soon ran into an old acquaintance from home, Snalfy. Well, Jason obviously shit himself when they saw one another, because he knew that Snalfy would probably tell Carl. Or even if he didn't tell Carl he might mention it to someone else who might then tell Carl. If I was Jason I would have been thinking, 'Fuck, if they know where I am they can come and get me here easier than in Australia where I know people to protect me and support me.' He came back to Australia.

And what did he do next? He put his kids in the school where my kids went. So if you think about it, everything Jason said he was doing was all bullshit. He reckoned he was so scared for his life that he had to leave the country, but when he is seen overseas he comes back and puts his kids in the same school as mine. That isn't exactly the behaviour of someone who's living in fear of Carl.

What it meant, though, was that every day I was faced with Jason Moran's ugly face and stinking breath. Every time my kids saw his car at the school, they'd refuse to get out of the car. They would freeze in the back seat and cry and I couldn't get them out until Jason had driven off. They didn't know all the background of what went on between our families but they had been with me when Jason mouthed off at me and it scared them. Jason used to come up to me in the street and say, 'Get your fucking kids out of school, you fucking whore.' And we were the ones whose kids were in the school before he came along.

At this stage Carl was out on bail and this pissed him off so he rang Jason to warn him off. 'Keep it up and I'll get Roberta to kick the fuck out of your wife Trisha,' Carl said to him. That got Jason really shitty. 'If she fucking touches my wife, I'll be down there to fucking cave her head in, OK?' he said back to Carl. But he was all talk.

I didn't plan to kick the shit out of Trisha Moran, because I knew it would just bring a shitload of trouble down on us, but in the end I couldn't help myself and I snapped. It happened one day when I was dropping the kids off at school. I was still wearing my pyjamas because I had Dhakota in the car and I didn't think I would have to get out. It was all going to plan when I saw Trisha dropping her kids off. She looked across at me and she just started in mouthing off at me from across the street. 'You fucking scumbag whore,' she screamed at me, and other dumb stuff like that.

'What did you say?' I yelled back. Which is a bit stupid because the whole fucking neighbourhood could hear what she'd said. But it was just one of those things you say in those situations when you are, like, daring the other person to repeat what they said.

'You fucking scumbag,' she yelled back again.

I just thought, 'I can't just jack this shit anymore.' Not in front of everyone, not in front of my kids and all the other mums. I'm not going to have her talking down to me again and abusing me and treating me like shit, like I should be the one to go scurrying away and hide like some rat too scared to stand up to those stupid people. They'd always talked down to me and treated me like I was some trashy street kid that they were better than and I couldn't take it anymore. I didn't want to take it.

I hated the fact that it was all happening at school because it looks shit to happen in front of the kids and all, but then again it was the fact that she was abusing me in front of the school that got me really angry, because I thought they are talking down our family in front of all these other people, all of the kids' friends. And I probably thought in the back of my mind, if the other kids see me getting pushed around and talked down to like that by that dirty skank then maybe they'd talk down to my daughters and push them around as well. And that just got me furious. So I had all these thoughts swirling around in my head and I wasn't thinking clearly about what was going on. I forgot that Dhakota was in the back of the car when I pulled up in the middle of the road and got out. I also forgot I was in my pyjamas but right then I didn't give a shit.

I got out of the car and charged over to front her. She shit herself and whacked me in the face with an umbrella. It didn't hurt but if I wasn't going to hit her before I was now so I attacked her and I smashed her head in. I had been put down by the Morans my whole life and I'd had a fucking gutful of their shit and I suppose it all came spilling out that day. She pushed me to my limit so I punched her head in there in the street. And it wasn't like she wasn't fighting back or anything. I know that sounds really bad to be beating up another mum in the street outside your kids' school like that, but I just snapped. She wasn't badly hurt or anything, she only had a black eye or two and some cuts and bruises, because she just lay down on the ground like a dog. I turned around and hopped back in my car and drove off. Fuck her. Fuck the Morans.

When I got back in the car Dhakota was hysterical — it's not every day a baby watches her mum get in a fistfight with another woman in the street. I might have been in pyjamas but it was no pillow fight. I tried to calm her down but then I started to get more concerned that while I was laying into Trisha someone might have rung Jason to tell him what was going on and he might turn up any minute and then I would be in deep shit. So I took off and the whole drive home I was looking over my shoulder thinking, 'He's going to pop up from somewhere.' I rang a contact who I'll call Mr Y, because I wanted him to be out the front of the house when I got there. I wanted protection and he was *the* guy in Melbourne. I knew that he would have a gun and would be able to defend me if I turned up and Jason was already there or if Jason turned up after me. I knew Carl probably didn't have a gun at that time and I knew Mr Y would come armed. If I had to get out of the car with my daughter he would be there armed to do whatever he had to. When I told him what had happened he said without hesitating, 'I'll meet you at your place. Ring Carl.'

Mr Y was thinking the same thing I was — that Jason was going to snap and that this could spark the full OK Corral shootout. I was shitting myself thinking, 'What the fuck have I done?' Carl was at home waiting for me when I got there and we were all thinking the same thing. Jason had already warned us that if I touched Trisha he would be around to fix me up. Well I had touched Trisha, I had beaten her like a dog, so now where was Jason? We all sat there and wondered what the fuck was going to happen next. But then it just went quiet. Nothing happened. Carl couldn't work it out. He walked around the house trying to look out the windows. 'If they did that to you I'd be at their house, I'd be waiting at the school for them. They wouldn't get away with it,' he said. But nothing happened.

Hours passed and we saw and heard nothing from the Morans. The next morning Carl and Mr Y came with me when I dropped the girls off at school, because we thought there might be dramas. They were both armed, of course, but there was no sign of Jason or Trisha. A full week passed before I finally saw him. I nearly shit myself. He saw me too and of course he chased me. He drove over to my car and he was mouthing off through the window telling me to pull over. I was thinking, 'Why would I do that? I know you're going to bash me if I do, I'm not stupid you idiot.' I stopped in front of some shops where I thought he was less likely to pull a gun because of all the people around, and he came charging up to the car. I wound the window down the tiniest bit.

'Tell Carl there's not a problem. I don't want this drama, I just want to get on with my life,' he said through the window at me.

'Whatever, we only want peace too. So tell that scrag of a wife of yours to stop mouthing off at me when I'm dropping my kids off at school,' I said back.

When I got home I told Carl what Jason had said to me. He laughed. 'What a fucking liar,' he said. We all knew Jason was full of shit and all his talk about wanting peace was just talk. He didn't mean it. He was going to get Carl any way he could.

A week later we had our proof when Carl and Mr Y pulled up at Red Rooster in Gladstone Park. They saw

Jason and started to follow him, even though at the time they only had a screwdriver on them as a weapon. They figured that if they caught him they'd just bash his head in. Jason saw them, took off in his car and raced around the streets. He popped the hatchback of his car up and started shooting at them through the hatchback like he was some big James Bond hero. I think he had seen too many movies.

Carl and Jason obviously hated each other's guts by now. There were a whole bunch of reasons why Carl took off after Jason to bash him even though he only had a screwdriver on him. Until he saw him that day in Red Rooster Carl hadn't laid eyes on Jason since the day Jason shot him. He also knew that I had kicked the shit out of Trisha and Jason might have wanted revenge for that so Carl was going to get in first. And he knew Mark and Jason had lagged to the jacks about the pill press and that he'd been caught in the flat with the drugs, so he wanted to get him for that. Then of course there was the outstanding million dollars. Mark Cole might have been dead but it was the family business and Jason could still pay up.

Jason got away that day, but he would not always be that lucky. There would always come a time when he would let his guard down.

CHAPTER 17

JASON

When I look back on it now a lot of things Carl was doing at the time leading up to Jason Moran's death make more sense to me. As everyone in Australia probably knows, Jason was murdered on 21 June 2003, while he was sitting in his car watching his kid play Auskick football. Before it happened there were a lot of meetings between Carl, Mr Y and Mr Z. The three of them would go for drives and have lots of talks but never in the vicinity of my house because of police listening devices.

Naturally I knew they were cooking something up because I could feel they were into something but at the time I wouldn't have asked questions and no-one ever volunteered information or talked about what was going on. When people are in the drug trade they behave like that anyway. It doesn't make you think they are going to kill someone, so I figured it was some sort of drug deal they were trying to work out.

Carl wasn't one to sit there and big-note or brag anyway. Since then I've read other people's statements about Carl and listening device transcripts where they say 'Carl used to sit there and have a few drinks and talk about these things,' but that was bullshit. Carl wasn't one to sit and talk about what they were going to do because firstly he wasn't the type to do that and secondly he knew, or thought, our place was 'off' [meaning there were police listening devices in the house]. Carl would always keep to himself what he planned to do and only ever discussed it with the people who were going to do it. He would never talk in the house or anywhere where there might be a listening device, so they would go on these drives to find somewhere to talk. And as it turns out they drove to the Cross Keys Reserve so Mr Y and Driver could check their entry and exit routes, and they'd talk about when and where it would happen.

The day Jason was killed Carl was booked in for a blood test along with Snalfy. Obviously that was to be their alibi for when the jacks came around after Jason was done. Carl knew that as soon as Jason was murdered the jacks would be at his door wanting to know where he was, so that was going to be their alibi. I didn't know what they were up to. I was just doing the same thing the Morans were doing that day, being a taxi for my kids to get to their sport. I had taken the girls to netball.

The first I knew of Jason being killed was when I got a phone call from a guy called Travis, who was in prison at the time. He said Jason and another guy had been killed at the Cross Keys. Well, I didn't even know what the Cross

Keys was. Travis thought the other guy was Tuppence, Jason's uncle — Lewis Moran's brother. It turned out that it was Pat Barbaro, not Tuppence. Tuppence was murdered years later and his lovely ex-sister-in-law Judy was charged over it.

Carl came home a few hours after Jason Moran was killed. A close friend called in to our house before Carl got home, because I had his girlfriend's daughter from netball. I talked to him about what had happened. He didn't say a lot about it but I remember saying, 'Who gives a fuck he's dead? It's one less arsehole in the world.' You know — yippee.

The media rang me and I said to one of them, 'We'll be partying tonight.' That might have seemed heartless to some people, but that was how we felt. He wanted to kill us and he was killed before he got the chance, so yeah, there was something to celebrate and we did party that night. We went to the Flower Drum for dinner, and it was a huge night. The boys were toasting Jason and clinking glasses and drinking. Everyone hated his guts so we were celebrating big time, doing coke and drinking and whatever. It was a huge night. Huge. Nothing was spared that night and everyone had fun.

We saw Judy Moran plastered on the TV news and we thought it was laughable. I don't care what anyone thinks of that — we were laughing at her because she was such a hypocrite. She didn't give a shit when her boys shot Carl. I thought she was full of shit when she was playing the innocent grieving mother. Sure she was upset her boy had died, but she was no innocent.

I remember thinking at the time that Andrew Veniamin seemed quieter than normal — in fact he seemed to be in absolute shock that Jason had been knocked. Originally Carl had wanted Andrew to set Jason up, luring him someplace that Carl or someone he hired could ambush him. The reason he chose Andrew was that he was still associating with the Carlton Crew and was still friends with the Morans at the time, so he was sort of playing both sides of the fence. Andrew was a friend of Mick Gatto's so Jason would trust him and go wherever Andrew said to go. Andrew had agreed to do it a few times but each time it never worked out and Andrew would always have an excuse. Now I realise Andrew was going back and warning Jason off. That was why Carl cut Andrew out and went off and did something else with Mr Y.

Obviously Carl never told Andrew anything about his change of plans, probably because he suspected Andrew would tip Jason off but also because he only wanted to tell people who needed to know, so Andrew knew nothing until after Jason was killed. Given Andrew's reaction on the night it happened, the penny dropped for me that Carl had burned Andrew's bridges with the Morans and Andrew knew it. The Carlton Crew accused Andrew of being with Carl prior to Graham's Kinniburgh's death. Whether he liked it or not, he realised now that he was tied to us, because Mick Gatto would think he might have knocked Jason himself, or at least knew about the plan to do it, and he did nothing to warn them. Andrew's days of playing both sides were over and he knew it.

At the time I didn't know for sure that Carl had organised it, but I would have been very fucking surprised if someone had knocked Jason and Carl didn't know about it. I mean, I would have been stupid to think that Carl hadn't had something to do with Jason's murder, but he had been getting a blood test done that morning so I knew he hadn't done it himself.

Despite what *Underbelly* tried to make out, I wasn't the one pushing Carl to kill Jason. That was bullshit. Carl knew without me telling him that Jason wanted to kill him and that if he didn't get in first it would have been Carl's funeral next. But the day before Jason was killed the police said there was a phone call from Mr Y to my mobile phone from the public phone box near the Cross Keys where Jason was shot. Mr Y had rung Carl's phone and couldn't raise him so he rang my phone and the jacks tried to say that that proved I knew about the plan to kill Jason and that I was in on organising it. It was bullshit. Mr Y rang my phone because he couldn't get Carl on his and when I answered I handed it over to Carl and that was that. I didn't know they were going to kill Jason.

Having said that, I was not surprised Carl did it and I am not embarrassed or shy about saying that I was happy Jason was killed. I hated his guts and I hope he burns in hell for what he did to us — what he did to Carl. But that doesn't mean I was happy about how it happened. The really sad bit was that Pat Barbaro, who was sitting next to Jason at the time, was also shot and killed. Pat was a lovely bloke who'd been a drug runner for them for years, taking drugs from Melbourne to Perth. Pat got pinched for drugs over in Perth once and the Morans just left him there and didn't give a fuck about him. They didn't organise a lawyer or do anything. Poor Pat got out of prison and came back to Melbourne to the only thing he could do and the only people he knew. He offered the Morans loyalty and he got killed because of them. That was terribly sad.

It was also horrible where it all happened. To do it at an Auskick clinic, for God's sake! Whatever the media reports say, I don't believe the children were in the van, they were out playing on the field and that's why Jason was still sitting there watching, but it is horrible that it happened there with the kids around. I saw the crime scene photos of him slumped over in the van with half his face blown off and it made me think, why didn't they just follow him home or wherever he was going and get him later? It would have been less risky and it would not have outraged people the way it did. Everyone agrees that it was out of line to shoot them in front of little kids.

Having said that, Jason and Mark always used to carry on in front of their kids and didn't care what their kids saw or heard. When Mark threatened my life and Carl's life at school one morning when I was dropping the girls off, his own daughter was standing right there next to him and he didn't give a fuck about her listening to him threaten my life. Obviously Mark's children were used to his violence and madness. I know Jason used to give his nephew a little .38 to hang on to and run around the house with, so even though I thought it was terrible that these kids had to see people killed in front of them, I think the Morans had never hidden violence from them in the past. To me it looked like the kids were used to the madness.

The whole saga makes me angry. When I look back at everything now, I wonder if things could have been resolved differently, but then I remember the night our house was shot at and our car was shot and I think it was always going to end that way, if it was going to end. One of us was always going to be shot, and frankly I was glad Carl got in first.

After Jason was killed Carl knew that Lewis Moran and the Carlton Crew would be after him and that our house wasn't safe so he moved into a new apartment building in the city, but he left me and the kids in the house. He didn't give a fuck about whether we were safe, he just organised an apartment for himself and sent us back to the house. I was too scared to go back there after Jason's murder so I started to plan to sell the house, meanwhile renting a place in Essendon.

Eventually I moved into the same apartment building as Carl but I moved into a flat on the 19th floor and Carl and Andrew Veniamin stayed up on the 30th floor. Carl said it was safer for him not to stay in the same place as the kids and there wasn't enough room for us all in the one apartment. We were broken up by then but we were still seeing each other all the time because of the kids.

Before I moved into the apartment Carl got arrested on some bullshit charge that he had threatened to kill jack Stuart Bateson and his girlfriend. Bateson was one of the main coppers investigating us and the one that used to wind

Carl and I up more than any of the others. But to say Carl had threatened to kill him and his girlfriend was a load of shit. Carl called me one night and he was drunk and blabbering on with his bullshit and I was just going along with him, saying, 'Yeah, yeah.' I knew the phone call was tapped and I was embarrassed because he was being stupid, going, 'Where are you? Who's in my bed?' He knew Dhakota slept next to me, so he was just being a total fucking moron. The next thing, he goes, 'If Bateson or anyone else comes to the house, you know what to do, don't you?' I was just going, 'Yeah, yeah' — it was like 3 am or something. He said, 'Just grab the gun from under the mattress and shoot him in the head.' So I hung up on him.

I don't know whether it was before or after that that Mr Y rang from jail. He was locked up for Michael Marshall's murder. Carl got on the phone to him and they started talking about Bateson — they used to call him 'toilet basin', because it was rhyming slang, like 'peppermint patty' is a fatty and 'Mickey Mouse' is grouse. So they start talking about Bateson's girlfriend and they say, 'Oh yeah, I'd like to whack her up,' which basically means they wanted to fuck her.

We hated Bateson, because right from the word go he'd come to our house and try to push us around. He used to walk into our house like he owned it. He was a cocky smartarse from the start and we really hated him because no-one pushed us as hard as he did. He had a job to do, and that's all good and well, but I thought he went beyond what he should have done as a serving police officer. They weren't all like that in Purana, just him and Michelle Curley. She interviewed me early on and tried to suck me into hating Carl by telling me about all these girls Carl was supposed to be having affairs with.

We tried to give each other shit about Bateson all the time. I used to tease Carl and say, 'Stuart Bateson's so sexy, he's so good looking.' Carl would say, 'Don't even fucking say that.' So in this phone call with Mr Y Carl was putting shit on Bateson and saying he wanted to whack up his girlfriend but the Purana task force detectives reckoned he said 'chop her up' not 'whack her up'. When the phone intercept was played in court you could clearly hear it wasn't 'chop her up', and after the judge heard that she gave him bail. At that stage the jacks just wanted any excuse they could find to pick Carl up, so that is what they did. They arrested him in Beaconsfield Parade, St Kilda, and put him in jail for talking crap on a wire and the dumb shit coppers took it seriously.

Dhakota's christening was on the Sunday after the bail hearing so Andrew was sitting next to me in court with his arm around me, supporting and comforting me, because he knew I was stressed about Carl getting bail in time for the christening. I had Dhakota in court and I was holding her bib in my hand squeezing it and praying that he would get bail. When the judge heard the tape and gave him bail straight away, I sobbed so loudly I had to put Dhakota's bib across my mouth.

We left court that day and the journalists were in our faces trying to get us to talk. Andrew was saying to me, 'If you fucking say one word to them, I'm going to kick the shit out of you — I'm going to smash your head in.' That's why in all those photos of us that were in the papers I'm looking the other way, not showing any expression, because he was going to strangle me.

So Carl was out of jail for our little girl's christening. Some people might think it hypocritical that we were so keen to have our daughter christened when Carl was a drug dealer and was allegedly involved in some murders and I had convictions of my own. But all I can say is that our beautiful little girl Dhakota had not done any of those things and we wanted all the right things for her. We also wanted to have the biggest party of all time to celebrate her christening. Really it was to celebrate the fact that we had her. I had been through so much, having to have operations so that I was able to have kids and then the difficult labour, that we wanted to have a big party to celebrate Dhakota's birth. Carl was so proud, he just wanted to show her off.

The christening was held in the Palladium Room at Crown Casino and we had 150 to 200 guests. I think it cost about $200,000, although I'm not sure of the final figure. I know it was a lot of money because we had Vanessa Amorosi sing there, which cost $20,000 on its own. She did a whole concert, every song, and of course we got to meet her and have photos with her. I had Brian Cadd come down from Queensland to sing 'Little Ray of Sunshine' and we had to pay for flights for him and his band and we put them all up at Crown. There was every food you could imagine

— lobster, prawns, everything — and all the best wines and drinks.

Dhakota's cake was four tiers high and she was wearing the most beautiful christening gown that we'd had made. It cost $4,000 and my outfit, which was made by this top designer as well, cost like $7,000. We had everything, including a balloon machine. Dhakota was mesmerised by bubbles so we had this electronic machine that made huge balloons with little bubbles inside so the whole room was filled with bubbles and balloons. The comedian Marty Fields did his act, and there was heaps of other entertainment. It was just the best night.

It was worth it for all the trouble I went through to have her. She was a miracle child to me and I just wanted no expense spared for her. At the time we were lucky we had the money to be able to do that.

CHAPTER 18

ANDREW

I know it sounds bad, but I didn't really pay much attention when a lot of the people were killed. The truth is I didn't know a lot of them any more than anyone else in Melbourne did, so why should I get upset about them? To me they were just people you read about too. People like Michael Marshall or Willy Thompson, I didn't know them, they were just names. Some of them I had heard about in different circles but I didn't *know* them.

Because of that it was a shock to me when I heard in court all the stuff that Carl and his friends and associates had done. I had no idea about most of it. I know people might think, 'Bullshit, you're just saying that now to make yourself look good,' but honestly, a lot of the shit they did I had no idea about. They weren't, like, coming home and telling me, 'Oh we knocked this bloke or that bloke.' I knew there was a lot of drug dealing going on, obviously, and I knew Carl wanted to kill Jason and that they did that, but they weren't coming home and talking about it.

I met many people through Carl and some of them were the most beautiful people you could ever meet — like Andrew Veniamin — and others, like Mr Y and Mr Z, you wouldn't spit on. I had known Mr Y for a long time through Carl but even before he decided to give evidence against Carl I hated his guts. What he did in the end just showed that all along he was a dog who never cared about anyone other than himself.

I didn't hate Mr Y because he gave evidence against Carl — though that didn't help — no, I hated him because he was rude to my daughter. Tye even had a go at him once because of the names he called Danielle. He went out with my sister and he treated her like shit and I hated him for that too. So he disrespected my kids and my sister — why would I like him?

He used to come to our house and I warned Carl there was something about him I didn't like and he shouldn't trust him. 'You just don't like me having friends,' Carl would say. It wasn't that, because I didn't think they were friends anyway. I thought Mr Y and others like him were scum that were clinging on to Carl to suck what they could out of him. Carl should have known it was not personal, it was business. They weren't his friends, they were his drug-dealing associates or his employees or whatever you want to call them.

I put Mr Z in the same category. I hated his guts too. I always thought he was a creep because he used to lurk around and you never knew what he was doing. Maybe it was a female thing that I could pick the creeps, but he'd always look at me funny and make me feel weird. And this was before I found out he was a convicted rapist and before he gave evidence against Carl. This one time — and you could say it was all in my head but I know what I felt — I was pregnant with Dhakota and I was in the shower and I just knew someone was watching me. I could feel someone's eyes on me. You know how sometimes you have an instinct that you are being watched, well someone was definitely watching me while I was in the shower. I didn't see him looking at me, but I felt it was him. When I came out of the shower he was in the lounge room. You might think that sounds like shit, but he was that kind of guy. He was a creep.

I had been introduced to Andrew Veniamin years earlier but I didn't really meet him properly until one day when I was at the shops with Carl and Snalfy, and Andrew came up to talk. I was swinging Dhakota by the arms, playing with her, and Andrew later told me that he wanted to whack me because he thought I was going to pull her arms out of their sockets. I knew what I was doing, though; I'm her mum, and I was just playing with her. She was laughing and loving it so I don't think she was getting hurt but Andrew got really upset about it apparently, though he never said anything at the time. I just said hello that day and not much else because his friend Faruk was there and I hated his guts from the moment I saw him. I don't know why, I just hated him.

Andrew used to come to our house but he would never drink or eat anything. I don't know why. In an accident some time before Carl and Andrew became friends, Andrew had gone through the windscreen of a car. From that he suffered terrible migraines so he'd chew Panadeine Forte tablets all day. When he came to our house he'd drink water from the tap across the road. I have no idea why he wouldn't come inside and drink from a glass but that was what he did. He and Carl used to walk around talking and Andrew would get on the ground and guzzle water from the tap and swallow his pills.

Andrew and I became really close. I know everyone thinks we had an affair — the jacks think we did, I think Carl thinks we did and *Underbelly* made out we did — but I can honestly say we didn't. There is no reason for me to bullshit about it. In the end Carl and I got divorced and he was rooting around on me the whole time we were married, and is in jail now anyway. Andrew is dead and I am with someone else now, so I have no reason to lie about it. All I can tell you is the truth and the truth is, nothing ever happened. He was like a brother, not a lover. I wish I had had sex with him, then I could have rubbed Carl's nose in it for all the affairs he had behind my back when we were together. But I never did. Pity, it would have been worth it for that reason alone.

Carl would have hated it more than anything if he found out I had had an affair with Andrew, and he always thought there was something wrong about us being so close. I suppose anyone would get jealous if their wife or husband had such a close friend of the opposite sex, but we were just friends. We got on really well and we used to muck around together. He was grouse with the kids and was really close to my daughter Danielle — he used to take her everywhere with him.

Once Carl got arrested Andrew stayed with me and his friend used to come over and stay the night to check that I was alright. That was probably what got Carl thinking that something might be going on. Carl and Andrew were really good friends so I think in his heart he knew nothing would happen, but then Carl doubts everything.

Andrew would do anything for you, but he was also a big practical joker. I met a lot of weird people during this time. One of them was Greg Domaszewicz, the bloke who was the babysitter charged with murdering the toddler Jaidyn Leskie in Moe and got off. It turned out that Greg's cousin lived next door to the house we had in Hillside and he used to go there all the time. Andrew liked him and would talk to him a bit and he seemed alright to me even though I thought he was an idiot. He was really stupid but he seemed harmless. Because of what happened with that little boy, though, I was always a bit wary of him and would never have left the kids with him.

Andrew used to tease him, calling him Kid Killer, which was a bit sick. Andrew would say to him, 'You fucking knocked that kid, Greg, didn't you?' And Greg would just look back at him with this stupid smirk on his face because I don't think he knew how to take Andrew. We can all pass judgment but I believe that if he did kill that little boy, he didn't mean to do it. He used to try so hard to be nice around my kids but it was always like he was trying too hard. I remember one time we went out and left Danielle at home with Andrew and it turned out Greg was over at his cousin's fixing his car in the front yard. Andrew went out to him and said, 'If Roberta and Carl come home, don't tell them I've got Danielle with me.' So when we came home Danielle wasn't there and I was freaking. I raced out to Greg and yelled, 'Have you seen Danielle?' 'No,' he said. All of a sudden Andrew walked out from the back yard with Danielle, laughing his head off saying, 'Ha, ha, I got ya.'

Another time we went out while Andrew was at home with Dhakota and Greg must have come over. Anyway we rang the house to check on Dhakota and Greg answered the phone. I asked him what he was doing there and where Andrew was. 'Andrew went out and asked me to look after Dhakota for you,' Greg said. 'It's no worries, she's fine.'

I hung up the phone and turned to Carl and I must have been as white as a sheet. 'That fucking idiot has left Dhakota with Greg,' I said. Carl slammed on the brakes and floored it back to the house. We ran inside and there was Andrew, sitting there with Dhakota on his lap and pissing himself laughing. Greg was in the corner giggling. Andrew was like that — he used to love practical jokes. I'd want to kill him at times because he drove me mad, but I loved him to death at the same time.

About eighteen months after I met Andrew we found this house to buy in McPherson Street, Essendon, but with Carl in jail I had to go to the auction without him. Andrew came along with me and we were bidding but bidding against us was this smartarse guy who we reckoned was a dummy bidder just trying to jack our price up. Andrew walked over to him and got in his face and said, 'Mate, if you're going to bid against me, bid for the right reasons. Otherwise, fuck off.' People sort of knew our faces by then because we'd been on the TV news a bit, so I think this bloke realised who it was and just shit himself. He turned around straight away and left in his car and we were able to buy the house.

When I got divorced from Dean I used my divorce settlement of $90,000 as a deposit for a house and borrowed the rest. Then I sold that place and used the equity we had built up for the deposit on this place. Carl's mum and dad got a loan for the rest. A lot of people think that Carl was rolling in money at the time what with all the drug dealing, so he'd have heaps of cash for the house but in a situation like that it's not like you can just turn around and pay cash for a house or else the jacks will be at your door wanting to know where it all came from. Sometimes it just looks better to go and get a loan. So Carl's dad got a loan.

Near the end I felt closer to Andrew than Carl and something sexual could have come of it, but it didn't. Before Andrew died we had lots of fights because he got this girl pregnant and he wanted her to have an abortion, which she wouldn't do. One night we were having dinner in Lygon Street a few doors down from where the girl worked and Andrew said to me, 'Come on, you're going for a walk with me to tell this fucking moll that she's not having my kid.'

I said to him, 'Just leave her, she's pregnant, just let her be.' He was going mad and saying that I was going to have to raise the kid for him. Naturally I would have looked after the baby if that was what they wanted but then I'd make him laugh by saying how funny it would be to have this baby that would call me Mum and him Dad.

When she eventually gave birth at the Mercy in Werribee, I dragged Andrew along to the hospital to see the baby. I remember the baby was crying as he picked her up and when he started rocking her she stopped. He was so happy, he loved that baby. We tried to get the girl to put Andrew's name on the birth certificate, but she wouldn't do it.

I knew Andrew had a nasty side, but we never really discussed all that shit and I never saw it. Afterwards I was surprised at the amount of stuff Andrew had done.

I didn't trust Andrew at all at first. I just thought he was a car thief because that's what comes out of Sunshine — car thieves. The boys in Sunshine steal cars and grow dope. I knew he was tight with Gatto and that he still dealt with the Morans so I didn't trust him and used to warn Carl about going anywhere with him because I was worried he would set him up. I loved Andrew to death in the end, but early on he could have been bought. If somebody had said they'd give him $250k to kill Carl he would have done it without blinking. Further down the track his loyalty switched to us but for a long time there he was sitting on the fence.

Andrew just used to spend more and more time with us and we formed this really good friendship. Much later on after he had become tight with us Andrew reckoned the Morans had once asked him to kill Carl and me and that he even hid out, off and on, in our roof for four days. He said he heard me rocking Dhakota to sleep at night and he just couldn't do it. When he told me about that I remembered exactly when it would have been because I remembered there was this time when I had a feeling that something wasn't right and I heard noises in the roof. We thought it was possums. Fucking big possums as it turns out.

The first time I had any inkling that Andrew was anything more than just your average Sunshine car thief was when Snalfy's wife said to me once that Andrew killed somebody then went back to their house and ate pizza with them. I thought she was kidding because she was a little stuck-up bitch and it just didn't seem to me to be what Andrew was like. She was serious but I only found out much later down the track, through Carl talking to me and telling me bits and pieces, that she was right.

Since he has been in prison Carl has enlightened me about lots of different things that have caused me to nearly fall off my seat. At the time these things happened I had no idea. It's not like I could have gone up to one of the boys and said, 'Well, did you kill anyone last night?' It doesn't work like that. With everything I know now and from what I have heard from Carl and the police, I think Andrew probably killed at least ten people. But it was just a job to him. I think he could just treat it as going to work and doing what he had to do for his living and then he could switch off.

Early on Carl knew that Andrew was still friendly with the Morans and that he did business with them and Mick

Gatto. At that time in the drug trade that was how things were — you often had to do business with lots of people who had associations on both sides. I mean, these people are all drug dealers so they are all dodgy and untrustworthy. I don't think Andrew was loyal to Carl full on at the start but he became devoted to Carl about eighteen months before he was killed.

What eventually changed it all was that Mick Gatto thought Andrew had killed his best friend Graham Kinniburgh. It was the final straw on top of the Carlton Crew suspecting that Andrew had something to do with Jason's death. Despite what Mick thought, and no matter how many people Andrew did actually kill, Graham Kinniburgh wasn't one of them. The police knew he didn't do it because they had heard him on a listening device at the time of the murder and he was in Taylors Lakes, nowhere near Kinniburgh's house in Kew.

Mick Gatto and Andrew were fairly good friends until then, because Mick used to be a boxer and so did Andrew. Even though Andrew was working with Carl Mick was OK about it. I think Mick used Andrew to his advantage but then thought, 'This is getting a bit dangerous, Andrew might get me.' One night Carl and Andrew were in Chinatown and Gatto and someone else were getting in their car. Andrew crept up behind the car and jumped up in front of them to give them a scare. That was when Mick realised, 'He could really get me if he wanted to.' Andrew was just playing, but Mick thought, 'Shit, what happens if he decides to stop playing one night?'

After Kinniburgh's death in December 2003, Carl and Andrew had a meeting with Mick at Crown Casino. Gatto wanted to meet Carl somewhere in Carlton to talk to him about the murder. When some friends — who can't be named — heard that Mick Gatto wanted to meet Carl they said, 'We're coming too,' because they knew there was going to be a drama. Carl said to Gatto he would meet him anywhere he wanted but not at his restaurant in Carlton because that was his turf, so they agreed to meet at Crown because they knew that with all the security cameras there they would be safe and no-one would try anything. The jacks said there was a lip reader there, but what they claimed was said wasn't accurate.

Mick always used to call Andrew 'Tricky' because he reckoned he was a bit tricky. So when Andrew and Carl arrived at Crown Andrew turned to Carl and said, 'Watch, when I go in he'll call me Tricky.'

'Yeah, when he says that, you say "You're the fuckin' tricky one, cunt",' Carl said back.

They walked in and Andrew kissed Mick hello and shook his hand and of course Mick called him Tricky. Mario Condello was there too but Carl wouldn't shake his hand because he thought he was an arsehole and he hated him. In fact he hated them all.

'I hear you were involved in Graham's murder. Do you know anything about it?' Gatto said to Andrew.

'I heard the Asians had something to do with it,' Andrew said and started laughing. It was a dumb thing to say but Andrew was probably thinking how stupid it was to think he would kill such a good mate of Mick's.

Carl then piped up and said to Mick, 'You want drama? We'll turn it on, too. You aren't the only cunts who can turn on the drama.' So there was a bit of a thing there in the room after he said that. They got a bit shitty and it had to be calmed down. Carl then looked at Gatto and said, 'Why the fuck would we have anything to do with it? I didn't even know Kinniburgh. I had no idea who the fuck he was.' And he didn't. Until Kinniburgh died Carl didn't know who he was and Andrew certainly had no reason to kill him.

Andrew had gradually got closer and closer to Carl and become more and more loyal to him in the months before this, but this was the time their friendship was sealed. He couldn't be close to the Morans or Gatto anymore because he knew that Mick thought he killed Kinniburgh. He also knew that there was no bullshit with Carl — he was what he was. He was true, loyal and honest and didn't want Andrew for anything other than to be his friend. I mean, they did business together and I am sure Andrew probably killed people for Carl, but that was business. Carl was always straight up with him and he really liked the kid, so I think that made Andrew think, 'Hang on a minute, I'm being used to kill people and being thrown $100k or $150k or whatever to do it, but then these people just want to sit and eat with me and have a coffee for no particular reason other than they like me.' It made Andrew loyal to us as his friends.

CHAPTER 19

COME TO MY OFFICE

It was like Carl and Andrew knew something was going to happen. They both stayed in the apartment and had been really quiet. They hadn't really seen many people since the meeting with Gatto at the Casino. It wasn't that they were hiding or scared of Gatto or the Morans, they just figured that with Carl having blown up a bit at the meeting, it was better to let things cool down and keep out of the way for a while. But it was my birthday so we were going out to celebrate.

While Carl, Andrew and I were on our way to Carl's apartment to get ready to go out, Andrew received a phone call from Gatto telling him to come and meet him. Carl had always said to Andrew that regardless of what Mick might say, do not go and meet him alone anywhere. Carl knew that the Morans had gone through Gatto previously to try to get Andrew to kill Carl. According to one plan Andrew

Me in a rare happy moment in the back yard at Seaford as a young girl. I spent a lot of time there when Mum locked us out of the house half the night.

I always loved kids and animals. Here I am with a couple of puppies. How is that haircut! Who doesn't look back and laugh at photos of themselves as a teenager?

This is me (on the left) and my sister Michelle.

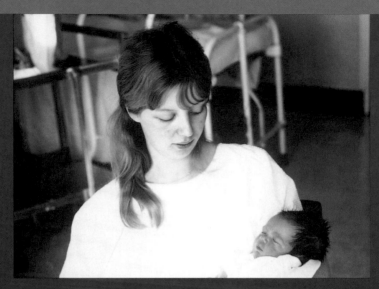

The media said Carl was baby-faced. Well, here he is as a baby in the arms of his mum, Barb.

He never could get the smile off his face — Carl on his dad George's knee as a baby.

Butter wouldn't melt in his mouth. This is Carl as a boy.

A normal happy family. Here is Carl (on the right) with Barb, George, and his brother Shane, who later died.

My first husband Dean and me. I said I always liked the tough guy look and Dean was a tough guy. Unfortunately, I felt the pain of what a 'tough guy' he was.

This is me on the day that I married Dean. That's my sister Sharon holding Breanane in the background.

Dean and I had been friends with Carl for years. People tried to say Carl and I had an affair but that was bullshit. We were not together until long after Dean and I broke up. Here we all are on holidays in happier times.

This is Dean and I, out at a Darwin Cup dinner with Carl. We used to go up to the Darwin Cup as an annual family holiday with Carl and his girlfriend at the time.

This is a photo of my mum and dad's wedding. I wonder what my life would've been like if he'd lived …

Proof of one of our happier days — the marriage certificate from Carl's and my wedding.

You can kiss the bride ... Carl was
not the most romantic type but he
had his moments. He proposed
when I was in the bath then we
had one of the best weddings ever.
That was one of the happiest days
of my life and it was sealed with a
kiss. I had a beautiful gold dress
by a well-known local designer
that cost Carl a small fortune.

Carl in Europe on holiday; he travelled to Greece and Turkey in the early 1990s and had a terrific time. Met up with the local police!

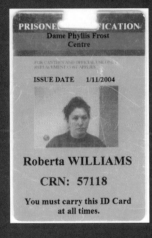

PRISONER IDENTIFICATION

Dame Phyllis Frost Centre

FOR CANTEEN AND OFFICIAL USE ONLY
REPLACEMENT COST APPLIES

ISSUE DATE 1/11/2004

Roberta WILLIAMS
CRN: 57118

You must carry this ID Card
at all times.

Not the most flattering picture of me — my ID card from prison.

Before the trouble started. One night out at a party the boys posed together. That's obviously Carl on the left but the one on the right with the Michael Bolton hair and wearing a cow jacket is Mark Moran.

One of the stressful moments captured by a media photographer at the scene of Andrew's murder.

Newspix

Andrew was more one of our family than just a friend. We had this photo collage made up as a tribute to him. I still cry just looking at it.

Andrew

loyal and loving friend

Sorry I never told you
All I wanted to say
And now it's too late to hold you
'Cause you've flown away
So far away

Never had I imagined
Living without your smile
Feeling and knowing you hear me
It keeps me alive

And I know your shining down on me from Heaven
Like so many friends we've lost along the way
And I know eventually we'll be together
One sweet day

Darling, I never showed you
Assumed you'd always be there
I took your presence for granted
But I always cared
And I miss the love we shared

Although the sun will never shine the same
I'll always look to a brighter day
Lord I know when I lay me down to sleep
You will always listen as I pray

Zarah Garde-Wilson began as our lawyer but became much more. We were so close for a while we were like sisters, but later we had a falling out and, sadly, we no longer speak.

Carl and Dhakota. Carl wasn't a typical dad and didn't fit in with normal family life, but he loved all my kids.

Carl and I were friends from the first time we met, but only got together years later. He always made me laugh — even those times when I wanted to hit him.

George cuddling Dhakota. He always loved his little girl, but Barb dying has brought George and Dhakota a bit closer together, I think.

Barb just loved Dhakota — here they are laughing and carrying on.

Barb and I had our moments — mainly because she rode the bumps of Carl's and my relationship and like any mum sided with her son — but I loved Barb and still mourn her death.

Here's Barb, just after Dhakota had done her nana's make-up.

The day Barb died was a shocking day and her funeral was just so sad. I delivered a eulogy and said that she was like the mother I never had. I miss her terribly as does Dhakota, who bravely carried a photo of her nan from the church.

Newspix

Newspix

Underbelly meant everyone instantly thought they knew me and what I was like. Kat Stewart played me and Gyton Grantley played Carl. At first I hated the show and how they made me look, but then I realised that they were just actors saying their lines. They ended up winning Logies for their parts so some good came of it.

Newspix

For years, we could barely step out the door without the media being on us and shoving microphones in our faces.

Carl and his girls. Here he is with Dhakota on the left arm and Breanane on his right. I always loved that Carl treated my children like his own.

Carl and Dhakota on Danielle and Breanane's Communion day.

Despite all the tears and dramas that happened over the years we had a lot of laughs as a family. Here is Carl and I smiling for the camera and the girls carrying on mucking around.

My new partner Rob (on the left), pictured here with a friend. Rob and I have spoken about having more kids.

This is my beautiful son, Tye. Having my children has been my proudest achievement in life.

My three gorgeous girls on Danielle and Breanane's Communion day. That's Danielle on the left, little Dhakota in the middle and Breanane on the right. How beautiful do they all look?

Roberta is consoled by a mourner outside St Theresa's church before Carl's funeral service begins.

Newspix

Roberta follows Carl's gold-plated coffin, carried by eight pallbearers, out of the church on 30 April 2010.

would convince Carl to go somewhere to see Gatto and when he arrived Andrew would be over the road waiting and he'd shoot Carl. Of course Carl never turned up to that meeting and it saved his life. He found out about it later, of course, from Andrew.

Andrew also told him that when Carl met Gatto once in Lygon Street, Andrew was waiting to shoot Carl — the idea being that as soon as Carl went inside the restaurant, Andrew would run in and shoot him and run away. But Carl refused to go inside. He said, 'We can talk here on the street, I am not going in your restaurant. Whatever you have to say to me you can say here.' Andrew later told Carl about that plan too, and Carl realised how close he had come to dying and each time it would have been at the hand of a man who turned out to be one of his best friends in life. But it meant that Carl always said to Andrew, 'Just don't go and see Mick Gatto on your own, even though you think you have history with him and you can trust him, just don't take a risk. You just can't trust the bloke.'

As soon as we arrived at the apartment and I opened the door I could smell Andrew's aftershave. I said to Carl, 'That little shit's gone off to pick up chicks.' We had only just walked inside and put our bags down when I got a phone call from someone in the media. They said, 'Roberta, there's been a shooting in Carlton on the corner of Rathdowne and Faraday Streets and Andrew's involved.'

I was a bit shaken by it because I thought, 'Oh, here we go again.' Naturally I thought Andrew had shot somebody. It didn't even enter my head that Andrew was the one who had been shot. My first reaction was to try to go down there and help him. I told Carl what had happened and he just said, 'Quick, we better go and get down there.' If I think about it now we probably should have twigged that Andrew might have been the victim not the shooter, because if Andrew was going to shoot someone Carl would have known about it, unless it was some random spur of the moment thing. But Carl knew nothing about it. We also should have twigged from the address in Carlton that if there was a shooting and Andrew was involved, it was also going to involve Gatto.

We got downstairs and as I drove out of the underground car park into the side street I got another phone call from a different media person. This time they told me it was Andrew that had been shot. I just started screaming and yelling at Carl, 'Andrew's been shot. Andrew's been shot.' I didn't know how bad it was at that point. I was just saying, 'Please God, let him be alright.' My head was spinning so much I couldn't work out which way to go. They told me the street name but I couldn't work out where it was even though it was somewhere I had driven a million times.

Carl was trying to direct me and he couldn't think either. We were both so upset and confused. Eventually I got onto Lygon Street and we drove up there until we saw the right street and stopped the car. Before I'd even put the handbrake on I was almost out of the car and running down the street. There were police there and they were yelling out to each other, 'Roberta Williams is here ...' I was going crazy asking what had happened to Andrew. Then I saw the ambulance and thought, 'He's alive, they must be helping him.' I thought that you didn't need an ambulance if someone was dead, so maybe they were still working on him and he'd be OK. We couldn't get sense out of anyone and the jacks at the line were just trying to keep us away. The media were closing in around us the whole time getting in our faces. I went back and sat in the car.

One of the Purana task force detectives, Andrew Stamper, came over and knelt down next to the car to talk to me. He was always one of the nicer ones and he said, 'Look, Roberta, I know we come from two different worlds but you've lost one of your own and I'm really sorry for that.' That was when it really hit me that Andrew was dead. I don't really remember a lot of what happened from then on.

Carl just sat in the car straight-faced and didn't say a lot. He was quiet and stared straight ahead. We drove around the corner to Rathdowne Street and parked again because I wanted to try and get in to see what the fuck was going on. I still sort of didn't believe it, or I didn't want to believe he was dead. So we parked the car and walked up again to try and get through to get some answers. By now there were media just everywhere and it was totally insane. We finally talked to some copper who said they had someone in custody.

'Who?' Carl asked.

'Mick Gatto.'

I was beside myself. I think I knew it would have to be Mick because of the address. We knew that was Mick's restaurant or the restaurant Mick was always at and when we heard Gatto was in custody I think it really sank in that

Andrew was dead. Gatto might have been his friend once but I knew if there was a shooting involving Mick Gatto and Mick Gatto was still alive, then the other person was going to be dead. The other person in this instance was Andrew.

We went back to the car to try and get out of there. I was so hysterical and in shock I couldn't even get the door of the car to open. The media were closing in on us and suffocating us so Carl just pushed through them and walked away across the road and into a service station. He went inside, went into the toilet and just closed the door. He needed peace and the only place he could get away from everyone was in a fucking service station toilet.

Eventually he realised he couldn't stay locked in a toilet for long so he walked out and just hopped in the first car he saw in the driveway of the service station. By coincidence it was being driven by a cousin, or a relative of some sort, of a close friend. Carl was lucky he got into the car of a friend because most people in Melbourne at that time would have been terrified of Carl Williams trying to get in their car, but this guy was great — he just drove Carl off down the road and I finally got the car door open and drove off as well, and we met up a short distance away.

We phoned a good friend of Andrew's called Frank to talk about what had happened. We met up with him on Lygon Street and talked. It was hard for Frank because he was a friend of Mick Gatto's and Andrew's, and he didn't know what to think. He sort of had to sit on the fence even though he was really sad about Andrew.

Eventually Carl said, 'What the fuck can we do here?' and we went back to the apartment. We got inside and Carl opened a bottle of Johnnie Walker Blue and sat down and drank his guts out and barely said anything. He just sat there staring straight ahead. Andrew was his closest confidante and Gatto had killed him. He was probably thinking that he would be next. No doubt he was thinking of what he needed to do and who he should kill to get even.

I went back home because I knew that by now the kids would know what had happened from watching the news and they would be upset. My daughter Danielle was really close to Andrew and she would take it hard. I spoke to my sister Sharon and she came down and picked up the kids for me. I went back to be with Carl but I don't remember much of that night. The phone kept going crazy but someone had given me a Valium to calm me down so I was pretty out of it.

The next day there was a court appearance for Gatto and I went along but remained outside. The media were all there and I was obviously emotional, really on edge and angry. I flared up a bit at the courthouse. George Defteros was there representing Gatto and I was so angry and upset I just wanted to bash someone, and he was the one I could get to so I went after him in the foyer of the court. He hid behind a security guard while I verbally attacked him. Finally, I just had enough and left, emotionally and physically drained.

We were trying to get Andrew's body released for the funeral and we were still trying to find out what was going on. We organised a funeral parlour in Sydney Road, Fawkner, to handle the arrangements. Andrew's family were overseas but they got in touch with them so they could get on flights from everywhere. Everyone helped and did whatever they could. I was on medication and was like a walking zombie, really.

A lot of people had died leading up to this, but no-one close to me. In fact I'd never really lost anybody who was close to me. Nobody was like Andrew. I didn't know my dad and I'd fallen out with Dino Dibra a while before he died. We'd had a big dispute and Carl was really angry about the way he spoke to me. Carl and him became friends again but I was never as close with him as I had been. Andrew, though, was like a brother to me and the kids idolised him. It was like he was a part of our family because he was so close to everyone in the family, and we spent so much time with him. We spent Christmas and birthdays together — all the fun things. I bought Andrew aftershave for one birthday and he sprayed it all around the house because he knew it would give me migraines. He was just like a naughty little kid. I know he killed a lot of people, but the Andrew I knew was just cheeky like a kid.

When the funeral company called us to say Andrew's body had arrived we went down there to see him. He had just been delivered from the morgue and they wheeled him in on this trolley with a white sheet over him. Carl was on one side and I was on the other and Carl and Andrew's mates were there behind us. They stopped and we pulled the sheet back and Carl rubbed Andrew's face and said, 'You're alright now, little buddy.' I'll never forget the expression on Carl's face. He was just devastated. I was a mess. Having to look at him there on the trolley and confront the reality of his death was shocking. I couldn't believe the injuries; there was a gunshot wound on his neck with a two or three inch wide powder burn. It was like the gun had been held to his throat.

I always thought there was so much about the whole shooting of Andrew and Gatto's version of events that didn't make sense. It was stupid to think that Andrew would have gone in there carrying a gun. He knew the police were following him, listening in to his phone conversations and pulling him over all the time for supposed random checks, so he wouldn't have carried a gun on him or had it in his car because it would have been too risky. He knew that if the jacks caught him with a gun on him he was fucked.

He was still in the same clothes he had worn to court that morning. He was filmed going in and out of the Magistrates Court by that many TV crews for the news that night and you could see clearly that they were really tight-fitting clothes. He had on his three-quarter length Adidas or Nike tracky pants that were a pretty tight fit and he had a body-hugging T-shirt on, so if he was carrying a gun when he walked into the restaurant I think Mick and his men would have seen it.

Then there was the fact that Andrew walked into Mick's territory and threw his car keys down on the table while he went out the back with Gatto. If he went there planning to shoot Mick Gatto would he really plan to do it in Mick's 'office' with his boys still sitting at the front of the restaurant? Would he throw his car keys on the table that Mick's boys were sitting at while he went out the back to talk to Mick and shoot him? He would have had to walk back to the front of the restaurant again and say, 'Can I have my keys back, please? I've just shot your mate and now I want to leave.' That seems ridiculous.

I think Andrew was smart enough not to confine himself to a particular space or to go on someone else's turf.

I wrote to Mick Gatto once about Andrew's death, but I never sent the letter. I don't know why. I suppose I knew it would be a bit of a waste of time. I think just writing it made me feel better. As I wrote in that letter to him, I didn't want to know what happened on that fateful day — 23 March — I just wanted to know why. I told Mick that right to the end Andrew always classified him as a friend and would never let a bad word be spoken about him, so I just wanted to know why.

When I was trying to work out which clothes to put Andrew in in the casket all I kept thinking about was that I didn't want his mother to see the gunshot wounds. I pulled part of the cloth from the inside of the casket over his head to cover the bullet wounds as best I could. I know how devastating it was for me to see him with these holes in his head without his mum having to see him like that. I buttoned his shirt all the way up to his chin because the powder burns on his neck were horrific. I couldn't believe it. There is no way I could have done anything like this for someone else.

They put shoes on him that were too small. I don't know who picked them or even whose they were because they were just too small to be Andrew's.

Carl and I sat at the funeral place day and night with him until he was buried. It was the last time we'd see him and spend time with him and we didn't want him to be alone. All the boys came down too and we all hung out together and waited there with him.

I'll never forget when his mum came in and first saw him. She was screaming in Greek, and it was heartbreaking to see and hear a mother go through that. It was heartbreaking for us all to go through that. We organised for Andrew's body to be taken home to his family's house that night for a viewing so his friends could come and see him and spend time with him. It was really nice.

Underbelly said that I stayed in bed and refused to get up after Andrew died. Yes, I was heartbroken and I hated what had happened, but that was bullshit. I was with Andrew every minute I could until he was buried. They said I didn't go to the funeral, which just shows how much shit they made up in that show because I was in the front row with his family and the priest came over to me during the service and consoled me. So don't take my word for it, or *Underbelly*'s, take the priest's.

CHAPTER 20

FRIENDS AND ENEMIES

It was eight days after Andrew was killed, the day after his funeral, that Carl had Lewis Moran shot and killed in March 2004. Carl pleaded guilty to it later on and, unlike Mark Cole's murder, I won't argue about this one. Carl definitely organised for Lewis to be killed.

I still remember that night really clearly. We were getting ready to go out for Greek food in Nicholson Street, Fitzroy, just me and the kids. We had Dhakota's godmother's son with us and Carl was sleeping at his mum's house. The phone rang and I answered it. It was a journalist friend of mine, Adam Shand. 'Lewis Moran's been killed,' he said. I was a bit numb. I knew Carl would be behind it, but I'd had no idea about it until then.

At the time I was driving from Moonee Ponds to Fitzroy, to the restaurant we were going to. I kept getting lost because the streets were blocked off and there was traffic everywhere. Then the phone rang again. It was a close friend looking for Carl. I just started whingeing because I was stuck in traffic. He asked where I was and when I told him he said, 'Fucking get out of there — that was where Lewis Moran was killed.'

I was upset when I heard Lewis was dead. I think it was because we'd gone through all that hell with Andrew and now someone else's family was going to have to endure what we had. As much as I hate that family it was still sad to think of his grandchildren grieving for their grandfather. It was odd because I expected my first reaction to be, 'Good, fuck you.' That might have been how Carl thought of it — well obviously it was how Carl thought of it — but it wasn't the way I thought of it straight away. Don't get me wrong, I wasn't crying because I was sad that a Moran had died — I think I was probably crying for Andrew more than anything, because it brought that home to me all over again. I think I also just felt, 'Where is it all going to end?' I suppose the rest of Australia was thinking the same thing at the time.

Lewis was killed because of the feud between us and the Morans, there's no doubt about that. But not everyone who died was killed because of a war between the two families, or between us and the so-called Carlton Crew. They died because of a fight between drug dealers. Most of the time it was drugs or money that got people killed, not revenge. Like Mark Cole. He was killed over those drug chemicals of his that were stolen and not because Carl and his mates wanted to get him.

At the time it wasn't always clear who was on which side anyway. Like with Andrew — early on he was on both sides. And then there were always dirty jacks in the middle of everything working with dealers and taking their bit right from way back. Dealers had police in their pockets left, right and centre and it wasn't a shock to know someone was going off to meet a jack down the road or some other dirty jack was coming to pick up his envelope of cash. I never personally witnessed that stuff — jacks being given money — and I didn't know the names of the jacks that were dirty other than those that I'd read in the paper like everyone else, but you'd overhear talk and you'd put two and two together and you knew there were jacks involved.

It wasn't hard to work out that some people were getting help from the jacks and some weren't, or else they were getting help from different coppers. You couldn't really back it up with anything concrete but you just knew. Everyone knew. Somebody would come and say, 'Oh, he's working with the police,' or 'Here's the info he got from that jack he worked with.' Some of it was about giving information to the jacks and getting information back, it wasn't about passing money or dealing drugs. That was how Carl came to find out that Lewis Moran had a hit out on him.

The bloke who turned out to be a grass in another big criminal case (who I can't name for legal reasons) had a meeting with Lewis Moran in someone's garage and he was wired up by the jacks. Lewis wanted him to find someone to knock Carl and offered him fifty grand to do it. The bloke said to Lewis, 'I'm not going to do it for fifty grand, I'll see if I can find someone else.' And off he went to the police with his wire.

Anyway, that so-called Supergrass also lagged to the jacks a heap of shit about how I was supposed to be doing a heap of drugs at the time and so was Carl, and he listed about sixty other people who were supposed to be doing all this shit. A lot of it was crap because I know I wasn't doing drugs at that time. I have already been honest here in talking about the drugs I did but at that stage I wasn't doing drugs. All the information he gave them was transcribed onto a piece of paper which Carl ended up getting. I am not sure how he got it, but he got it. Maybe the senior jacks knew that Carl was going to be told about Lewis trying to get a contract on him and they agreed that he should be told so as to warn him. I don't know. But wouldn't that make what Carl did in organising to kill Lewis self-defence? I mean, even the jacks knew that Lewis wanted to kill Carl and was trying to hire someone to do it, so if you are in fear of your life that is self-defence, isn't it?

Although the police knew Lewis Moran was chasing up someone to kill Carl they did nothing about it. They didn't arrest Lewis and charge him with conspiracy to murder or anything else, they just left him on the street to try and find another hit man. So all Carl knew was that Lewis was trying to kill him and that, despite having that information, the jacks were doing nothing about it. I think at that stage the police would have been quite happy if someone had knocked Carl to get him out of the way and maybe end their 'underworld war'.

In the days after Andrew died there was a lot of stuff going on. There was a guy whose daughter went to school with the daughter of a friend of ours and he started to ask through his daughter if he could get in touch with us. When she came back and told us that he wanted to reach us we just thought he might be another hit man that Lewis had tried to hire, and that he was trying to find out where Carl lived in order to kill him. It turned out we were half right, but he wanted to help Carl, not kill him. He *had* been approached to kill Carl but it wasn't Lewis Moran doing the hiring this time, it was another of the Carlton Crew — that slimy lawyer Mario Condello.

Condello had approached the bloke and asked him to kill Carl. The guy used to transport guns around Australia and one time when he was transporting weapons from Adelaide to Melbourne for Condello he got caught and jailed for it. Condello didn't give a shit about him and didn't look after him then, but it didn't stop him going back to him again when he wanted something — someone to kill Carl. But because Condello didn't help him out when he was in jail this bloke thought, 'Fuck you, what better way to get you back than to tell Carl Williams.' So he was trying to get in touch with Carl to warn him. This bloke was a very good sniper, apparently, and Condello wanted him to sit across the road from our apartment block and shoot Carl when he was downstairs in a café, or when he was walking in or something. He didn't care if it was while Carl was sitting down with all of us family in the restaurant or not.

We didn't meet with the bloke because we thought it was a trap but word got back to us that that was the message he was going to give us, so we stopped eating with the kids downstairs after that. It started to feel like it was too dangerous to do anything. I mean, at the time we didn't really need to be told that someone wanted to kill Carl because you didn't need to be Einstein to work that out, but it was still a bit upsetting to find out how someone had planned to do it and that they didn't care if Carl had his kids around him in a restaurant in the middle of the city.

Carl never showed any fear about any of that. He knew people would want to kill him and that they were trying to hire people to knock him but he just never showed any fear about it and that made me more comfortable. 'If it gets you, it gets you. There's nothing you can do about it, so there is no point worrying about it,' was what he would say.

It made me think, 'If he's not scared, why should I be?' He was never concerned about anything. When all the dramas were going on I always had it in the back of my mind that one day I would get the phone call. I would always wonder when I was going to get the call to tell me that this time it was Carl who'd been shot. I honestly thought Carl would have been killed before Andrew. I knew their numbers were coming up because of all the madness happening around them, but I never thought Andrew would have been killed the way he was. And not before Carl.

Sometimes I thought about myself and whether I'd be shot. I asked Carl about it several times in normal conversation and he was dismissive. 'Roberta, if someone was to kill a female — you — or a child, it'd be a whole different ball game. It'd be open slather then,' he told me. It might have seemed like it was open slather already, but he reckoned it would have been much worse if they'd killed a woman or child.

CHAPTER 21

IN THE SLOT

I went to prison on 19 October 2004. It was the start of the longest six months of my life. I had been in prison before, but not like this. I was treated like I was some sort of terrorist in Guantanamo Bay.

I knew I was guilty and there was no real use fighting the charges — trafficking ecstasy — so two days before I was due to stand trial I decided to plead guilty. Most of the time you figured that if you are found guilty when they sentence you, they will credit you with the time you have served on remand so you might as well fight and maybe you'll get lucky. In the end, though, I knew it was going to be a pointless fight so for me it would be better to just get it over with, plead guilty, try and get a discount for saving the court time and get out as fast as I could. By that stage I'd had just about enough of courts and lawyers and jacks, and all I wanted was to know what my sentence was going to be and to serve it and get back out again to my kids as quick as I could. It had already dragged on for three years and I didn't want it dragging on any longer.

I was taken out to the prison van and there were all guys in one part and they were all saying things to me, like keep your chin up and generally just offering encouragement and support, as they walked me through to a little isolation section. I just sat there and cried my eyes out. I was scared and stressed because I knew I wouldn't be with my kids for a long time. I didn't know when I would see them next. I knew Barb would have Dhakota and Dean would have the other kids, but I was really stressing about it because I wanted Dhakota to see her brother and sisters and I knew that Barb and Dean didn't speak so it was going to be hard to arrange and awful for them. I just wanted to cuddle my kids. I had never been apart from them for any length of time and I didn't know how I would cope, let alone how they would. Dhakota was only three and her Dad had been in jail since she was two months old and now her mum was there too. I was embarrassed as well as upset.

We did a few drop-offs at other prisons before we got to the women's prison at Deer Park. When we got bundled out of the van there was an older prison officer there who sort of greeted us. Anyway, he must have previously worked at Fairlea when I ran over the prison guard because he looked at me and said: 'I hear there is a prison officer that walks with a limp these days because of you.' I thought he was letting me know that he was going to get even or something, but he had a smile on his face and was making a joke to try to settle me in.

They normally send you straight in to have a shower when you arrive but they knew I wasn't a druggy or anything and it was late by the time I arrived so they just strip-searched me — which was not pleasant — and chucked me into prison clothes — the blue tracksuit, white T-shirt and runners, even the prison issue bra and undies — and left me in a little cell.

I didn't know Deer Park at all. I'd been in Fairlea and all the youth centres but I didn't know Deer Park and what sort of sections they had. They said to me, 'Look, we are going to put you in the slot for the time being until we can work out what to do with you.' The slot is solitary confinement, a little single cell where you're supposed to be locked down for only 23 hours a day but they don't ever really let you out. They told me they would put me in there for the first 24 hours until they decided what to do with me and where to put me.

Even though I'd broken up with Carl they thought that because I was his wife maybe someone would try and get me while I was in jail. They didn't know if the Morans had friends in the prison or if there was going to be a problem. So even though I was supposed to be in there just for the first day, I ended up being in the slot for seven weeks before I was even sentenced. I think the whole time I was there I only got out for five to ten minutes a day. You are limited to ten phone calls a week, one visitor a week, plus your kids can visit once a week, so I was let out for those visits but otherwise I was alone in this cell all day and night. I didn't even get out for meals because they just passed them through the slot in the door. Inside the cell was a bed, a shower and a toilet, with some little shelves. There was a TV but it didn't work for the first few nights, which made the nights seem even longer. Even bad TV is better than no TV at all when you are alone in a cell.

I mean, I was in there waiting to be sentenced on an ecstasy charge and here I was in the slot for weeks on end like I was some kind of terrorist. Every morning I'd be woken by the intercom telling me to get up for muster. We had to be up and out of our beds for them to come around and see us. Then I'd get breakfast delivered — cold toast, butter and jam. Every day, cold toast. It got so that I was looking forward to a piece of hot toast as much as I was my phone calls. We were allowed to make tea and coffee and Milo in the cells and I would make that. I was just so hungry, especially at the start, that I would eat any disgusting thing they brought us for meals, and so quickly I didn't have time to think about it: sausage rolls or dim sims with no soy sauce and fried rice.

There were other women in the unit — Management Unit A1. There was one woman there who had been sexually molested as a kid and had then sexually abused a little kid herself. She was in there for her own protection, but I knew no-one would be trying to get me and I could handle myself anyway. I wasn't scared of some slag trying to get me so I didn't see why I should be in the slot. Every day I kept crying, thinking that Carl and the boys had already done five months in the slot and I didn't know how they could have coped.

Eventually my lawyer subpoenaed Brendan Money and Wayne Blyth, who both worked below the prison's governor and basically admitted that there was a directive from above that that was how I should be treated. After seven weeks I was moved to B4 section where I was locked up for 12 to 13 hours a day but Blyth said to me that because of who I was I would never be moved to a cottage or out to Tarrengower, which was a low security prison. He made it clear that I would never be treated like other prisoners would be that were in there with my sentence and my record. So I was doing harder time because of Carl. It was like I was serving part of his sentence.

I wrote a diary during my time in prison. I wrote in it every day and when I read it back now it breaks my heart. It takes me back to when I was there — every day the same as the one before. And it reminds me of all the shit that went on with the prison officers and not being allowed to go into mainstream for so long. It reminded me how much I missed my beautiful husband Carl and the pain I felt in my heart being apart from him. It also gave me a lot of time to think about Andrew and how much I missed him. I used to dream about him and it always felt so real, I felt really close to him, and I would wake up and be upset all over again that he was gone but I would want to know I could see him again in my dreams.

I used to sit in my cell every day and cry, and at night I would rock on my bed and sob because I felt so alone and

I was stressing about my kids. They had to call the psych nurse on four occasions to give me extra medication to calm me down because I was stressing so badly. I also had three different panic attacks while I was in the slot where I felt like I couldn't breathe and I would get all hot and sweaty like I was going crazy. I was on a lot of drugs to calm me down.

I knew I was being picked on by the guards in the prison because of who I was. Blyth said I would be treated differently because of Carl and that was how it was, but it got me really angry when they treated my kids differently too. Once when Tye came to visit me early on, they made him wait nearly three hours before they processed him. Then they brought in the dog squad and had the dogs sniff him before they took them out to the car Tye had driven in and sniffed all over that looking for drugs. Then when they came back inside he was strip-searched before being allowed in to see me. All of this because a seventeen-year-old kid wanted to visit his mum. I was lucky he was a tough kid and was still prepared to come back again to visit me.

Because they never let me out of my cell I thought I'd just have to exercise inside it. I was normally a fit person so I wanted to exercise and I started using water bottles as weights and doing push-ups and sit-ups, but it was so hard to do in such a small space that in the end I thought, 'Fuck it, I can't do this,' and I went to the other extreme and started ordering lollies and chocolates from the canteen. I started eating and eating to pass the time because I was so bored. Obviously I started to stack on the weight. I was on a heap of drugs too — they gave me Avanza at first and then Prozac, and I was taking Imovane and Valium to sleep.

When I moved into B4 unit I still just used to pig out on shit food all the time. I got money put into five different girls' properties (the jail equivalent of a bank account) as well as my own so I had the maximum $120 a month in my own property paid in by my family, but I also got $120 put into each of these five other girls' properties and they would keep $40 each and I would get $80 so I was on $520 a month that all went on lollies, chocolates, soft drinks and chips. They said I used to live like a queen in there and I did, I had everything at my feet, but the problem was I was starting to struggle to see my feet. I was putting on a lot of weight.

I had been sentenced to 18 months with a minimum of six months and 12 months parole. Any sentence was going to be shattering because I knew I would be away from my kids but when you hear the exact amount of time you get it is still heartbreaking. I suppose six months is what I should have expected for the drugs involved but my record was mainly for things I had done as a juvenile so that does not count against you as an adult.

I figure the courts never give enough of a discount to someone who pleads guilty and saves everyone the time and grief of a trial. Even for someone like Carl — who admitted to killing four people — to still get a minimum of 35 years I don't think reflected the fact that he saved the state millions in the cost of trials. I think he should have got a lot less than that. It wasn't Osama Bin Laden they were sentencing — yeah, he'd killed people, but they were all drug dealers.

In prison we'd pass the time by getting up in the morning and then either being allocated or choosing a job. But I didn't want to work. I thought they could jam the job up their arse. What were they going to do, put me in jail? So that meant I did fuck-all. I got up, had a shower, socialised with other people, sat on the step having coffee, then somebody would cook us a nice lunch and we'd eat as well as we would have in a restaurant outside, then I'd make my phone calls, if I had any I was allowed to make, then we'd get locked in our cell for the night. Every Sunday I had a 10-minute phone call with Carl, which was all we got because he was in jail also, at Barwon.

I wanted to do an educational course while I was in jail but the woman in charge of education said, 'Look, we are only funded for a certain number of people and we can't fit you in. You can't do it.' They had something like 210 prisoners in the jail but they only had funding for 120 places in the courses. So there was always this huge waiting list, which meant it was really hard to get in any of the courses. Prison is not about rehabilitation. It is not what people think it is or would like to think it is. It is about locking people away and letting them out on the street again when they have served their time but they don't leave with any new skills to help them change their lives. And because they get out with a criminal record it is so much harder for them to get jobs and do anything other than commit more crimes to survive.

Don't get me wrong, I know I broke the law and was going to be punished for it, but I don't believe the system should be all about punishment. It should also be about trying to stop people making the same mistakes again. When you only fund enough places for half the girls in the prison to do an educational course then it means that only the girls on the longer sentences ever have a chance to get in a course. Wouldn't you think that the girl who goes inside for her first stretch, which would probably be short, should be the one to do one of these courses to lessen the odds of her going and committing more crimes and ending up back in again on a longer sentence?

It is the same with the drug courses and rehab. They say they have all these rehab programs in the jails but they don't have enough places for all the girls who need and want to go in them. Nearly all of the girls who go to prison go in with some sort of drug problem and when most of them get out of prison their drug problem is worse because the drugs are nearly as available in prison as outside and you can't get into the rehab courses even if you want to. From what I could see the people running the courses had no idea either. They weren't ex-addicts or ex-cons so they could only teach people what they had read in a book and they didn't know what the fuck they were doing.

It was never violent for me in jail but the longer I was in there the more stressed I was getting because I had these other charges coming up and I was pleading guilty, but I was worried they would add time to my sentence and I wanted it served concurrently. The longer I was away from the kids the worse I was and the worse the kids were. Danielle had always been a good student and she started to struggle at school.

A forensic and clinical psychologist, Jeffrey Cummins, had spoken with me and the girls over a few years for different court matters and he saw us again at this time and wrote a report for the court. He said in one of his reports that in his opinion both Danielle and Breanane had been 'forced to mature in a precocious manner because of their parents' circumstances'. That broke my heart to read that because even though I had tried my hardest to be a good parent to them and not repeat the same mistakes as my mum, they were still suffering from things I had done. They had not suffered the way I had with my mum but they had been forced to grow up too soon because of me.

It made me feel better to read in the report that I was a responsible and caring parent and that it would be better for the girls and for me to be able to see them more. I felt so much better that this expert had seen us together and knew that the best thing for my girls was to be with me. It upset me when I read that he thought while I was in jail the girls' behaviour had regressed, or got worse, and that he reckoned that was because I was not in their life as much and so was not able to discipline them. Finally he wrote:

'In conclusion it is my opinion Ms Williams is doing it hard at the Dame Phyllis Frost Centre. It does appear as a result of being sentenced to the offence of trafficking in a drug of dependence and simultaneously being isolated from her daughters, including her daughter Dhakota, and from her family network, she has been forced to reflect more so on her future and particularly on her husband Carl Williams' future. In my opinion and based on her comments and presentation at interview it is correct to state she is currently severely depressed.'

No shit.

He added that in an earlier report he had described my mental state as 'being reflective of Adjustment Disorder with Mixed Anxiety and Depressed Mood'. I am not altogether sure what this meant but I knew I was depressed and anxious so I suppose he was right. 'In my opinion there has now been an exacerbation of Ms Williams' symptoms so she would now be diagnosed as having a severe Adjustment Disorder with Mixed Anxiety and Depressed Mood', he wrote. He said the fact that I was being seen weekly by a psychiatrist and a psychologist was more proof of the trouble I was having in jail.

What really upset me, though, was when he spoke about my girls: 'In my opinion her daughters Breanane and Danielle do display some symptoms reflective of separation anxiety disorder and no doubt Ms Williams' observations of her daughters' changed behaviour also serves to exacerbate her current feelings of helplessness, powerlessness, isolation and apprehension about the future,' he said. So even the doctors agreed prison was badly hurting me and my kids.

I was finally allowed out of jail after six months and when I walked out the door I was a big fat cow. I had stacked on 22 kilos — none of my clothes fitted and I looked disgusting. I had never looked like that in my life. So when I came out I had liposuction because what the fuck else could I do? I had liposuction and a breast reduction. I had had breast reductions before because I hated having big boobs and this time when I stacked on the weight in prison my boobs got massive again — and I hated that and having every bloke staring at my tits as much as I hated having a huge fat arse.

CHAPTER 22

CAN'T LIVE WITH HIM, CAN'T KILL HIM

In the end the very thought of touching Carl made me feel physically sick. We were still sharing the same bed a lot of the time but we had not 'slept together' for months before I finally decided that enough was enough and I was ending it with him. I knew then that our marriage was over. You can't be married to someone who makes you want to vomit when you even think about touching them.

One day I finally told him. It was 21 January 2003, and out of the blue, not after a fight or anything, I just turned to him and said, 'Carl, I have had a gutful. I can't do this anymore. I want a husband, not someone who drops in whenever they feel like it. I'm selling the Hillside house and moving.'

I always wanted a husband who would go to work, come home, I would cook his dinner and we would sit and have our family time together and be happy. It was sort of how life was going with Dean — we weren't in crime or anything, we were just living a normal life, going to work and living in the house, being like normal people. But then that all went to shit because, like I said, Dean became a prick and would beat me. I never had the beatings with Carl, but I never had the family life I wanted either. Maybe I should have known better and known that Carl was not like that and he was never going to live that life.

Carl got married — and maybe he did that because he wanted to make me happy more than anything else — but he never lived a married life. Or if he thought he was living a married life, his idea of married life and mine were very different. I didn't expect Carl to become a choirboy or suddenly run for the local council, but I thought getting married and planning to have kids would settle him down at least a bit and make him feel like he wanted to be at home more often. But to Carl, getting married was just a matter of having a wedding then carrying on like a single bloke. He was always out and about and having his scummy friends meeting him to go for drives and taking drugs and dealing drugs. I got to a point where I grew out of it. I just wanted a normal life. He was driving me crazy.

One day before I told him I wanted out of the marriage he pushed me so far I snapped and attacked him with a pool cue in broad daylight in the city. I had driven in with him to drop him off at his apartment. Carl had already moved into the apartment block in the city before we split up, because it was much more secure and his life was in danger. I knew it was also convenient for him because he could take his skanky hoes in there and root them whenever he wanted without worrying about me and the kids because, like I said, he was living the life of a single bloke.

So this one day he was being really cocky as we drove along and he was smart-mouthing me as he got out so I jumped out of the car and went after him with a pool cue I had in the car. I wanted to smash him across the face with it and swung it at his head but he ducked and I hit the side of my car with it. I dented the car and snapped the pool cue in half. Carl laughed at me because I'd missed and damaged my car and that only got me angrier so I kept going at him and attacked him with the broken cue. He ran away inside the apartment building but he realised I could get into the building and he knew that when I did I would wreck everything and attack him in the middle of everyone, so he rang me to talk to me on the phone through the glass doors and I calmed down.

I was so angry because I knew he was trying to get rid of me but didn't have the balls to tell me. He was trying to be such a prick to me that he would force my hand to be the one to end it. And it worked, because I got so absolutely sick to death of him it made it easy to tell him it was over. He was such a coward and a child that his way of dealing with things was to just not deal with them and to just be a prick about it, so I made the decision for him. Carl wouldn't have cared that we weren't having sex by then because he had been fucking everyone else the whole time we were married anyway — when he was with me he was probably glad of a night off.

We were never a lovey-dovey couple. Carl was never one to touch me much, hold my hand or give me a kiss and a cuddle. Months and months went by without Carl even kissing me or hugging me. And I was always a tomboy right from childhood, so I wasn't into being all cuddly either. In fact I am not even a sexual person really. I could have no relationship with anyone and not sleep with anyone for the rest of my life and it wouldn't worry me at all. I am just not a sexual person like that. It's one of the reasons I have had the breast reduction operations — as I said, I hate having blokes staring at my chest the whole time. I hate it. I am just as happy without sex. My kids keep me happy and that is all I worry about. Rob, my boyfriend now, won't like reading this, but he knows what I am like and we make each other happy.

Before I finally ended it with Carl I had so many nights when I just lay there on the bed sobbing myself to sleep because I was so unhappy. Sometimes Carl was lying next to me but he'd never ask me what was wrong, why I was crying and upset. I suppose he just didn't care. That really made me wake up and realise I wasn't in a marriage anyway — no husband would happily roll over and go to sleep night after night when their wife is crying.

A lot of the nights Carl wasn't there, I would cry. I wasn't crying because I was alone, I was crying because I felt like even when Carl was lying right next to me I was still alone. There's a saying, that you can feel loneliest in a crowded room, well that was how I felt in my marriage. I was married but I felt I was the only one in the marriage, because there was no relationship. Not a real relationship where the other person cares more about you than they do themselves. Carl has never cared about anyone more than himself.

It was like there was this loneliness in me that I had come to expect to be part of my life. I had my kids so I didn't feel lonely in that way, but I didn't have a husband. Carl would just go out and get himself a girlfriend, go and fuck Grace Arico or Nicole Mottram, but I am not the sort of person to go and search for another partner at parties and clubs or whatever. I had battled with depression previously so this all made it worse. For a long time I just put up with it.

Because of the abuse I had copped from Dean and my mum's boyfriends, I sort of came to think that that was how relationships with men worked — you just had to put up with being beaten or abused or treated as the bottom of the food chain. That was why I was attracted to Carl in the first place — he was gentle and was interested in me and he was the first male in my life that I had a close relationship with that didn't beat me. After a while, though, he became distant and bored, I suppose, and then he just treated me like shit. He'd be nice and charming when he wanted to, then he'd just ignore me and not come home for days at a time. In the end, then, it was just the same as all the other relationships I'd had with males, only without the bruises. Strange, isn't it, that the one male relationship I had where I didn't end up with broken bones was with a murderer.

When I told Carl I'd had enough and that I was going to sell the house to move somewhere closer to the kids' school, he couldn't have cared less. Carl and Andrew already had the city apartment so to him it wouldn't change his life much one way or the other.

I moved with the kids into a rental property in Essendon. Even though I had broken up with Carl he was still going to come and stay with us now and then because of Dhakota, so it was not like I was cutting off from him completely — I couldn't have even if I'd wanted to. But the house I moved to had all these trees in the front yard and Carl didn't like it because he said it was a perfect place for him to be ambushed by someone late at night. So he got sensor lights and stuff set up everywhere in the front yard, but it didn't make any difference, Carl still refused to come there anyway.

Later on when things were getting out of control with all the stuff going on with the Morans and Gatto and Condello, we decided it wasn't safe for the rest of us at the house in Essendon either, so we moved into the same apartment block as Carl and Andrew but on a different floor.

After breaking up with Carl I was suddenly 'single', but as with Carl's lifestyle, my life didn't change much either, being on my own. Even though I had been married to Carl the closest relationship I had with a male was not with Carl, it was with Andrew Veniamin. I felt so close to Andrew, it was like he was my brother or soul mate. I felt connected to him in a way that I never felt with Carl. He understood me better than Carl and I thought I understood him too, but then maybe that was all a lie as well because I didn't know half of what he had done in his life, and was still doing.

218

We had split up in January 2003 but when Carl was arrested in June 2004 I felt duty bound to go back to him. He needed someone and I was the mother of his kid and still technically his wife, so I felt I owed it to him to be there for him when he needed me most. I would take Dhakota in to see him, but I was never allowed to have contact visits with Carl because when he had been in jail before there had been an issue with a gun being smuggled into the prison. It was supposedly brought in to shoot Lewis Moran and the jacks said I organised it all.

One of the prison guards smuggled the gun in along with drugs and other stuff and he was caught. When he was questioned about it — he was later jailed for it — he gave evidence that I had met him and given him the gun. The jacks were obviously feeding him all his lines, because it was bullshit. The truth was they were doing what they could to set me and Carl up with anything at the time. I had never seen this prison officer before in my life — I do not have dealings with police or prison officers because at the end of the day they always have more to bargain with than you have. Anyway, they claimed it was me but it was bullshit and they knew it. All they had was the prison guard saying it and they knew that wouldn't stand up in court because they had worded him up. Even though they didn't charge me they did make life hard for me and stopped me having contact visits with Carl.

But it didn't last. How could it? He might have said all the right things and asked me to help but I wasn't the only one he was laying the charm on. I only discovered that that tall blonde girl, Renata Laureano, had come into the picture when his trial started and she turned up. That's when I thought, 'I am sick of your bullshit, Carl.' He was still trying to say to me, 'She's just a friend,' but I ended it then and there. Finally.

The huge turning point was the day I walked to court and saw her arriving with Barb and George, Carl's parents. Sadly, the whole thing was caught on camera by the TV crews and everyone could see how angry I was. I could have strangled Renata that day, and I could have slapped Barb. I probably would have too if the cameras hadn't been right in our faces. That just hit me in the heart, not because I was so in love with Carl or anything, but I felt betrayed and cheated because I had gone back to help him out when he asked me. I didn't want to go back to him but I did it out of a sense of duty to him and Dhakota more than anyone, and here he was shitting in my face.

In court Carl strutted around like some big stud calling out to me that he could still pull chicks when he was in jail. That was it, we were finished. The sad thing is Renata is gone now, and I am still visiting him and taking Dhakota in. Carl has another girl now and she sometimes takes Dhakota in. I get along OK with her, but I do think, 'What the fuck are you doing, you girls?'

CHAPTER 23

TRYING AGAIN

A few weeks before Carl was arrested for the murders we had bought the house in McPherson Street, Essendon. It was just an empty shell but we planned to do it up for me to move in with the kids. Carl would be able to stay at times as well, so he could see Dhakota.

We started to fix it up and we needed a plasterer so I spoke with my friend Beau Goddard who I had met through Dhakota's godfather, Tommy. Tommy and Beau had been in prison together and we became great friends with Beau. He used to come and eat and laze around at our place and I just loved him to death. His brother Brendon plays for St Kilda and we met him through Beau too, and he was a fantastic guy even though we didn't have a lot to do with him. Beau wasn't sleazy. You could walk around in a bikini top or walk out of the shower in a towel and not feel uncomfortable. So I told Beau I needed a plasterer and he organised a young mate of his to come over and give us a quote.

This car pulled up and Beau's friend Rob got out with his beanie pulled down low and he was all cocky and I thought to myself he was cute. He was with his brother, who was the main plasterer, and they quoted the job at $2,200. It was heaps cheaper than the other prices we'd been quoted so I hired them. They started on the job and two days later Carl got pinched. All the work on the house stopped because there was all this drama with the media and jacks around and they probably didn't know if they were going to get paid, so everyone disappeared for a few days. They eventually came back to work and then Rob realised I was on my own with young kids, so he rounded up all his mates who were tradesmen and they all came around and fixed the place up in three weeks for fuck-all money.

On one particular day I had money on me to pay the floor sander but he had done a shit job so I refused to pay him. When I drove off down the street Rob was on the side of the road because his car had broken down. We pulled over and he was stressing because it was a new car but it was out of warranty and it was clear he had no money. Well, he had helped me out so I rang up Carl's dad George and got a mechanic friend of his to fix it up for $1,800 and I just paid it. I used the money I was supposed to pay the sander. Rob was really thankful.

With Carl in jail I had no access to any money. He never ever left me access to large amounts of money because he knew I would just spend it. So that meant that from the day Carl got pinched I had nothing; his parents barely gave me a cent. All of a sudden I was living on Centrelink payments after having had more money than I knew what to do with. I was desperate and Rob was there for us straight away. Even after the work was finished he used to just hang out at the house and we would have a laugh. I got back with Carl when he was in jail because I felt sorry for him, so Rob and I were just mates at that stage.

After all the Renata Laureano stuff I dumped Carl and after a bit Rob and I got together. Rob was shitting himself about what Carl would think when he found out we had got together. He was virtually in tears stressing about it the first time. I asked him what the matter was and he said, 'What do you mean, what's the matter? I'm fucking Carl Williams' ex-wife — wouldn't you be fucking stressing?' I suppose I would, but I never saw Carl the way other people saw him.

No-one knew Rob and I were seeing one another but that wasn't surprising because we hadn't been together for long. Rob is nine years younger than me and he can be very immature, and at the time it gave me the shits. He had spent a few years in prison when he was younger and it was a bit like that time had taken something away from him. It was like he never had the time to be a kid so he was making up for it.

I knew he had been in jail and I knew shadows of the situation of why he had been in jail but not the whole situation. The bits I had heard didn't tally with what I knew of him. You might know by now — it was all over the front page of the *Sunday Herald Sun*, after all — that Rob had done time in jail for killing someone. It was true, but the story painted a different picture of it than the one I got and the one I believe. The story they told was that he was among a group of blokes who tortured and killed a 14-year-old boy before rolling his body up in a carpet and throwing him in the river. Which was right except that from everything I was told Rob was not there when the kid was killed or when his body was dumped.

Rob used to smoke bongs and hang out at the house of this drug dealer, Lance Franklin (obviously not the Hawthorn footballer). When Franklin went out Rob would stay in the house and do his heroin deals for him. One day this 14-year-old kid arrived, walked into the kitchen and asked Rob who else was in the house and where they were, and then he just left. A few minutes later two blokes came running through the place with balaclavas on and they bashed Rob and took all the drugs and jewellery in the house.

Lance Franklin and Rob and the others all presumed the kid had come into the house to check it out then gone outside and tipped off the blokes for the run-through, so they grabbed the kid and his older brother one day and took them back to the house. The brothers admitted they had been involved in the run-through, so they drove the older brother to where the drugs were supposed to be and kept the younger brother at Franklin's. When the older one got to where the drugs were supposed to be he escaped and did a runner.

Rob wasn't with them at this stage but he came over to Franklin's to smoke drugs and he walked into the room and found the 14-year-old kid tied to a chair. The others were bashing him and Rob hit him a few times with the baseball bat and left — he didn't care about this kid or the drugs being stolen, Rob was just a young kid who smoked bongs. That's what he told me and that's what the other blokes that were involved in it have told me.

The next thing, the kid had died so they rolled him up in a carpet and dumped him in the river. The crime is bad, I know, but I honestly don't think Rob was involved in killing the kid and dumping his body. Yes, he hit the kid a few times, but the kid had been involved in a run-through during which Rob was bashed. That didn't matter to the jacks, though, because they were all arrested and Rob was charged with murder like the rest of them. He got bail with a night-time curfew but one night he was pulled over just after his curfew time and he was remanded in prison for 18 months. Just before his trial his lawyer came to him with a deal to plead to involuntary manslaughter instead of murder. He did that and got seven years with a four-and-a-half minimum.

Rob was only eighteen at the time but he looked about twelve. He was probably two stone wringing wet so he could have found it tough in prison but his dad knew a lot of people — even though he had never been in trouble himself, he knew enough people to reach out to to make sure Rob was looked after in jail. It is a crime that haunts Rob to this day: I know because I have been lying next to him when he has woken up from having nightmares about it.

I met Rob four years after he was released from prison and I didn't know his background at the start. It was months after meeting him before I found out, not that it would have made any difference to me. I wouldn't have judged him because of that. I had been in prison so I was not going to hold that against him and I would have wanted to hear something from the horse's mouth rather than believing innuendo and rumour. So I wasn't upset that he had been to jail, I was more put off that he was still acting like a child. When I went to jail he hung around with Tye and even though at that stage Rob and I had not done anything, it felt a bit weird that he was suddenly good friends with my son. I had had Tye young so he and Tye were not that far apart in age. When we did get together Tye would tease Rob that he was that kid from *American Pie* who does the business with the mother.

Rob would visit me in prison even though we had never been together. He is a very loyal person. Since Beau got locked up for ten years for heroin trafficking Rob visits him all the time and helps him in whatever way he can.

Carl was a bit freaked out at the start when he found out Rob and I were together but he realised Rob was great with the kids and really good with me so he got used to it and it was OK. But Carl was never OK with me seeing Mohammad. I was with Mohammad after Rob and Carl hated Mohammad from the start. I don't know whether that was because he was Muslim, but Carl just hated him.

I had met Mohammad through Beau as well, and I really liked him so I started seeing him at the same time as Rob. Neither of them were serious relationships at that stage so I didn't see the harm in it. Mohammad and I would go out to eat and he started coming over and then we went to Queensland together and the friendship developed on that trip.

Carl hated that we were together. Mohammad was married when I started seeing him and Carl would say to me that I was fucking another woman's husband. He didn't care less that Nicole Mottram had been doing the same thing to me with him. He was a hypocrite that way. The point was it was different for me with Mohammad because he was open about the fact he was married. He told me he actually had two wives and they both knew about me and they were happy about it too. He explained to me that in his religion it's normal for a man to have more than one wife. I didn't like it, I thought it was weird, but I liked Mohammad and I was trying to be respectful of his religion and understand his culture. After a while I realised it was all bullshit — he was the same as any bloke and just wanted to be able to justify fucking anyone they wanted.

My sister Shaz also knew Mohammad and she thought he was a really good guy. And he was at first. Early on he seemed really nice but then as we got closer he started pushing this weird thing on me saying that in his culture when you're a 'proper' couple no-one's allowed in the woman's house. He said that I wouldn't be allowed to communicate with anyone but my family and I'd have to give up my friends — in fact, I couldn't have any friends because friends put things in your head that your husband may not agree with. It was crazy and I'd tell him it was bullshit and he didn't like that.

One night he left my place after we'd had an argument but then he came back soon after saying he had forgotten something. I let him back in the house and because it was really late I went to lie down on my bed while he got what he had left behind. The next thing I know he's sitting on top of me punching me in the face and yelling stuff about Rob. He suspected I had been seeing Rob and he was freaking out.

I was getting claustrophobia and panicking because he wouldn't stop hitting me and I couldn't defend myself. I was saying, 'Please, Mohammad, get off, I can't breathe.' But he just started mimicking me and said, 'Once I finish with you you'll need more than plastic surgery.' He kept punching me for a while, then just stopped, got off me and walked away.

After Dean I was never going to put up with anyone hitting me again so I wasn't going to have anything more to do with Mohammad after that and I told him so.

I've told a lot of lies to people about the time that I shaved my head but I can say now what honestly happened. Mohammad was the one who shaved my head. He was angry because he kept saying that I was seeing Rob — and he was right, I *was* seeing Rob at the same time as him, but the physical attack on me wasn't right. He wanted to cut my hair to make me look ugly so Rob wouldn't be attracted to me. He then took me to my hairdresser and Mohammad shaved my head in the salon. I was embarrassed about it so I told the kids that I shaved it because my sister had cancer (which, sadly, was the case) and I had cut it short in sympathy with her. The kids would have freaked out if they knew the real reason.

That was what Mohammad was like: he just wanted to have this life where he controlled the women in it. He was like a stand-over man with women in the way he made them do what he wanted no matter what they wanted. He believed women were like possessions and once they were with him they were his and he owned them and could do what he liked with them. He fitted the image many people have of Muslim men but that is not an accurate picture. Even though I had a bad experience with Mohammad it didn't make me think badly about the religion. Mohammad was just a fucking idiot but that doesn't make the religion wrong.

I had never really known about the Muslim religion until one night early on when we were in this café and he just started speaking about it. It intrigued me and what he was saying really made sense so I sort of hung on every word he said. I liked the idea that the women wore scarves to keep their beauty only for their husband's eyes. Why should other men get to look at a woman? I always thought the women who wore the hijab were made to by the men — and obviously Mohammad made his wife do it — but a lot of women choose to wear it because they like to be covered up so the only person that sees them is their husband. I had always hated being looked at and it was one of the reasons I had always had breast reduction operations — I hated men staring at my tits all the time when I walked down the street.

Mohammad got me books on the religion and I read up on it and I'd talk to this other girl that Mohammad had introduced me to who was instructing me in the religion. I had never been to a mosque, and I still haven't, because I didn't think I knew enough about the religion and so it wasn't respectful for me to be there. I had been brought up Catholic but I eventually decided I wanted to revert to Islam. They say revert to the religion, not convert, because the idea is that everyone is born a Muslim so if you have been brought up in another religion, when you finally come to Islam you are reverting to your true faith.

I sent Mohammad a text one day asking what I would have to do to become a Muslim and he wrote out all the words to say and I did that. There was some controversy among my friends because some of them were angry with me when they heard I did it. People were bagging me but I didn't care. People judge all Muslims by what a few people do and it is not fair, people should look into the religion before they bag it.

Despite my bad experience later on with Mohammad it still hasn't changed my views on Islam.

After Mohammad assaulted me I left him and got together properly with Rob. We are still together now and it is going well, even though a lot of the time he's still a bit of a child.

So the main relationships I've had with men have all been with violent characters, I suppose. Dean was a criminal and beat me. Carl is in jail for murder, Mohammad beat me and now I am with Rob and he has been in jail for killing someone too — even though it was involuntary manslaughter. I suppose you could ask why I surround myself with violent men and criminals, but the fact is that the lifestyle I have lived has not allowed me to go out into the community and be around normal, everyday people. After living the life I have lived you can't just fit into that circle.

As much as right now I am trying to get a business up and running and do normal stuff, I still tend to have friends that have had a criminal past and who are now also trying to work in the normal everyday community. People like Rob. And that is why I end up around them, not because we all want to commit crime together, but because they are not judgmental. If I went into some squarehead person's life and tried to fit in — even if I had not been in the media spotlight — it would be difficult. If I don't tell someone at the start that I have a criminal background and they find out later, they will think I have lied to them and won't want to be my friend, but if I do tell them at the start they are wary of me and judge me and don't want to be my friend anyway. That has been my experience of it, so it means the friendships and relationships I have all tend to be with people with something in their background.

CHAPTER 24

LAWYERS, GUNS AND MONEY

I saw Lewis Caine the day before he was killed. The kids and I had all been sitting downstairs eating in the café at the bottom of our apartment block when Lewis walked past. He came in and said, 'I spotted you, Roberta,' and he had this big laugh. He had a big coat on and I hugged him and said he looked like a polar bear.

The first time I met Lewis, which was through Carl, I thought he was related to the Morans because his name was Caine and there were Kanes that were related to the Morans. Jason's wife Trisha was a Kane — her dad was Les Kane, he was an old crook who was involved in the 1976 great bookie robbery with his brother Brian. Both the brothers were killed. So when I heard Lewis Caine's name I presumed he must be related to Trisha. When my sister Michelle said she had been hanging out drinking with Lewis Caine I was furious. One night when Carl and I were at Crown Casino — this is before

Andrew died and Jason Moran was killed — Lewis came up to Carl to hit on him for cash. Lewis never had any money and he was chasing Carl for some. Carl told me he was going over to talk to Lewis and his girlfriend and I said, 'Don't fuckin' bring them anywhere near me.' So I walked off while Carl talked to them and gave Lewis some money.

Lewis's girlfriend, Zarah Garde-Wilson, was a lawyer. That's how they met: she defended him on some charge and they ended up going out together. Neither of them ever had any money. They could never pay their rent, they had nothing. Carl met them in Chinatown one other time because once again they didn't have the rent money. I could never understand it because Zarah was working as a lawyer and even though she was only a young solicitor working for George Defteros, she was still being paid.

Carl used to meet Lewis a lot. I presumed from the fact that he used to look after him with bits of money here and there that Lewis had done some work for Carl. But we also knew he was friends with Mick Gatto and the other side. Like a few other people, he tried to keep friends on both sides of the fence, but that was never going to last. You had to pick your side at some point. I knew Lewis had done time for killing a bloke years earlier. Lewis knew karate or something and I think he kicked the bloke to death.

Gradually I got to know Lewis and through him, Zarah. One night Lewis came up to Carl's apartment for a drink and I said to him, 'Come downstairs and have a look at my place,' because I'd just moved in with the kids. But he was really paranoid and kept looking over his shoulder the whole time, thinking that I was setting him up or something. I didn't know what he was doing at the time but later I realised what he was thinking and I couldn't believe it. Once I had gotten to know Lewis — after initially thinking he was a Kane not a Caine — I was nothing but a friend to him and Zarah and it really saddens me that he would think I might have set him up. Anyway, he looked around the apartment really quickly and left.

A short while after this Carl and I heard that a body had been found, but it meant nothing to us because we didn't know the name. Lewis was born in Tasmania and his real name was Adrian Bligh, but I think he hated his dad, who was a copper or something like that, because he never used that name. He was only ever known as Lewis Caine. It meant that when the police said the body had been identified and it was someone called Adrian Bruce Bligh, we had no idea who they were talking about.

A few people in the media rang us to ask if we knew him and what we thought about it, but the name honestly meant nothing to us so we obviously said no we'd never heard of him. We rang around to people we knew to try and find out who this person was. I didn't even think to ring Zarah. Then Adam Shand rang me out of the blue and said, 'Do you know a Lewis Caine?'

I said, 'Yeah, of course. Why?'

He said, 'That's who Adrian Bligh is, that's who has been killed.'

I was stunned. I rang Zarah straight away. Carl was stunned, but for different reasons — he knew that Lewis had been killed because of him and that they would be coming for him next, but I didn't know anything about this at the time.

Zarah was beside herself, she was so upset. She had no-one with her and she had locked herself away in her apartment to grieve. Eventually she'd come around to our place and just hang out. I think she just enjoyed being around friendly faces. We became really close for a long time, so much so that we were like sisters.

When I went to jail on the ecstasy charges Zarah had been my lawyer and the one I would see all the time. She was my saviour at that time. I always knew she was looking out for me and she was always there on the end of the phone and coming in to visit me. She was the one who went in fighting for me when they had me in the slot for weeks on end and only let me out of my cell for less than an hour a day.

I was glad to be able to repay her by being there for her when she needed me. We were really close and I felt like we would always be friends, and that as time went on we would only get closer and closer. I loved her so much and thought she was wonderful, but looking back now I can see Zarah and understand that she was a little obsessed with the 'gangster' image. Lewis was a great bloke, but he was no big gangster. I think it's like she wanted to be in *Goodfellas* because she seemed very excited by the glamour of it. Zarah is a very smart girl, but I think she is also very immature in that way and she got completely sucked in by the so-called excitement of the criminal lifestyle.

I realised all of that later but at the time she was a girl who was really upset because her boyfriend had died. And she had been a terrific friend to me. She was really distraught and I was glad to be able to be there for her.

You might be aware already that Zarah and I had a falling out and I don't have anything to do with her now. I felt badly betrayed by Zarah. When I went to prison on the drug charges she stayed in my house, borrowed the car and filled it up with petrol every day on our card. She lived in my apartment and damaged it so badly I lost my bond. Obviously I didn't know at the time because I was in prison, and I thought she was terrific because she was my contact with the outside world and I enjoyed seeing a friendly face come in during my low times when I missed my kids and was desperate to get out.

After I had broken up with Carl, Zarah and I went away to Queensland together. I was seeing Mohammad at that time but for one reason or another I didn't want Carl to know about it. Zarah knew this, but she'd leave the room and go down the hallway and secretly make phone calls and get word back to Carl. Then she'd come back in to me and play the act of, 'Oh no, Carl has found out. I feel so sorry for you. How did he find out? Will he cause trouble for you?' Carl told me later that she was the one who told him.

It was about then that I started to realise Zarah wasn't the friend I thought she was. We had a big argument and didn't speak for a long time after that. I rang her a few times, going crazy and telling her I was going to punch her head in — which I was going to do — but then because she's a weak person I thought, how am I going to bash her up if she is cowering and crying? So I calmed down and eventually I just missed her friendship, so when things had cooled down enough I rang her and we started talking again.

I was so upset because we'd been so close. We used to have these long deep and meaningful conversations on the couch at my house and I thought she was my best friend. I even bought her a big diamond ring as a sign of our friendship. When I got it for her — it was my sister's ring and I bought it from her — I was all excited and rang Zarah and said, 'I've got a present for you.' We used to muck around and say, 'We're getting married now.' One night when she stayed at my place Zarah said to me, 'Roberta, if anything happens to me, would you look after my kids?' I said, 'Of course.' But then I had to find out on the grapevine that she was pregnant.

The thing was, even though we had had our big argument we had started speaking again but to have to then find out on the grapevine that she was pregnant was heartbreaking for me. I rang to congratulate her on the baby and she just went on about the father of the child and everything, and I thought there just wasn't any room left in her life for me. She rang me a few times asking advice on what to buy for the baby, and I told her that to me the top of the line pram was the Emmajunga because it was the one I had when I had Dhakota and it was great. But I didn't want to get drawn in to being close to her again because by then I knew what she was like — she was a user.

After Lewis died and Zarah went through all that thing in the courts about wanting them to let her have Lewis's sperm so she could get pregnant we had big discussions together. Even though we thought it was a bit weird we were pushing for it because we knew Lewis and how much she loved him and wanted his kids and thought it would be a good thing for her, and then she went and had a child to some loser who ended up getting pinched for spraying handbags in a Versace store because he was upset he couldn't get a refund. It was just stupid. Like, what sort of person is that? And what was she thinking being with him?

When she finally rang me and told me about the baby I was hurting inside because I had imagined myself being there to help her with the kid and suddenly I wasn't part of it anymore. The hard part was that Zarah didn't have a clue.

Zarah wasn't the person I thought she was and I think of the person I thought she was and I want that back. If Rob or the kids see me upset over her, they get angry and say, 'You should have realised she wasn't your friend.' I thought finally I'd found somebody who really was my friend and who understood me, but it was a lie.

I spoke to my friend Danielle Maguire, and she said, 'You should have heard how she bagged you around us, calling you a loud mouth and saying how she was sick of you and bagging your kids.' That upset me even more, of course. Admittedly it was hard to know what to believe with Danielle and Zarah, because both of them used to tell me things that the other one said behind my back. I think they both used to play each other off against me. It is funny, though — Danielle was a store detective at David Jones. Some of the boys — Carl's friends — didn't like that when they found out. We all went out to dinner one night to a Chinese restaurant and Andrew wouldn't sit at the same table as Carl and me because Danielle was there. He said, 'You can sit with dogs if you want to but I am not.' All because she was a store detective at David Jones, and to him that was the same as being a jack.

I think there was some truth to what Danielle said about Zarah, though, and that upset me because my eldest daughter Danielle and Dhakota idolised Zarah. Breanane never got along with her but the other two loved her. They rang Zarah about the baby a few times but she was stand-offish. Zarah used to take Dhakota down to the beach for the day. Her pit bull used to sleep on the bed with Dhakota from when it was born. I always thought we would be friends forever and now I know I'm never going to have this tight bond with her child that I would have had, and that saddens me.

I still can't believe that after all we had been through and how close we had been that she could have had her baby and not even rung to tell me. At one stage she'd wanted me to be in the delivery ward with her and then all of a sudden I was not even worth being told that the baby had arrived. That was low and I said so when asked by a reporter from the *Herald Sun*. They thought something might have happened to Zarah's baby because they saw her in court a week or so after she was due to have had it and she looked normal. They wondered what had happened to the baby and asked me whether I knew and I just said, 'I wouldn't have a clue because we don't speak anymore.'

I know some people don't like it when I am in the newspapers saying things about people, but the fact is I don't ask the papers to ring me and I don't ask them to print what I say. If they think what I have to say is interesting then that is up to them. The thing is, after all the shit I have been through I just say what I think and people either love me or hate me for it. So if the newspaper wants to ring me and ask me what I think of Zarah then I will happily tell them what I think. And I would do it again tomorrow — I would tell them that I was badly hurt by Zarah, who used me.

I think of Zarah quite a lot now, and I know this might sound like bullshit but it is true: I have a cry about her. I cry because it is like I am grieving for her and the friend I have lost. I suppose I should have known we were different — here I was having breast reductions and she was just tits in a tight skirt.

I didn't know it at the time but Lewis Caine was killed because of Carl. Not because Carl ordered him to be killed, but because of what Carl wanted him to do. This was at the time when things were going crazy out of control. It really started big time with Graham Kinniburgh being killed. Because of that Mick Gatto and all those Carlton Crew wankers thought that Carl and Andrew did it so they knocked Andrew. Gatto was on remand for the murder of Andrew so he was out of the way and with him in jail Carl obviously went after the other Carlton Crew.

Like I said, Carl knew that Lewis Moran, who was an enormous tightarse, had offered a bloke fuck-all to knock him, just $50,000. The bloke said no then told the jacks about the offer and word got back to Carl, so Carl had Lewis Moran killed. After that I think he figured that with Gatto in jail he would go after the Carlton Crew, because he knew they would be coming after him. Carl never actually told me that at the time but it was obvious because Carl knew the Carlton Crew wanted to get him more than ever and he had to get in first. Carl had lost his friend in Andrew but he also lost his hit man, and with Mr Y in jail he had to find someone else to knock them.

Carl was friendly with another old fence-sitting crook who I can't name for legal reasons, so I'll just call him The Snake. He was a rat-faced crim who was a complete snake because he was trying to suck up to both sides and make money out of everyone — play both sides to his own advantage. It was getting ridiculous, how many people were involved. At the time I had no idea what was going on, I was too busy dealing with my kids.

Things got bad after Lewis Caine was killed. He was suckered into a meeting at a pub. He was shot in the eye. I don't know if they were trying to be smart and say it was an eye for an eye or that he should have kept his eye on the ball and he should have seen it coming.

Carl obviously panicked a bit when he found Lewis had been knocked because he knew he would definitely be next.

CHAPTER 25

PINCHED

Carl had slept at his mum's house the night before he was arrested for murder. We weren't together by that stage but I was still his wife and we were still close and talking all the time. It wasn't unusual for Carl to stay at his mum's place even when we were together. I knew it was a scam — he pretended he was at his mum's but really he was rooting Nicole Mottram or Grace Arico or someone else. Anyway, it meant that the first I knew of him being pinched was when the phone started running hot.

I grabbed Dhakota and the dog — Dhakota never went anywhere without the dog, Simba — and raced over to Carl's mum's house. I found out on the way that Tye had been arrested too, as well as another friend called Chinaman who was a friend of Andrew's.

I had to get to Barb's to find out what was going on with Tye more than anything. I arrived at the house and there

242

was a jack at the front door trying to stop me going in, and I just said, 'My daughter wants her grandmother, get out of my fucking way,' and I went to push him, but he just cleared my path. Other police came out and again tried to stop us going through and speaking to people and I said to them as well, 'Fuck off, this is my daughter's grandmother's house. She wants her grandmother. You just do your fucking job, she's staying here.'

I asked them where Carl was and they said, 'We've already taken him,' so I rang Purana and they told me they had Carl and Tye. Tye had been arrested because he was at Carl's apartment when the police searched it. When they took Carl away they took Tye with him because they thought he might have been connected or something, I don't know why, but when I rang Purana they told me they had Tye there and that I could come down and pick him up.

I went to Carl's apartment in the city after the jacks had arrested and removed Tye because I wanted to make sure it was OK. I found a bag of speed in there and just grabbed it and stuck it in my bra because I didn't want Carl to be pinched with it. I didn't even think about this bag of speed when I went to the jack shop to pick up Tye, because I thought I was just walking in and walking out. But as soon as I got there they arrested me and I realised that it was all a stooge to get me down there in front of the media for their big publicity stunt. So that's where the news footage came from of me trying to fight the police — two jacks grabbed an arm each and they took me upstairs. I was pissed off and shitting myself because I thought they would definitely find the speed.

Upstairs this jack said to me, 'Have you got anything on you? Any weapons or drugs?' I said, 'Why the fuck would I come down to the police station with drugs on me? What kind of a fucking idiot do you think I am?' But I was wondering the same thing. I thought for sure they would strip-search me and find the speed and I would be stuffed, but they didn't. They grabbed my handbag and looked through that but they never actually searched me. Some dumb copper didn't know how close he was to pinching me.

They had us in the Asian squad offices, I am not sure why — maybe they thought Carl was Asian! I could hear Carl and Tye calling out and saying they were starving because they hadn't eaten anything. I handed the jack $100 and said, 'Can you get the boys some food? They're hungry.' One of the jacks went out and got everyone food and brought my $100 back because they were supposed to have fed them already anyway. Whatever, the jacks don't pay for McDonald's anyway, do they? They gave me my money back and took me into an interview room and started questioning me about Mario Condello and the Carlton Crew.

Condello was a slimy lawyer who I am told was Gatto's best mate after Kinniburgh. Gatto had him handling all of his business while he was in jail on remand for killing Andrew, so they were obviously tight. I always thought he was a wanker. Too smooth. He thought he was in *The Godfather* or something, the way he walked around and spoke.

I asked to go to the toilet because I was going to flush the drugs but when I went in there the plastic rustled really loudly and someone was standing outside the door, so I thought I can't get it out here or they'll definitely catch me. And then I thought that if they hadn't found it by then, they were not going to find it so I left it there. I went back into the interview room with this bag of speed in my bra and they started questioning again.

I didn't know what the fuck they were on about. I had no idea about any plan to kill anyone but it seemed they thought I did. Eventually the jacks let me walk because I wasn't saying anything and they had nothing on me. I got outside and there were media everywhere. I think the whole thing was just a big scene for the cameras to show off that they had Carl Williams in jail and they had arrested his family as well.

I drove up to my sister's house in Frankston because I knew Carl wouldn't get bail given what Purana was going to charge him with. What was happening didn't really sink in to me until I was sitting in the car in traffic looking up ahead and there above Young & Jackson's pub the big screen said, 'Carl Williams caught'. You would think they'd caught Osama Bin Laden or something. I just broke down crying. I was sitting there in my car in Flinders Street sobbing.

I knew that it was going to be a long rocky road ahead and a long stressful period we had to get through. I rang Zarah — this was obviously all happening well before I had the falling out with her — and she was trying to be really calm about it, saying, 'Everything's going to be alright, Bert, don't worry about it. He'll be fine.' Unbeknown to us the jacks were working on Mr Y and Mr Z to get them to roll over and lag on Carl and make shit up, and they had all this other information.

All this stuff was going through my head and I could see what was coming and I was freaking out. Everything was building up and I had no money. I knew I was going to lose the house in Essendon we'd bought when Carl was first arrested. The jacks put a caveat on it to stop us doing anything with it because they were going to claim it and other assets of Carl's as the proceeds of crime. It was our family home! So I had all this stress and I thought I was going to lose everything I had. Carl didn't give a fuck about me and the kids by then — he didn't leave us with any money or anything like that, he was only ever concerned about his mum and dad. I could see what was going to happen and that I was going to lose the house and I couldn't give my kids somewhere to live. I felt like I had let the kids down and couldn't look after them the way I wanted to and I hated it. It was terrifying and embarrassing and just kept building up.

Later on in court I found out all this stuff about Carl and Andrew and the boys that was news to me. At the time of all the bullshit going on everything was so crazy you wouldn't ask questions about a lot of things and other things you didn't even know had happened. I didn't realise the significance of everything until I heard it in court — like Michael Marshall being killed and his kids being there and his wife getting up and giving evidence. To hear that and then think you've been sleeping next to the person responsible and had no idea what they were up to was shocking to me. I had never given a second thought to a lot of the things that had happened but when it was spelt out in court it was like, 'Fucking hell, what was going on?'

It all became too much and I ended up in the Melbourne Clinic for ten days. I just couldn't cope and had a breakdown. My GP put me in the clinic because he thought I was ready to commit suicide. I don't think I was quite that bad but I knew I wasn't coping at all. I wasn't sleeping or eating, and I was worried about protecting my kids like a crazy woman. It wasn't healthy for anyone. At that point I probably could have killed anyone who looked like they were coming near my kids. It was just an overload and my doctor looked at me and said, 'Roberta, you're going into hospital today. You need help to deal with this.'

I got through but when I was in there I couldn't do any group sessions or programs because of the media interest — all they needed was someone to go and talk to the media and they would have been out there waiting to get pictures of me coming out of the nuthouse and writing stories saying, 'Look, Roberta really is nuts.'

I was getting through the days and with the medication I really felt like I was getting better and that I was actually coming to the end of my stay. I felt I could have gone home when the next thing I get is a phone call from some media outlet saying, 'Roberta, what do you think of Carl pleading guilty?'

I just flipped again. I was just frantic. I went up to the nurses' station and said, 'I've got to go home now. I have to protect my children.' They were at home with Rob but I needed to be there with them. As I got my stuff together, I was crying and stressed out so they gave me two Valium before I left to try and calm me down a bit. I drove home and found the media already there out the front of the house. My kids had egged them [bombed them with eggs] before I got there and I thought, 'Oh shit, that's all I need now, footage of the kids hurling eggs at the media.' It was a dumb thing for the kids to do, but they hadn't done anything wrong and the media were hassling them so I suppose they reacted.

I rang one of the TV reporters I knew that was sitting out the front of the house and said, 'Please don't put it on the news, because my kids will get their arses kicked by their dad and I don't need that shit.' He just said, 'They should get their arses kicked.' And they ran it, but that was the least of my worries at the time.

The media were insane with us. When I got up the next morning and looked outside the streets were lined with media everywhere. Rob was taking the kids to school and I walked out and told the media to turn their cameras off and said, 'If anyone films my children, I will have nothing to hide. I will go after you.' I went back inside and the phone rang. It was Carl.

CHAPTER 26

PLEA

Until I heard it from his mouth I had no idea what made Carl change his mind. I wasn't going to believe what other people said about it, all I could think was that some dog copper had something on Carl or his family and they were using it against him. I was confused. I mean, I had pleaded guilty to the ecstasy charge because I just wanted to quickly serve my time and get out but Carl would have known there was no way he was doing quick time on these charges. If he went down he was going to go down for a long stretch. I knew Carl wouldn't have pleaded because he was scared of other crooks. The fact was he *wasn't* scared of other crooks. There had to be another reason. And there was; one that I discovered later. I was confused and could not work out what he had been thinking, so I picked up the phone and it was Carl. 'G'day, Bert.'

'What the fuck have you done? Why, Carl?' Zarah had been telling us the case against Carl wasn't strong — and at the time we used to believe what Zarah was telling us — so I couldn't understand why he would turn round and change his plea.

Look, it might well be that Carl shit himself when he heard that those two lying dogs Mr Y and Mr Z had flipped on him and agreed to talk to the jacks and say a lot of shit to get themselves out of trouble, and he decided to cut his losses and try to make sure he got a decent minimum sentence. But that isn't what he told me. Carl said that when he walked out of the courtroom and the police were taking him back to his cell he saw jacks escorting a female prisoner down and he looked at her and thought of me and of his dad and the rest of his family. Until that point the jacks were still threatening to charge me. He said, 'I thought I will go two years without seeing you and talking to you while you are on remand trying to fight it and in the end they'll just fuck you over like they're trying to and I just couldn't do that. I couldn't let that happen.'

He said he just looked at them and said, 'Take me back into court.' They took him back in, called his lawyers, got the judge — the lovely Betty King — back and everyone. It was really late but they turned the prison van around and there were lawyers and jacks and judges going everywhere and no-one really knew for sure what he was going to do until Carl got in court and opened his mouth. I mean, obviously he must have said to someone what he wanted to do or else they would never have gone to all the trouble, but I think they were all still a bit worried that Carl was bullshitting and he would get them all in there and have a laugh. But he wasn't bullshitting. They got back in there and Carl did it, he looked at them and said he was guilty of another two murders.

He'd made a deal with them that his dad wouldn't go to jail for anything he had done; they also wouldn't charge me with anything. And he wanted to get a minimum sentence, because he knew if he went down for these two murders — he had already been sentenced from an earlier trial for murdering Michael Marshall — he would get life with no minimum. Carl wanted to know that at least he might get out of jail one day. The jacks and lawyers — the DPP [Department of Public Prosecutions] — agreed to it all, so Carl pleaded. And then he got 35 years as his minimum. Some incentive. I just couldn't think why he did that.

Before Carl cut his deal and before I had my breakdown, I met with Mick Gatto. I rang and set up a meeting because Carl had told me to go down and see Gatto and tell him Faruk Orman (a friend of Andrew's who was also a friend of Mick's) was going to be charged with Victor Peirce's murder. (Victor Peirce was one of four men charged, and later acquitted in court, of the Walsh Street police shootings in 1988.) So I went down and saw Gatto and said what Carl had told me to say. Mick wouldn't have a bar of it. 'No way,' he said. 'Nicola Gobbo told me there was no chance whatsoever that he would go down for the murder.'

Everyone knew that Nicola got information from police, the lawyers, the judges, whoever, and that her information was always right. For instance, just before Carl was arrested Nicola met him at a coffee shop near the court and they went for a walk. When Carl came back he told me that Nicola had told him he was going to be arrested. 'Maybe I should fuck off overseas,' Carl had said.

'Don't be ridiculous,' I told him. 'They've got nothing on you. You haven't done anything wrong, you should stay here.' To this day Carl says to me, 'If I hadn't listened to you and I'd fucked off overseas when Nicola told me I was going to be arrested, I wouldn't be in jail now.'

Carl had also told me to tell Mick that he knew what gun was used to kill Dino Dibra. I didn't know what the relevance of that was because I was just passing on a message, but I think he was trying to tell Mick that he knew who had killed Dino and that Mick was behind it.

Mick Gatto had written letters to Mr Z pushing him to make a deal and to say stuff about Carl to have him put away. Mr Z actually wrote to Mick saying, 'Is that money up for grabs? I've done the same thing as killing him — I've had him locked away for life — it's the same thing, basically.' Scumbag.

I don't know how many people Carl actually killed, or had killed. He pleaded guilty to three — Lewis Moran, Jason Moran, and Mark Mallia. Carl had already been sentenced over Michael Marshall's death.

But I have my doubts that he did all of those. I don't think he killed Mark Mallia despite the fact he pleaded to it.

Pleading guilty to something doesn't mean you actually did it, it is just part of the negotiation process. They charged Carl with Mark Cole's murder too, but they dropped those charges when he pleaded to these other ones. Like I said earlier, Carl didn't kill Mark Cole, Mr Z did.

I was in a Target store one day after Carl was sentenced and I had just gone through the register with my kids and was walking out when I got a tap on the shoulder. I turned around and this lady who worked there was looking at me and I thought, 'Do they think I've shoplifted?' But she just looked at me and said, 'Don't you know who I am?'

'No.'

'I am Mark Mallia's sister,' she said. 'I just want to know why my brother was killed.'

As soon as she said it I remembered seeing her every day when Carl was in court. I looked at her and said, 'I can't answer your questions. Mark was Maltese, he was the same nationality as me, we were friends. I don't know why he died.' I felt sorry for her because I wanted to be able to tell her something, but I didn't know what to say. I didn't know why Mark Mallia had been murdered. She really started crying then and I hugged her. This other girl came up and I said, 'Fucking go away, we're talking.' When she first started crying I told Bree to take Dhakota outside because I didn't know what she might have done — if I'd been her and I thought I was talking to the wife of the guy who murdered my brother, I would have attacked me.

I couldn't answer her questions. I couldn't say why he died, I didn't know what went on. Afterwards I spoke to

Carl about it and told him what happened and asked him what I should have said to her. He just said, 'Tell her the reason he was killed was that her fucking brother was trying to kill me.'

Carl admitted to it, I know, and maybe what he said to me that day would make you think he did do it, but I am sceptical about whether Carl committed that murder. The picture I get is, maybe Mr Y and he did it together, or Andrew did it with Mr Y. I don't know. Mark Mallia had a meeting with Andrew and Carl at Crown one night and he was hanging around for ages beforehand trying to suss them out and suss out the area. We'd been told on the grapevine that Mark Mallia had killed Willy Thompson, who was a friend of Carl's and dealt some drugs. So when Carl and Andrew walked into Crown to meet Mark at this little café, Andrew grabbed him and walked out with his arm round his shoulder and said, 'If I hear one more word that you're looking out for us or hanging round where we are, you're going to jack it before we do. Do you understand?' Next thing I hear, Mark Mallia is dead.

The weirdest thing was that out of everybody that was killed, Mark Mallia was never spoken about at all. Other murders, alright, no-one went into big detail talking about them, but they might say something about it. They would say how they knew them or they were happy they'd been killed or whatever. But it was funny, with Mark Mallia nothing at all was ever said. His body was found burned in a rubbish bin in Sunshine and I think they identified him through his tattoos.

As I said, in the end I am not sure who Carl killed or had killed. I don't know how many. I accept he had Jason Moran killed because he hated Jason's guts and I knew he was behind that one. And he organised for Lewis Moran to be killed because he knew Lewis was trying to have him killed and the jacks knew as well and were doing nothing about it. And he admitted to the Michael Marshall murder, but I saw no other indications of him being involved in other murders.

People tried to say Carl had something to do with Nick Radev's murder, but that was bullshit. Carl clearly said in a phone conversation with Nick not to go to a meeting with Snalfy because he knew Snalfy had organised to kill him. Carl only recently told me that Snalfy wanted Andrew Veniamin to kill Nick at Dhakota's third birthday. Carl said to Snalfy, 'If anything goes on at my daughter's birthday I'll kill you both, because you won't be doing shit like that where my kids are.' When Snalfy turned up at Dhakota's birthday without his own children I had no idea what the reason was. Carl only recently explained to me that that was the reason — Snalfy came with Andrew because they both planned to murder Nick at my little girl's birthday party. That made me feel sick.

Snalfy wanted Nick dead because Nick had been going through Snalfy to get his amphetamines cooked. Snalfy knew the cook and was jumping on the gear [cutting it] before he passed it on to Nick and before long Nick realised the gear he was getting was shit. Snalfy would just say, 'No, mate, that's how I am getting it,' but Nick remained suspicious so he wanted to meet the cook himself. Snalfy had no intention of letting Nick see the cook, so he got in first and knocked Nick.

Snalfy had it set up for Mr Y and Andrew to kill Nick. On the day of Nick's murder he made three separate phone calls from public phone boxes to confirm that Nick was going to be at the meeting place. When Nick arrived Mr Y and Andrew got there and, apparently, Mr Y emptied his gun into Nick and when he was on the ground dead Andrew emptied his gun into him too. They were laughing about it afterwards, calling him 'Swiss cheese', and I wondered what they were talking about at the time. I later realised what they meant.

Carl was friends with Nick and he says even now that Nick should never have died — he should have listened to Carl and not gone to meet Snalfy. Carl rang him that day to tell him not to go and he still went. Nick thought he was a bit of a tough guy and he wouldn't be intimidated by Snalfy or anyone. Mr Y had an incident with him in prison where Nick was going to pour petrol from the lawnmowers on Mr Y and set him alight and Carl stopped him. He said, 'Mate, you can't do that,' and pulled it up. Mr Y found out about it later and always had it in for Nick after that. Mr Y and Nick still crossed paths a bit — like the time Mr Y was at Nick's house snorting coke in the kitchen while Nick and Carl were out in the back yard doing business.

Carl had his issues with Mark Cole, but so did others. I mean Mr Z lagged in that Carl killed Mark but Mr Z himself had his issues with Mark over those stolen chemicals I spoke about. When there are drugs involved, I realised, people turn very nasty because it's always a case of 'who wants to be king of the castle.'

Poor old Dino Dibra. We've heard lots of stories about poor Dino. He and Carl were close friends and one day Dino went up to Fulham Prison to visit his mate Mark Morrison, who'd been charged with killing a jack when he rammed a car. Dino met him in prison while he was in for various serious offences and they became friends, and Dino used to visit him. On one visit a guy called Crabbe and Graham Kinniburgh and someone else were up there visiting Jason, and they all got into a bit of an argument outside the jail over Carl. Dino stood up for Carl because they were friends and there was such a commotion that the jacks came and they found a gun in Crabbe's car and he got charged and convicted over it.

I think they realised that day that Carl had some strong loyal people around him and that eliminating Carl's people was at the top of their list. That's the impression that I got. And if you look at it clearly, that's how it turned out. Dino was at a mate's place in Sunshine and someone rang him and said, 'Move your car.' So Dino ran out to move his car and the next thing he gets shot. He didn't die straight away because a friend called the ambulance paramedics. We thought he would survive — he'd copped a few gunshot wounds in the past and lived — but he didn't that time. They say Andrew was involved with that, and he was playing both sides then so it is possible.

Carl had nothing to do with the death of Victor Peirce, who was a friend of ours. Like I said, my sister had been married to an armed robber called Graeme Jensen and he had been a good friend of Victor's. The jacks charged and tried Victor, along with other blokes, with murdering two jacks in Walsh Street, South Yarra back in 1988, as revenge for the jacks shooting and killing Graeme.

Andrew killed Victor but that was before we knew Andrew. Victor was a good friend of Frank Benvenuto, who was killed in Beaumaris in 2000. Frank's brother, Vince, wanted to get the person who killed his brother. The Benvenutos were a big sort of mafia family — their dad, Liborio, was said to be the Godfather. It's confusing but apparently Victor found out that Mick Gatto had ordered Andrew to murder Frank Benvenuto so when Gatto found out that Victor knew, he had him killed and he got Andrew to do it. That is what they say, I don't know. Faruk was also charged with the murder because he was the driver when the car pulled up next to Victor's and they shot him in the street in Port Melbourne.

Then there was Paul Kallipolitis — PK. I met PK years ago — his brother used to be the garbo on our street — but I never really knew him. They say Andrew murdered him. I don't know what it was about, but that was the talk.

The couple, Terry and Christine Hodson, were in witness protection when they were killed in Kew. The police reckoned Carl killed them, but from what I can gather Carl didn't have anything to do with that and the jacks know it. The impression I got was that it was obviously someone they knew because there was no forced entry — they'd opened the door. They were under police protection so unless they knew the person, why would they open the door? If you ask me, it was obviously a police officer that did it. That is one suss case that proves there are dirty jacks.

One day in January 2009 I was surprised to read in the paper that Carl and George [George Williams was sentenced for drug trafficking and was released in June 2009] were out of jail and had been out of jail for Christmas. The article said the jacks had taken them to a secret destination to interview them about all the dirty jacks they knew. It was news to me and when I spoke to Carl it was news to him too. I spoke to Carl on Christmas Day and when the phone went it had that same recording you get on every phone call to Barwon Prison which says, 'This call has originated from Barwon Prison, our phone calls are monitored and recorded, it is illegal to divert a phone call, if you wish to continue stay on the line, if not hang up.' When I retracked my days I remembered hearing that message, so I wondered how he could have rung us from outside the prison with that message.

There was a photo in the paper of Carl and George eating and they made it look like they were out of jail at Christmas time and eating chicken and chips. But the photo was five years old. We had a laugh because they included a quote from the guy in the chicken shop saying, 'I would have been scared if Carl came in but I would have been more afraid if Roberta had have come in.' We joked that I should go there with a few of the boys to shake his hand and tell him I am nothing to be afraid of.

I eventually spoke to Carl about it and he said that he didn't go anywhere. If Carl had gone anywhere and had that privilege and agreed to speak to anyone, he would have got extra visits from his daughter. He said it was all bullshit and he hadn't gone anywhere or talked to the jacks. I don't know if he was lying to me but I don't think so because I couldn't care less if he lagged in jacks and neither could anyone else. Good on him if he did lag in dirty jacks.

How can police investigate police? They all stick together. One time when we were arrested Strawhorn, the police officer who is now in prison, actually went to Carl with another jack and said, 'All we want is a little cut of the action and you have got the green light to do as you please. We will come to you with any information we know of any investigations of you and whatever and you just have to give us our little pay packet each week' or month or whatever it was. Carl said to him, 'See your mate there? You might as well go and suck his cock because I am not sucking it for you. You are getting nothing out of me.' After that they went hell for leather on him. The Morans were paying them off and they had done for years. They used to meet above Ted's Camera Store in Elizabeth Street in the city and hand over money and get information.

So Carl pleaded and now he is doing 35 years in jail. I know he thought he would get a better minimum sentence and if he knew what he was going to get as a minimum he might not have pleaded to it. I always thought it was a dumb decision for him to plead. It never works out the way you think it will so I don't know why you would gamble on the rest of your life. I know Carl is thinking the same thing now.

CHAPTER 27

A BELLY LAUGH

One day Rob and I were shopping at Moonee Ponds Central shopping centre, which is where we always went to shop, and we were driving home when we saw people filming. It was a bit unusual — not a lot of people film in Moonee Ponds. So we stopped to have a sticky nose just in case it was Nicole Kidman or Hugh Jackman or someone. A girl was crossing the road from the filming so I called out to her and asked what they were filming. She said, '*Underbelly.*'

By then I was aware that there was a TV show being made called *Underbelly* that was going to be about all the people that died and I knew Carl would be in it. I had also heard that someone would play me in it but I didn't know who and I didn't know how much I would be in it. I didn't think I would really be in it at all.

Even so I was shitting myself — imagine how you'd feel if you found out someone was going to play you in a movie or on TV. You'd be curious, like I was, but you'd be shitting yourself about what they would make you out to be like. I had no idea how we were going to be portrayed. I wondered if they would use real names. I thought they would ring us and ask us questions and maybe the actors who were going to play us would want to meet us to talk so they could get to know what we were like before they did it. But no-one rang me or Carl (though Carl was in jail and meeting him would have been a bit hard).

What pissed me off was that apparently Mick Gatto was talking to them as some sort of consultant through all the filming. As you can see when you watch it, they make Gatto out to be the best person going. He was like some cool Mr Fixit organiser who sorts everything out, which was bullshit. The show was very sympathetic to him and I reckon it was because they were scared of him. Why wouldn't they have raised any questions about how Andrew was killed in the show? Gatto was found not guilty of killing Andrew because the jury said there was some doubt there. But I thought that Gatto's story didn't stack up. *Underbelly* didn't touch that, though, because it didn't suit them.

So when we saw them filming and the girl said it was for *Underbelly* I was naturally really curious. 'Is there anyone who plays me there today?' I asked the girl.

'Who are you? Are you Roberta?'

'Yeah,' I said, but she wouldn't believe me until I got out my driver's licence to prove it. She was laughing and couldn't believe it that they were doing a show with me in it and there I was sitting in a car and she didn't recognise me. Then she went over and got one of the other guys in the crew and I asked him if the person who was playing me or the person who was playing Carl were in any of the scenes they were filming there that day. I was curious to see what they looked like. He said they weren't there that day, they were just filming walking and talking in the park scenes. We said 'no worries' and left.

The next thing I pick up the paper and it says we somehow found out where filming would be that day and stormed on the set demanding to see Kat Stewart who played me. They said Kat was hiding or scared or something. That really pissed me off. I mean, we were out shopping at our local shopping centre where we went all the time and they turn out to be filming there. We didn't go looking for them, we were looking for our groceries. But when I ask an innocent question, which was a question I reckon anyone would have asked and anyone would have been curious about, suddenly I am some mad stalker who is going to go shoot them all or something.

I spoke to Carl about it and he laughed. He thought the whole idea of *Underbelly* was stupid and knew he was going to be made out to be a dickhead. I mean, Carl was in jail for murder, they were not going to make him look good, were they? He wrote to me about it from jail before it came out. This was what he thought at the time:

'You're 100 per cent right, they're going to paint me in a bad light in this upcoming *Underbelly* series — something like a brain-dead goose — but I expect nothing less and I don't really care what they say or do as I am now above that (ha ha). The facts are there which no-one can dispute — all my enemies are dead and I am still alive. I am the king of the castle and they are all the dirty rascals. They can all talk the talk but as proven no-one can walk the walk like Carlos the Jackal. As the old saying goes those who laugh last laugh the loudest and from what I have seen old Judy certainly isn't laughing, that's for sure. They don't mind dishing it out but let me assure you they don't like it when it is served back up to them hard and fast. They learnt the hard way — don't bite off what you can't chew.'

The funniest thing was a year or so before the show came out I saw an ad in the paper for people with big two to three storey houses, maybe with swimming pools, that would be prepared to let them be used for the filming of a TV show. Well, I rang up and said, 'I live in a three storey place, do you want to use it?' I thought I could earn some extra money from it, so I gave the guy my details and he never got back to me. How is this? It was for filming *Underbelly*. How funny is that? Back then I was not even aware there was a series being made — I don't think many people at all knew. It was a house I was renting at the time so it wasn't like it was my place and it wasn't a place I had lived in with Carl or whatever, so if they used it it wouldn't have been one of the actual houses we were in for the period of time the show was about.

When we finally got to see *Underbelly* on TV there were heaps of family and friends watching it with me and everyone was just on the floor in fits of laughter. I was throwing things at the TV and going off like a crazy woman. I was going mad. I fucking hated it. Everyone was killing themselves laughing, especially at that ridiculous part where Kat's getting her nails done and she's talking on the phone to the bloke playing Carl, telling him she had nothing on and was vacuuming. It was awful.

And the other part where I am out the front of court doing the business with Carl in the car. Carl rang me and said, 'Fucking hell, when did you start doing head jobs? Do you do head jobs now? I wish you were doing head jobs when we were together.' Carl knew I thought head jobs were yuck. Every girl does what she does but that is something I won't do. I was fuming about that and about everything, because it was like they were trying to make out it was all accurate as far as everything that happened and what life was like, but then they just made all this shit up.

Carl thought the whole thing was bullshit. No-one has ever really heard Carl speak so they don't know how to portray him. He just laughed about it and thought the whole show was stupid. He said to me that they would portray him that way, as some sort of dickhead. In the show they had him walk up to some of the boys at a café doing gun actions and our friends now walk around the house doing the stupid gun actions, putting one under their leg and all that sort of crap, imitating Carl in the show, not Carl in real life. Carl in real life would never do shit like that.

So much of it just made me cringe. And some of it was just sick, like when she said to Carl something like, 'I have got your spoof inside me' — I mean that is disgusting. And my kids have seen that — the oldest ones. In the show they had Carl in prison when I was pregnant with Dhakota and then when she was born, but Carl was out the whole time I was pregnant and was at Dhakota's birth.

I suppose when anyone is going to be played by someone on TV or in a movie they think they should be played by someone gorgeous. I mean, I knew they probably couldn't get Angelina Jolie to play me but I thought they could have chosen someone better looking for it than Kat Stewart. I just thought they had chosen some ugly chick to play me at first but then I saw Kat in other things later on and I saw her in interviews and I realised she isn't ugly at all, she is actually quite good looking, but they just made her look really ordinary to play me in the show and that got me really pissed off. It is not that I think I am overly attractive but I thought they made her look uglier than I am. She looked rough and yucky on *Underbelly*.

And they put her in tracksuits all the time. Why did they do that? I think they thought if she wore a tracksuit all the time it would make her look like some big bogan. But I have never worn anything but suit pants and dressed immaculately to go to court. There was only one time I had my beanie and jeans on, because I didn't give a shit. But I don't wear trackies around all the time. Everyone has trackies they wear at times, slopping around the house, but I don't wear them walking around the streets every day like they had her in the show. They just tried to make me look like some big fat bogan doing that. Well, not fat — at least Kat was skinny — but the tracky thing really got me because I thought that was just trying to degrade me.

But even that didn't upset me as much as when I saw the way they portrayed me as a parent, because I am not like that with my children. I certainly don't call them sluts and awful names. I try to be the best parent I can be and I know I am not a perfect parent but I haven't met the perfect parent yet. I certainly tried to stop the cycle of child abuse in my family by making sure that I did not repeat with my kids what had happened to me. Sometimes I'll yell at my kids and I think to myself, 'Don't do that, you are being a Dorothy.' (Dorothy is my mum's name — I don't think I bothered mentioning that earlier.) And it upsets me and I tell myself to stop it.

I am so concerned not to be like my mum that I am probably a bit soft on my kids if anything, but they tried to make me out as some foul-mouthed abusive mother. They never spoke to me or my kids but obviously just thought, 'Oh well, we've heard her go off on the TV news, she is just some bogan and they all wear tracksuits and abuse their kids,' so that was how they were going to portray me whether it was accurate or not. That really upset me because I am very proud of the way I have raised my kids and the *Underbelly* people belittled me and misrepresented how I am with them.

I also don't think I am rough spoken the way I was portrayed in the show. I know I can get pretty rough when I get worked up and when I get angry I swear a lot. When I get wound up I am despicable and will say anything, in the same way as when I am wound up I will react with violence. That's how I am when I am angry, but it is not how I am all the time. When I am calm and speaking in normal conversation I am civil and well spoken, I think. My language just gets pretty rough when I get wound up, but they presented me as though I am wound up and abusing people all the time, and I am not like that.

On the one hand I think, well, they don't know me and never spoke to me to find out, so I know it is not accurate and is not what I am really like. They have decided what I am like from seeing bits and pieces of me on the TV news when I have been outside court and I have been emotional and angry. How can you decide what someone is like in the rest of their life from how they behave outside court when they are really emotional and angry? So I think if that is what they have based it on then it isn't real so don't get shitty about it.

But then on the other hand I think, why didn't they make an effort to find out what I am like? Why didn't anyone ring me to say we are portraying you in this show and we would like to come and talk to you to get to know you so we can be accurate in how we make you look. I would have done that. They did that with Mick Gatto, why not us? Maybe it was just easier to think they knew it all already.

At the time I thought that Kat Stewart was a filthy bitch for the way she made me come out and that was why when people in the media asked me what I thought of her and the show I said that if I ever saw her I would grab her by the throat and bash her. But I have calmed down about that now and realised that she was just an actor saying the lines she was given. She didn't write the script, she was just paid to act a part. She was doing her job and did the best job she could with the script she was given. So now that I have had time to reflect on it I am not upset with her at all. I think, if she didn't know me, how else could she play it?

And I saw her and the actor who played Carl do an interview on TV the morning after the Logies and the girl who was interviewing them was bagging me and tried to get them to bag Carl and me in the interview, but they wouldn't do it. They overrode it and kind of stuck up for me a bit and I thought that was nice and I thought, good on them, because they could have taken an easy cheap shot at me especially as that was what the interviewer wanted. So I respected her for that. And each time I have seen her since I like her even more, so she has nothing to fear from me. I wouldn't hit her if I saw her now, I would smile and probably shake her hand.

It was funny, though, because even though I didn't agree with the way they portrayed me and didn't think I was like the person they made me out to be, a lot of people did like the person they thought I was from the TV show. It got me a huge fan base of people who liked me in the show. Thousands and thousands of people send me emails every week now. I have 7,000 Facebook friends and I have 3,000 people waiting to become friends. I get messages all the time telling me whenever anyone mentions me on TV or radio. When I did an interview after Barb, Carl's mum, died, I got heaps of messages from people saying things like when I cried they all cried with me. So it was nice to know that even though I didn't think *Underbelly* portrayed me accurately, it created a huge amount of support for me among people.

I did a lot of media afterwards and it was odd because Channel Nine, who made *Underbelly* and didn't come to me before they made the show, came to me after they made it and got me to go on *A Current Affair*. Nine offered me a contract, not to be an employee, but a three-month contract of $3,000 a week or $12,000 a month to be available to go on their TV shows. I didn't sign it, though, because I didn't like a clause in the contract that said I had to give them any material, videos or photos of my family that they requested. I thought, I am not giving you my family stuff. They would have wanted my wedding DVD and no-one had ever seen that. I am using that in the documentary I am making about my life and I have included photos from the wedding here in this book, but why should I just hand everything over to Channel Nine?

They flew me up to Sydney to meet the big bosses of Channel Nine because we were talking about me having my own program in which I would help kids in need, troubled kids. I was really keen on that idea and that was my reason for wanting to be involved with Channel Nine, but now I think they weren't really serious about that idea. I think they just wanted to make sure I wasn't on another TV station.

CHAPTER 28

BYE BYE BARB

I knew something was up. It just wasn't like Barb. Every
Saturday morning I used to take Dhakota to a cooking class
for kids called Little Kitchens in North Fitzroy. It was just a
bit of fun where the kids learn to make things with this
proper chef. Dhakota used to love it and it was our routine
after the lessons on a Saturday morning that we would call
past Nana Barb's house and take her what Dhakota had
made or give her a recipe. It was nice Dhakota loved that
part as much as the class because she got to be a big girl and
show off to her nan. Anyway, this Saturday I rang Barb's
house to tell her we were on our way and going to drop in
and there was no answer. We rang and rang and rang but
she didn't pick up the phone, which was unusual, but I was
thinking to myself that she was busy and didn't want us to
call in. In my gut deep down I had a bad feeling because
Barb would never really do that; she loved Dhakota coming

over on a Saturday. But you never want to think the worst of situations, so I figured there must have just been a normal explanation.

So we drove on home where I got a phone call from someone in the media — again — telling me that they had heard that Barb had been harmed in some way. I just went into meltdown, I was shaking and panicking because I just couldn't comprehend that something would happen to Barb. Obviously my first thought was that someone had hurt her to get at Carl some way and I knew that that was way out of line.

I desperately tried to ring Barb's sister but I got no response. Eventually I was getting nowhere so I just said to Rob that we had to get over to her house and find out for ourselves what was going on. We arrived and there was police tape up and jack cars around the place and media there and I just thought it looked seriously wrong. I sort of got out of the car and just collapsed on the ground. I think my body went into shut down, I just could not cope with the idea that this was happening.

I went across to the house and the police confirmed to me that Barb had died and it appeared she had taken her own life with prescription drugs.

I found out later that on the mirror in the bathroom upstairs Barb had written 'I am sorry' in black eye-liner pencil. That made me sad because I think she had felt she had no other option, but there is help out there that people don't tend to search for. She didn't have peace, she had hell every day from various things in her life.

Barb and I had had our moments before she died but deep down I really loved her like a mother — I had always loved her. But at first I was just really angry at her, at how selfish it was to take her own life and deny my daughter her grandmother. That upset me most. I kept asking the police if anyone had told Carl yet because I didn't want him to find out about his mother's death on the evening news. The police told Carl and I'm not sure what he did but I'm told he didn't cope very well.

I remember the first visit I had with Carl after it happened and it was understandably a very emotional day. With Carl and me, there was no bullshit that you had to be sorry about what the other person would think, he could just be himself, so I think it was the first time he could really let himself go and grieve about his mum. He just broke down with me and we sat there and cried together; we just couldn't stop crying. Carl would never let other people see his emotions like that, but he knew he could be himself with me.

It was just an awful time because you are dealing with all these mixed feelings of anger and sadness and rage and guilt. I loved Barb to death but in the days before she died we had had a bit of a dispute because Carl had taken up with another woman and he was getting Barb to do his dirty work and ring up and threaten me and abuse me. At the time I got the shits with Barb for that, but with time — especially now that Carl has broken up from that dirty skank and asked me to do exactly the same thing he'd been getting Barb to do to me and ask me to ring this girl and threaten her and abuse her — I have understood that she was just doing what Carl asked. And besides, any mother is only ever going to side with their child, I know that better than anyone with my kids (not from my own mum, of course). So I have calmed down about those last days and know that that was a minor argument in the scheme of things and it would have passed. More importantly, I remember what Barb meant to me and the kids and how much we all loved her.

I remember right back to the first time I met Barb. It was back in 1994 when I was still with Dean and Carl rang us one hot day to come over and have a swim. The kids were only young and we drove over and got lost on the way and I rang and Barb gave us directions. When we got there she had cool drinks for us and something to eat, she was just so welcoming.

We all used to go away in a group together to Yarrawonga waterskiing. We all had jet skis and the kids have all skied since they were really little and are really good at it. I was trying to ski on this trip, because I had never done it and I was always really scared of water. Dean was swearing at me and yelling out at me, calling me a fucking slut and abusing me and telling me to just get up and ski. Barb told me a little while later that she couldn't believe the way Dean spoke to me. So right from the start she was really nice and great.

Years later when Carl and I got together, Barb would always be so nice to you whenever you went over. She would always be cooking you something to eat, making up bacon and egg rolls in the mornings. Their home was always welcoming.

When I fell pregnant with Dhakota I told Barb I thought I was pregnant and she said not to get too excited but to get onto the IVF doctor straight away. I did that and we found out I was pregnant and the first thing Barb bought me was a little pair of pink and white socks with the gumnut babies on them. I asked her, 'Why did you buy pink socks, Barb?' And she said, 'Because you are going to give me a granddaughter. I know this is going to be a girl.' Carl and I had convinced ourselves we would have a boy, but Barb had her mind set on it being a girl. Then she was there when I gave birth to Dhakota, and she was so excited she was crying and hugging everyone and taking photos. She never wanted to leave the hospital.

Those memories just made me angrier with her that she would then leave that little girl and deny her a grandmother by taking her own life.

My original thoughts were for Dhakota because I thought, 'This is all she has' — her dad is in jail, her grandfather is in jail, and now her grandmother has just died. The grieving process is first emotion, then anger, then disbelief, and then what if? I still get angry that she took her life. To me, Barb seemed like a really strong person so it is hard to comprehend that somebody who is strong could not deal with things. But then I think of her and think that she is a mum and she had lost one son to an overdose and one would be in prison for the rest of his life, and she was with someone she loved but who was telling her constant lies.

It was reported that she was heartbroken about being left alone while George was in jail and because Carl would be in jail for ages, and that was probably part of it — and the fact that her first son Shane had died of a heroin overdose — but it was also because she had had a fight with her boyfriend. She had been seeing somebody for years and she wanted him to move in with her and he kept promising to move in but never did. He was stringing her along and never had any intention of moving in. I think she realised that she would never be with him properly and she just felt very alone. I think it was a cocktail of everything that led her to that fateful day. As coincidental as it is, my dad died on the exact same day as Barb — 22 November.

It was hard to take. As I've mentioned, I'd sort of had my disputes with Barb at the time she died but with Carl and George in jail I obviously had to be the one to organise her affairs and the funeral. That was tough. It was a hard time but I gave a eulogy to Barb that day in church that I think best explains how I felt:

> Barb was the mother that I never had. I did not grow up in a family where there was a Mum like Barb and I wanted nothing more than that in life. I still want it. There is no greater champion in this world than a mother who wants the best for her kids through thick and thin. That is the legacy of love she leaves behind for us.
>
> She never stopped caring for us — George, Carl, Dhakota, myself, Danielle, Bree and Ty, it was all one big family, not stepkids and new kids, all one unit to be defended and protected. That's part of the sadness

that I feel today. She cared more for us than for herself. She stuck by us even when we were wrong. She stood up to our enemies, the police and even Supreme Court judges, because she believed loyalty was a lifetime thing, not just a luxury for when things were going well. She knew loyalty was a sacrifice and she was prepared to pay the cost. She loves us unconditionally.

Barb and I had our differences. We had some very big loud nasty arguments. I never knew a mother's love like Carl and his brother Shane did. And I will admit that I didn't know how to behave, how to back down without giving in. I thought when you were wrong, people turned away from you. But not Barb. Despite the sorrow of losing Shane, of missing Carl and splitting up with George, her love still flowed in abundance. The turn-out today is evidence of that.

Barb used to say to me: Bert, you don't know how to say sorry. Just say sorry and we can go on with life. That was Barb, no grudges, no bitterness, no second thoughts. She was with you all the way, forgiving, encouraging, always seeing the best in a bad situation. Well Barb, your passing has shown me the true meaning of sorrow. As you watch over us, please know that I am truly sorry for any harsh words that passed between us, there were plenty. I remember that she used to keep a swear jar at home and she used to say to Dhakota, make sure your mum comes here all the time, because we are going to have a lovely holiday on Mummy's bad words. I could fill that jar in a couple of hours when I got going.

These are not just words, but a lesson for us all here today. Let's honour and remember Barb's spirit in the way we deal with each other, the love and loyalty that we show to one another. Let's see the best in everyone and try to forgive and forget the worst. Let's look after the people who are there for us and who never ask for anything in return. Don't wait till it's too late, come straight out and say how much you love them, how grateful you are for the part they play in your happiness. Barb did not live in anger and regret, though she had every reason to feel that life had not turned out the way she had planned and worked so hard for.

But she had a way of turning negative emotions into positive ones, minuses into pluses.

During the worst of times in recent years, Barb provided a place of solace and sanctuary for her granddaughter, my daughter Dhakota. She made her feel safe and loved, made sure she could enjoy the same simple things that all little girls deserve.

She used to say that I had given her what she had always wanted in life, a daughter. I could go now, having done my job!

I will never forget how overjoyed she was when Dhakota was born, so happy she forgot how to say her name. She told a couple of people that she couldn't remember Dhakota's name, but it sounded like coyote.

The name didn't matter as much as the joy of her arrival.

Barb made sure that Dhakota had a childhood when the mistakes that her parents made had threatened to rob her of that right. She was patient and indulgent, the perfect grandmother, but all too often a substitute mother, when I couldn't be there. And she played father too after Carl went away.

She was there for all the important moments in Dhakota's life so far, her first violin lesson, her first day at school, and any other time that she was needed. She was never too tired or too busy to be there.

And in her hour of despair, it was to Dhakota that she turned one last time. She rang us and asked to speak to Dhakota, she said she couldn't sleep without speaking to her. Barb asked Dhakota to sing her favourite song, a tender memory of love and hope to take her to the hereafter. She leaves so many memories for us to cherish. We wish there were so many more, as if there could ever be enough. But we are truly grateful for the times we spent together.

I remember Dhakota playing dress-ups and beauty shop with Barb. Kota was smearing make-up all over Barb's face and making her hair into a huge mess and Barb would pretend that Dhakota had made her up like she was fit to meet the Queen.

But what I will be always thankful for is the fact that Barb instilled in Dhakota the power of love. It really was a miracle that this message was sent and received, considering how much hate there was in our lives because of the dramas we had got ourselves involved in. Barb would say to Dhakota that hate was a bad word, there was no need to waste precious energy on that emotion. See the best in everyone, she would tell Dhakota.

And the miracle does not die with Barb. It lives in my daughter's eyes and how we treat each other from here on in. The Bible tells us that God sacrificed the life of his only son Jesus Christ that we should know His love and mercy.

If Barb's passing helps us to see the abundance of love in our own lives, rather than the hate and jealousy, her loss will not have been in vain. And she will be watching over us, I know it.

At the time I not only had to organise the funeral, I had to pay for it. Carl reckoned he had no money because the jacks had seized assets and frozen accounts and everything, and George also reckoned he had no money, so it was left to me. I mean at the time I was angry with Barb because she had been pretty hurtful to me in the months before she died, and here I was having to be the one to reach into my pocket and pay for the funeral. It upset me then, but now I have got over that and I just miss her, and I think I understand the whole time a lot better now. Back then though, I wasn't exactly flush with money myself so I stupidly went on TV and did an interview when I was in no real state to be doing it, but we needed the money for the funeral.

What made it even more upsetting is that after the funeral I was tidying up her house and getting her things in order and I stumbled across some letters from Carl. I am not a nosey person so I would have normally by-passed them, but I had to know what was important and what wasn't so I had to read everything. I looked at this letter and I thought it might have been to Dhakota because it had a smiley face on the top of it like the ones Carl would put on the top of his letters to her, which he prints out on his computer in prison. So I read the first paragraph and I just couldn't stop. It was a letter from Carl to his mum, but it was about me. The more I read on the more horrified I became. He was telling her to buy a pre-paid mobile phone because it wouldn't be traceable and she and her boyfriend Connie should use it to harass me. He was calling me an evil bitch who had ruined their lives for years and now it was payback time. I realised at the time that the letters were not that recent but they were recent enough.

As for what Carl said in the letter all I can think is that because I had caught him out having his affair with Nicole Mottram, he knew they could never be together and he wanted to blame me. It was bullshit because as if Carl ever didn't get his way with anything in life. If he wasn't with Nicole Mottram, who was supposed to be his big sweetheart, it wasn't because of me.

It would have had more to do with the fact that her twin sister was a jack and her brother was a jack too, so you could imagine how happy the family would be to have Nicole turn up and say 'Oh here's my new boyfriend, his name is Carl Williams, you might have seen him on the news. He is a drug dealer and he might have killed some people.' Her family would never have allowed them to be openly in a relationship together so they used to sneakily see one another behind my back and behind her family's back. I used to find messages in the phone from her and I was not one of these women who would accept her husband having an affair, so I would have a go at him and he resented me for it. He wanted me to be some obedient wife who just did whatever her husband wanted and let him get away with all his shit and his other women. So in his mind he wanted to blame me for him not being with Nicole Mottram and it was easier in his own head if he could tell himself it was all my fault and I had destroyed that part of his life.

There was another letter from Carl among his mum's things, which was disturbing too in its own way. It was a letter from Carl in prison again and it was to his girlfriend. I am not sure which one it was because it didn't have her name on the top — I think it was probably that Renata Laureano. I don't know why Barbara had the letter; he must have sent it to her to get her to send it on to his girlfriend. In the letter he was telling the girl they were going to do IVF and now that he was divorced from me I had no right to say anything about it. He went on in that letter too that I was the one who ruined his life. There was no date on the letter so I don't know how old it was but it says in the letter 'you are not even 23 yet' so I believe it must have been Renata — she was only twenty-one when he was seeing her in jail.

It would be just like Carl to want to have another baby through IVF while he is in jail. The wanker. He showed with Dhakota that he was good at having beautiful kids, just not at being a dad. He already had one daughter who only knew her dad on contact visits and now he wanted another one. Fortunately, Carl broke up with that moll before any of that happened. When he did break up with her then got on to me telling me to ring her and threaten her and abuse her, I just thought then that this was what he did with his mum and it put the whole time before she died into a new perspective for me.

My heart hurt most for my daughter when Barb died, because she was another victim of someone else's actions. Adults can deal with their bullshit and make their own choices but these little kids don't have any say in it. I include the Moran kids in that as well — they go to school with my daughters and they are lovely kids and they shouldn't have to deal with the stupid things their parents did, which have left them all without their fathers. That goes for Carl too. Dhakota has basically been left without a father — sure, she sees him each week or whatever in prison, but what kind of relationship is that?

It is really sad and makes me have a little cry because each year she buys her dad a Father's Day present at the school Father's Day stall, and because Carl isn't allowed to get presents in jail, she puts them in her cupboard for when he gets out. She was being teased by a child at the school stall, who said, 'I don't know what you're doing buying Father's Day presents — your dad's in jail.' But she just brushes it off at the moment. It is always sad and emotional when she goes in and has to leave him behind. But that is the life she has now, that is the life Carl has given his daughter.

Carl is a different man now in prison in one way at least. He has lost 27 kilos and is down to 83 kilos now — when he went in, he weighed 110. He does weights, and runs 10 kilometres a day on the treadmill and he is eating better because he just realised life is too short to be a big fat pig and you need to eat properly and exercise and worry about the future — even in jail. I don't want him to die in prison of a heart attack or high cholesterol. I want him to walk from prison one day a free man into the arms of his daughter. He knows that he will have a married daughter by then and grandchildren. The sad reality is that his grandchildren will have to meet their grandfather in prison, and his son-in-law will have to meet him in prison. People will have to accept these factors, and I'm hoping that Dhakota does marry a nice normal working-class man and lead a normal life. That is my dream and I will hopefully lead her to that.

I remember there were times when I was about six or seven that I would get upset and cry for my dad, but if anyone asked me I would pretend it was something else that had upset me and brush it off. And just recently I was putting Dhakota to bed and she started wiping tears away and she wouldn't say what it was that had upset her, but I just know she was crying for her nan. And that made me leave the room wiping tears from my eyes too.

CHAPTER 29

WHO'S YOUR DADDY?

The letters I found from Carl in his mum's belongings said a lot to me about what Carl was really like. As the days go on I wish I could just say 'see you later' to Carl and cut him completely out of my life and never see or hear of him again. Obviously because of Dhakota I can't do that, but it doesn't change the fact that I wish I could. It is a misery that is ongoing and will continue to be ongoing in my life.

I know I look better in the public eye now that I have changed my life around and I am not involved in crime — I no longer see anyone from that time in my life — but I know that I can never completely get away from it because of Carl. When Dhakota is an adult she can make her own choices about her dad and she can be the one to deal with him if she wants to, because by then I won't have to. And one thing is certain: he will still be in prison so he won't be in my face.

I cannot say I wish I never met Carl Williams because we had Dhakota together and she means the world to me. I would not give her up for anything, but in so many other ways I wish I never had anything to do with Carl and wish I never had to have anything to do with him in the future.

He has dumped Renata now and has another young girlfriend who is twenty-one. When he started seeing Renata he wrote to me once from jail and said, 'I can still pull 'em even when I'm in jail.' I honestly don't know how he meets these women and why it is they are attracted to people like him who are locked up for life. They must be the kind of women who have an obsession with criminals, like those women who start relationships with prisoners on death row in the United States. The only thing that I can think is that these women like the glamour and the drama of it, and that they sometimes find it romantic — it's a stupid fucked-up idea of romance.

It is not just Carl. The other day I got a message from the girlfriend of this guy we used to know who was a big drug dealer and knew all the Morans and Carl and everyone. The boyfriend is in prison now and she has got a newborn baby and another child. I remember going to their house a few times and it was full of people. They had all the most expensive stuff in every room and there were drugs everywhere, and people were taking them and drinking and eating the best food. But when she rang she said she had nothing, not even money for her children for Christmas, and she was desperate. So I sent Rob over to give her $1,000 and she messaged me back saying, 'I can't thank you enough,' and I messaged her back saying that of anyone in the world I knew exactly how she felt, because I had been that person not so long ago. When the drug dealing is happening and the money is coming in everything is great because everyone wants to be your friend but it is all bullshit. They are not your friends. They all disappear when the money and the drugs run out. All of a sudden you are very alone.

I would love it if Dhakota didn't have to see her father in prison because I just don't think it is healthy for a girl to grow up going in and out of prisons. But of course I am not going to stop her seeing her dad and I would always take her. She doesn't get upset going in to see him because she doesn't know any different: she has never had Carl in her life because he went to jail when she was a baby. She doesn't really know why he is in there, although he has explained it to her in his own way. Carl's parenting is a lot different to mine — my idea would be to wait until she is sixteen or old enough to really understand and then tell her the full story, but Carl told her, 'Daddy is here because somebody was going to hurt him and he hurt them before they hurt him.'

I don't believe that should have been said to my daughter. The same as when Barb passed away, I didn't want Dhakota to know what had happened and he told her over the phone while I wasn't there. I wanted to speak to a counsellor and ask what would be the best way of going about it, particularly given the circumstances of how she died, but I never got the opportunity to do that because Carl just jumped in and told her on the phone. Carl has no parenting skills at all. He has been at home for Dhakota for maybe three months at best, then all of a sudden he is jumping up making decisions on parenting and telling me this is how we go about it and what we tell her and when and how.

I still speak to Carl on the phone a lot because he calls from jail to talk to Dhakota and me and the other kids. Some days we have good calls and other days shit calls. We argued a while ago because I think Dhakota needs to see a counsellor to deal with all the shit that has already happened in her life that is not like any other normal kid has had to deal with, and Carl disagrees. He will be Dhakota's friend more than a father because a father is there to tell you how to do stuff and to discipline you and talk to you and Carl will never be there to do that. But he will be there to be her friend.

Dhakota is allowed to have contact visits with him and she goes in and sits on his knee and I sit on the other side of the glass. It saddened me when I watched them one day and realised she had built a real bond with him. I mean, it is great but it is also very sad because I think she will never know what it is like to have a real dad and I know that feeling. No matter how much you reach out for it you will never grab hold of it because nobody will ever be your father. She lays her head on his shoulder and hugs him and she is always concerned about where he sleeps and if he is warm.

Regardless of what offence you have committed and whatever people say about prison being soft or easy, being incarcerated is a hard thing to have to deal with. People who have never been incarcerated, and victims of crime — who I do feel sorry for — don't realise that jail really is punishment. Carl watches every week as his daughter walks away and he knows he can't be part of her life the way he should be. He only has himself to blame for that, I know, but don't tell me that that is an easy thing to do. I nearly went insane when I was away from my kids for six months. Imagine doing 35 years.

What saddens me most is that Dhakota will spend her whole life being punished for her father's crimes. Carl is not the only one doing his time.

CHAPTER 30

FAMILY TIES

Family has been the source of the greatest happiness and the greatest heartache in my life. My kids give me my greatest joy in life but the death of my dad before I knew him and the death to cancer of my sister Sharon were obviously the saddest moments of my life.

I know, though, that with one notable exception — Susan — family will be the most important thing in what lies ahead for me. I have learned a lot of life's lessons the hard way. Nothing has been easy and even though I have moved on from a criminal sort of life and am trying to make my way building a T-shirt business, it doesn't get any easier. Criminal life was wrong, I know that, but for a long time it was the only thing I knew. Now I better understand my choices.

What has not changed in me is that I will defend my family to the death. My kids are my life and I will do anything to protect them. My brothers I love dearly. Maybe it is because we are getting a bit older but we have all had to look at one another and realise that life is fragile. Sharon's death obviously reinforced that more than anything. As I have said before, Shaz and I were really close and did everything together: when I went overseas she came with me. Whenever I did anything Shaz was a part of it. We had the same sense of humour and laughed together all the time. What upsets me most about her death is not just that I have lost her in my life but that a few months before she died we had a bit of a minor disagreement and didn't speak much.

The worst thing is, it was all my fault. I was out of control and being a complete bitch to people at the time. We were arguing about something small but suddenly it blew up into this big fight. We had lent Shaz $4,000 to help renovate her house and I said I wanted it back. Of course I knew she didn't have the money, or she wouldn't have borrowed it in the first place, but I was just being a vindictive bitch and I hate myself for it. We didn't speak for months after that but then my niece rang me and said, 'Aunty Berta, Sharon is really sick, you should go in and see her.' She had cancer of the ovaries and was in the Freemasons Hospital. I went in there and I couldn't believe it, she was half the size she had been just months before. I was shocked and really emotional but Shaz was laughing and she was OK. She had had a hysterectomy and massive chemo and we were told it was in remission so we thought she was going to be OK. She was always my indestructible older sister so I thought she would never die. I couldn't get my head around the idea that she might.

Sharon had always been like the mum of the family, because Mum certainly never was. But Sharon had decided a month or two before we had our argument that it was important for us all to try and rebuild our relationships with Mum, so she organised a big dinner for all five girls to have with Mum one night down in Mordialloc. We all went along and it was a really fun night. We had laughs and we were taking photos together and it was good. I mean, no-one really got along with Susan but we were all polite.

Mum died soon after that of a massive brain haemorrhage. She had gone to hospital complaining of shocking headaches and they gave her aspirin and sent her home. Then a couple of days later my phone rang and rang and I could see it was Mum on the phone and I just didn't want to deal with her, so I crunched the calls and she left messages on my mobile phone voicemail saying she had shocking headaches. It embarrasses and upsets me deeply now to think that I didn't answer the phone.

I went to Queensland on a holiday and a couple of days later got a phone call to tell me Mum had had the brain haemorrhage, was in hospital on life support and I should get there. I flew back the next day and walked in and all my brothers and sisters were around the bed. We said our goodbyes, and they turned off the machine. Even though she had been a bitch to me I was still upset. When I had had quiet time with Mum alone before they turned off the machine, that was what I said to her: 'Why Mum? Why did you treat me that way? Why did you always hate me? Why couldn't you love me?' I was really upset.

We had the funeral and we all went except Mick. He could never forgive Mum for the way she treated her kids. He hated her and never saw a reason to forgive her. I could understand his attitude, but I went along.

It was only months after Mum died that we found out about Shaz's cancer, but we were told she was in remission and we had a big dinner out in Port Melbourne to celebrate. The next thing I knew I got a phone call to say it was back again and this time it didn't look good for her. I took my time going into the hospital because I sort of felt like it wasn't real and if I didn't go in and confront it then maybe it wasn't happening. It is a bit childish, I know, but that was how I felt. I eventually went in and I was overcome with emotion. I just went up and hugged Shaz so tight, I had never hugged anyone like that before and I squeezed her and told her I loved her and she kept saying, 'You are going to have to step up to the plate now, Bertie, you are going to have to be strong.' She knew she was always like a mum to us. I was really close to Shaz and Michelle but Shaz was always like a mother figure and Michelle was always a sister.

I walked out and Michelle and I went to the tea room and hugged each other and cried and said, 'How do you say goodbye to someone you have spent your life with and means the world to you?' I look back now and I treasure every moment I had with Shaz and it breaks my heart that we stupidly wasted time we could have had together.

I rang Dean because he had known Shaz for a long time and always liked her and got along well with her. He was really good about it. He was understanding of my grief and was emotional himself. He said, 'She has always been the most stable thing in your life.' And he was right. That experience is why I have become even closer to Mick, Michelle and Laurie. Mick had a heart attack a while back — he is a truck driver and he has the diet of a truck driver — but when I heard that it had happened my heart jumped and I thought, 'I can't deal with this, I can't lose Mick now after losing Mum and Shaz within months of each other.' It really shook us up. Because of the age difference between Mick and me we were never really close when I was young — he was gone from the house when I was really little — but in recent years we have been building a really good relationship and we are now very close.

Laurie too has had serious battles but hopefully he has overcome them. Laurie was fantastic when he was younger, he worked and worked and built up a lawnmowing business and owned properties and did really well. Then someone introduced him to smoking heroin and predictably he and his girlfriend Margaret got addicted. I only found out she was on drugs the day before she was due to give birth to their second baby. I went over to their house and they had nothing for the baby at all. Nothing. So I called Shaz and we went out and bought them everything they needed — pram, nappies, clothes, everything. I was shocked because I knew Laurie had done well in his business so it was obvious where all the money had gone. And Margaret admitted to us that she had a problem.

We booked Margaret into rehab and organised for her to have a naltrexone implant. I paid the $6,000 for her rehab and to get the implant, but the money was not the issue — we had to get her off the stuff. I took her to see this wonderful doctor, Dr Kozminsky, in Brighton after she had had the rehab and she was sitting there saying she didn't know if she should get the implant when the doctor distracted her and just cut her and put it in. It saved her life but sadly she gave up heroin only to get on speed.

At the time Laurie refused to admit he had a problem. He admitted he was using but insisted he had it under control and was not an addict. It took years for him to accept it and he only really did when he ended up going to prison for a short stretch for some minor things. When he was in there he came to his senses and my niece rang me and said Uncle Laurie wants you to organise that implant. So I rang Dr Kozminsky to ask what my options were. He told me that since Laurie had been in jail and he'd done half a rehab program he wouldn't need detox, just the implant, which would cost $1,500. He said to me, 'Just get Laurie treated the second he walks out of the prison, that is the main thing.' He organised half a naltrexone pill for when Laurie was released and the half pill was shoved into him straight away. My niece took him to the practice the next day for implant. Laurie has been fantastic ever since.

Laurie has since said that he thinks it saved his life and he can't believe how good he feels now. He always felt like he could never feel as good as he did on drugs but now he realises that the drugs were what was making him feel shit the rest of the time and destroying his life. He is now more like the old Laurie and I am so happy about that.

I say all of this about my family to provide some background for our amazement when my other sister Susan came out in the newspapers attacking me. I spoke earlier about Susan and the shit she said about me. She had a go at me early on on *Today Tonight*. The gist of Susan's first TV interview seemed to be that she had watched *Underbelly* and believed it and said we had a perfect family. No-one in the family could believe what she was saying. I sent her a message asking her what she was talking about and why she was saying those things. And she sent me back a text saying, 'Fuck off scum.' I still have it in my phone.

She was paid for the interview — just a few grand and a few nights in a city hotel. No-one knew who she was before that because we don't have the same surname and we don't look much alike, but she was saying that I was to blame for her not being able to get a job. I know why she lost her job and it was nothing to do with me — she complained that they were underpaying her a few cents an hour and she quit despite them offering to backpay her.

The night after she was on *Today Tonight*, the people from the show had her packing boxes and saying she had to move out of her house because of fears for her safety — they presumed I would turn up there and try to attack her and they would film it. But I didn't go near her place. I didn't care. Channel Nine rang me to say come on and have your say, so I did. We got a private detective to watch Susan and we know she didn't move out of her house or go anywhere for four days, she just did her normal things.

I spoke to all of my family about it in the days after she went on TV and none of us could believe it. We were all trying to work out why she would do it and make up the lies she did about our 'happy' childhood. We worked out that it was probably because she was shitty with me because I didn't go to her fiftieth birthday party. Apparently she'd been telling all her friends that her sister Roberta, the celebrity, would be there because I was getting messages on my MySpace page from people saying they wanted to meet me and have a drink with me. And I just thought, 'What is this shit?' She was offended because she was probably embarrassed that I didn't turn up.

What amazed me was that she said I was living off blood money from the people Carl killed. She tried to make herself out as some innocent squarehead who didn't like the idea that her sister had been in jail and was married to a drug dealer. What a fucking hypocrite. Susan of all people should know that you don't throw stones in glasshouses. When we were younger Susan was always out and about with her boyfriends. She had one boyfriend in particular, who she lived with. He was a convicted bank robber and she went out with him for years and years and she lived off the proceeds of his crimes. He went to jail and she visited him and even took me in there as a young kid to visit him in Pentridge.

I used to stay at Susan's house when I had nowhere to go after Mum kicked me out. She was in her twenties and living in a house with her boyfriend. Back then Human Services paid about $150 a week to people to take on a foster kid, and even though I was her sister she got the money. But as I said earlier, she wouldn't let me actually stay in the house.

Susan was always jealous of Sharon because Sharon was beautiful and glamorous and Susan was — she was a bit fat and ugly. One day when my mum was bashing her, Susan came in and butted a cigarette on her back. We couldn't believe it.

When Susan piped up in the newspapers again after I was quoted having a go at Zarah for not telling me about the baby and for cutting me out of her life, I was furious. It seemed she was addicted to getting her name in the paper. I have already said what I think about Zarah but it really pissed me off that Susan bought into it with the lies and bullshit. Put it this way, no-one else in the family talks to her and she is the one saying that I should shut up and stop embarrassing the family.

If it wasn't so serious it would be funny, the shit that Susan has made up. She said in the newspaper that we had a good upbringing and that Mum didn't even have boyfriends let alone blokes who beat us up. So who was Theo then, the fucking postman? And what about Joe? Who was he? Whose name is on Robert's birth certificate as the father? It is not Dad. That sort of shit alone should be enough to make you realise what a liar she is and how she just made stuff up because she wanted publicity or something. Susan reckoned she was too scared to say anymore because I could pay a junkie $20 to hurt her. Well Susan should know me well enough to know that if I wanted to hurt her I wouldn't be paying a junkie $20 to do it, I would punch her head in myself.

The media was happy to publish all of her shit without asking a word about her background. I wonder if they might look now at who they are putting up there as the big poster girl of happy families. But I don't suppose they would be too worried about that, they just wanted to find someone to slag me off for some reason and Susan was the only one they could find dumb enough to do it. She has always wanted to get a slice of the action for herself.

It was the same when Mum died and, like I said, she left everything in her will to Robert and Josephine. But Susan fought it in court and asked every member of the family for affidavits and everyone signed what she asked and made the statements she asked us to make. I signed but I stayed right out of it because I thought, 'That's all I need, the media coverage of an inheritance fight.' Josephine and Robert didn't want to fight it and agreed to a settlement. Susan had always said that whatever was coming to one should be coming to all and that any money should be divided up equally. But she kept it all and by then no-one could be bothered going to the courts to fight for it. I never wanted any money anyway. I said to them then, 'I'm not going to fight a dead woman's will and take her money. If she didn't want me to have it, fine, give it to someone else. I don't want it.'

CHAPTER 31

TUPPENCE

All the madness and the bullshit of the so-called gang war had stopped when out of nowhere the news broke on 15 June 2009 that another Moran had died. This time it was Des 'Tuppence' Moran, Lewis Moran's brother. I knew one thing straight away — Carl didn't do it.

The media always boast that they are the first with the news and sure enough they were this time as well. The first I knew that Tuppence had been shot was when someone from the media rang me and told me there had been a shooting and Tuppence was dead. I rang Dean straight away, because I knew with his relationship with the Morans he would know if anything had happened to one of them, and before I even got to say anything, he just said, 'Yeah, yeah, yeah, it's true.' He knew what I was going to ask him.

I just said, 'You are fucking joking, Dean. What the fuck for?' Straight away we both said the same name at the same time — we both thought Judy Moran would be charged with the murder. I had never met Tuppence; I think he was one who just sat back and lived his life away from a lot of the shit, and so while I didn't know him I liked him, because the one other thing that I knew about him was that him and Judy didn't get along. And anyone that didn't like Judy was all right by me.

While Dean and I immediately had our suspicions of who shot Tuppence to death outside that café in Ascot Vale, so did the police. Funnily enough, the three names that immediately came to my mind seemed to be the names that came to the police's mind too, because they turned out to be the three people charged with the murder. I can't say much about it because these people have to go through the courts but I can say that one of the people charged with the murder was Judy Moran. Like I said it was well known that her and Tuppence didn't like one another. Whether she killed him, the jury can decide that.

All I really knew of Tuppence was that he used to be a debt collector or standover man with Lewis when they were younger but later on Tuppence sort of kept to himself. During all the bullshit of the gangland killings I never heard anyone mention him like they were worried he was involved in things.

The only time he sort of got involved was once in a newspaper article he talked about me having an affair with Carl and that sparking all of the gangland war. It was bullshit that we had an affair (like I've said before) but it was true that Dean thought we had and was furious about it. Carl has always believed that he was shot partly because Dean paid Jason to do it for him as payback for Carl being with me. There was the argument about the money Mark owed Carl as well but Carl reckons the fact Dean paid the Morans to get him meant that the dispute over drugs and the money got out of hand and they shot him where they might not have shot him otherwise. When they took Carl's bum bag off him that day it was Dean that ended up with it and the money and the gun that were inside it. Dean used to torment me about having Carl's bum bag.

As I have said a hundred times, it was not an affair because Dean and I had split up by then, but in Dean's warped mind because we were still technically married, even though we were separated, Carl had no right to be with me.

So that was really my only brush with Tuppence. If Judy is found guilty of being involved in the murder my feeling would be it would be likely to be over Lewis' money. The only other thing I will say is that I laughed my guts out when I heard she was charged with murder. After all the shit she went on with, with her acting all high and mighty and superior and making out she was above everyone else and acting like butter wouldn't melt in her mouth while her sons were killing blokes all over town, I was rapt when I found out she was charged and would be locked up. As Carl said, the one who laughs last laughs loudest. And I am laughing loudly now, Judy. (Hope you enjoy the Wella Balsam shampoo and the cold toast inside.)

One thing about Judy Moran really annoyed me — well, more than one thing to be honest, but one thing in particular. Judy wrote in her book that I bought a BMW to copy her. It got me so angry because it was just so untrue. The fact is that firstly it is not like me at all to compare and try and compete with people for what they wear or what they own; and secondly I know that I had already bought and sold my car before Judy bought hers. I don't know how you can copy someone when you are first.

She tried to make out that we were trying to keep up with her and her family with the cars we drove and it was bullshit because for another thing Jason and Trisha used to drive an old Holden Astra. For safety reasons you always know what car your enemies are driving and one day after appearing in court we happened to see it. This was well before Carl was well known so when we walked out of court there was no media following us and when we walked down the road and saw their car parked there, we thought, 'Fuck this,' and kicked in every panel of the car. If it wasn't a big enough bomb before, it sure was when we finished with it because I jumped on the roof and we smashed that car to pieces.

What people find a bit strange about my relationship with the Morans is that in the middle all of this my daughter Breanane has become close friends with Taylor Cole, Mark Cole's daughter. It is awkward because even though Carl is not her dad he brought Breanane up and she treated Carl like her dad and Carl and Mark were enemies. Obviously, Carl was accused of murdering Mark, so in that sense it is pretty strange that Carl's step-daughter would be best friends with Mark's daughter.

In another way, though, it is not so strange because Dean was Breanane's dad and he was always good friends with Mark Cole. But, really, Bree lived with me not her dad so she knew we hated the Morans and the Coles. In fact she was being cheeky recently and she brought home DNA papers and said, 'Mum, I look so much like Carl I want a DNA test to prove he is my dad.' She was only joking but it was funny because there *is* a resemblance there. And before you go jumping to conclusions, no, he could not be her dad. I think it is because Carl was around so much when she was growing up that she has picked up a lot of his habits and that makes her resemble him.

I really like Taylor. At the start she was a little bit stand-offish towards me, which I can understand because she was probably worried about how I would react to her but now she knows I love all kids and I don't blame her for what her parents say and whatever they have done. One time she needed our help because a boy had assaulted her at Highpoint Shopping Centre and Bree rang me to help. I wasn't able to go there so I rang Dean and told him Taylor had been hit by a boy and was hurt so could he get there. He sent Tye and someone else over and they helped Taylor. They also knew who the boy was so Dean rang him and threatened him — he was only young so Dean wouldn't hurt him but he did say to him, 'Mate, look out because you just can't fucking hit a girl and think it is OK.' He warned him that if he was a bit older he would be doing more than talking to him about it.

That boy's dad was actually already in jail for murdering his aunty (the dad went to shoot the mum and the aunt got in the way), so the kid has been brought up in a circle of violence, but Dean told him where he had to draw the line. What I was pleased about though was that Taylor knew us well enough and trusted us to ring for help and know that of course we would do anything to help her.

Breanane and Taylor are part of a bigger group of girls who hang around together and go to Macca's after school or to a café. When I see them I ask them all if they have money for food and drinks and sometimes Taylor is a bit short and I will give her $10 — like I do for any of the girls — just to make sure they all have the same amount.

When I first found out Bree was friends with this girl I was very hesitant because the Coles and the Morans are out-and-out enemies and the whole family knows that. They have been going to school together since they were in prep and at first they were not friends, for the obvious reasons. I heard at one point that Taylor was giving Bree dirty looks and I got angry but Danielle checked it out and found out it was a misunderstanding. When I calmed down I thought, well, even if she was, this girl is just a child who thinks my daughter's father has killed her father. I thought of it differently after that.

After a while it seems they just started to like each other and wanted to hang out together. I was surprised and worried at first but then, as I've said, she is just a child and whatever her parents and uncle have done is nothing to do with her. It took me by surprise and I suppose it took Antonella — Taylor's mum — by surprise as well. I am told she was a bit unpleasant to Bree at first when the two of them started being friendly but recently it has been different.

Antonella's brother Paul is married and I was going to kill his wife at one stage. It was just after Barb had died and I went to the school to drop off the girls and I saw her looking out the window and laughing at me. It got me so angry that you would laugh at someone because someone they know had died — how low is that? It disgusted me. I told Carl I was going to get her and he said, 'Roberta, if you are going to bash her and get pinched for bashing her, then leave some damage.'

So I rang Mick Gatto and said to him, 'Look, there is an issue. I don't know how to get in touch with Paul but get him to ring me or I am going to smash his missus's head in at the school with a hammer.' I thought I would let them know I meant business, and I had had enough. Mick said he would sort it out and within 20 minutes Paul rang me and said he would talk to his wife and pleaded with me not to hurt her. That was the closest things have been to a dispute between our families since everything settled down and since Bree and Taylor became good friends.

Antonella and I give the girls lifts to parties and they get ready at each other's houses, so there is no issue there. I would never myself go to the door of their house to drop her off or collect her. That would be too much and too fake. Imagine walking up to Antonella's door and saying, 'Hiya, you know me, I'm Roberta, here to pick up Breezy.' No. Not going to happen. She would never come here to collect the girls and I would never ever give her the time of day if she did. I don't like her and I don't care who I tell. Taylor knows that, everyone knows that. But it is not an issue between us and it is never discussed. I have every reason to be angry at Mark and Jason for what they did to Carl but I would never take it out on that child.

At the start I warned Bree to just stay away from Taylor because being a Cole — or a Moran — I thought you don't know if she will turn on you because it is in her blood. But Bree said, 'No, Mum, I really like Taylor — I think she is nice.' Then I started to think, well, I brought my children up not to judge a book by its cover and only to judge somebody by how they were to you, so it is fair enough that she makes up her own mind and chooses her own friend. I rang Dean when I found out they were friends and I said, 'You need to remember whose daughter she is and you need to remind them that she is your daughter, she is not Carl's.'

I know that Judy did their make-up for them when they went to the races one day. I hope she didn't let them leave looking like Barbara Cartland, like Judy did! Bree has even had a sleep-over at Taylor's house. Can you believe that — my daughter sleeping in the house of Mark Cole?

CHAPTER 32

GETTING MY LIFE
BACK TOGETHER

Since the night I literally came back from the edge of a cliff when Dean beat me and put the gun to my head, I have had six lots of surgery to repair the damage. My nose was so severely broken that the right side of my face and nose had collapsed. The doctors had to take cartilage from my left ear to build up the nose but it just keeps collapsing and I can't breathe. And when that happens it gets all clogged up and the infection sets in.

I've had some dental work, implants and crowns put on my teeth because they were knocked out when he beat me and my eye socket was broken on the brow bone, but that won't be fixed for a little while yet because the nose has to completely heal before they can even think about that operation. It is just such a long, ongoing mess.

I have had a bit of other work done, I don't deny it. I have had three breast reductions because, as I've said, I naturally have big boobs and I just hate them. I have had to keep having the reductions because every time I put on weight they get big again. I went to Queensland for the first reduction and the doctor found a lump that he thought was cancerous, so he sent me for a mammogram saying, 'There's a lump there we think is cancer, I am putting you in for surgery tomorrow.' It turned out it wasn't cancer but he was 100 per cent certain it was going to be. Anyway, he also did a breast reduction and he made such a mess of it that I had to have it fixed. He'd taken too much fat out of one side so that it left a hollow and so I had to have it refilled with some fat.

Also I wasn't stitched up properly after one of my kids so I had to have more surgery to repair that damage. It's been a hell trip. And then I got endometriosis really badly and they had to do a bladder repair because the 'endo' had grown around my bowel and bladder. That was the reason I had to have IVF when I had Dhakota. I want more kids still, I plan to have two more kids with Rob, and they will probably have to be IVF too.

Even though I have had operations to reduce my breasts because I don't like blokes ogling them when I walk down the street, I was proud of my new body so when *Zoo Weekly* asked me to do a photo shoot I thought, why not? It was just a bit of fun, and believe me it was actually a lot of fun because what girl doesn't want to be treated like a model? What girl wouldn't like someone else doing their hair and make-up and having a professional photographer take great pictures of them for nothing? When I did that photo shoot a lot of people said, 'Gee, they have done a lot of Photoshopping on those pictures,' but I can honestly say it was all me. Yes, the doctors had done a little bit of work to help me out, but I reckon that if you can get that stuff done and it makes you feel better about yourself, then why not do it?

The real reason I agreed to the *Zoo* shoot, though, wasn't to show off my body, it was for the simple reason that I needed the money. When Carl went to jail the kids and I were left with nothing. Part of the whole Purana investigation was to try and hurt Carl and his family wherever they could, and the state government had this new legislation about the proceeds of crime, so they took whatever they could. Suddenly we were broke. And being a kid from the streets who had no real education, I wasn't in a position to go out and get some high-paying job — I have had to rely on my own nose to try and get by. That is why I was prepared to do the photo shoots.

That's also why I did the first interviews with Channel Nine and, I am not going to lie, it was one of the reasons I decided to write this book and to be involved in the documentaries being made about this period. I stress this, and you can choose to believe it or not, but after having read my story now I hope you believe that I am honest when I say that while I did want the money, more than anything I wanted to write this book to put the other side of the story. I wanted to correct a lot of the bullshit that has been said over the years. I wanted to sell my story but first and foremost I wanted to tell my story.

The only other thing I will say now is that I have moved on, although I might bob up in the papers now and then because the police still have an unhealthy obsession with my family. They raided our house early in 2009 looking for Tye over some burglaries and, lo and behold, the media knew about the raid within minutes and suddenly there were TV crews and newspaper reporters all over our house and waiting for us at court to gloat and rub our noses in bad publicity.

The day that Tye was arrested I heard a lot of commotion outside. I looked at my alarm clock and saw it was 5.30 am and out my window I could see police everywhere. I ran downstairs and as I opened the door I found the police about to smash it down. The sergeant came in and said, 'We are not here for you, Roberta.' I asked for their search warrant and they didn't have one but said they were sorting something out. Then a sergeant arrived with a warrant that allowed police to enter the house if a suspect they needed to arrest was there but they had already arrested Tye outside and there were no other suspects inside the house so I said they could not come in. I knew I had not done anything illegal so I didn't see why they should be allowed to traipse through my house and upset my kids.

A police media officer arrived because there were so many media outside. He asked me if I wanted to go out and make a statement and I said no, I had nothing to say. He went out and told the media it was nothing to do with me but that two men had been arrested. One of them was obviously Tye and the media knew that so they were still excited that my son was involved. I can't go into many details of what happened because the case is waiting to go to court.

Because of all the media I didn't want to leave the house. They were coming up to the frosted glass in the door and trying to snap photos of us through that. We were going to throw flour on them from upstairs but I rang my lawyer to ask if I would be in trouble if I did that and she warned me not to.

Dhakota kept looking through the window at them. I warned her not to because they would take a photo of her and sure enough they took a photo of her with her dummy in her mouth and it turned up in *MX*. They were saying she was six and shouldn't still be using a dummy. They tried to make out she would become a drug addict or a criminal because she was too old to have a dummy, which made me furious. I always thought, well, what is a cigarette? That is just a prop you shove in your mouth for comfort, why can't she keep her dummy if she wants it?

Anyway the media stayed there all day. Tye's girlfriend was inside and she wanted to leave and not have to run through all the cameras and journalists, so she rang a friend to drive around the back and she jumped over the back fence and got in the car. Some of the media saw her go and they reported that it was me. Not true. I wouldn't jump a fence to get out of my own home. If I wanted to go out I would walk out with my head high — the public should know that about me by now.

The next thing I get this phone call from the finance company over late payments on my silver BMW. Tye had bought the car for me on hire purchase because I couldn't get a loan. Anyway, the repayments were a few months late and the guys from the finance company rang that day and I said to them that I couldn't talk because the police were raiding our house and there were media everywhere. So they turn up at the house and talk to the police and media out the front. Rob rang the finance bloke and said, 'If you want your money, come to the door and I will give it to you.' But the guy was too scared to do that thinking we would bash him or something, so he didn't get his money or the car.

Another car was towed away by the police — it was a car allegedly stolen in connection with the burglaries and was parked around the corner — but the media filmed that car being towed away and said it was my car being repossessed. It was bullshit, that car was nothing to do with me and I still had my car.

The finance company has since begun sucking up to me because someone — apparently some bloke from the Hells Angels — rang and threatened them over the way they had treated me. I knew nothing about it, although I know a few senior blokes in the Hells Angels, but I had not spoken to anyone about making any threats. If I wanted to threaten some piss-weak little finance bloke I would do it myself. And if someone is angry on my behalf at how I was treated and takes matters into their own hands, then that is nothing to do with me.

CHAPTER 33

REGRETS,
I'VE HAD A FEW

I have a lot of regret in my life. I regret I didn't do things differently and see things clearer and make decisions that I should have made. There is a lot of sadness. The biggest thing in my life I will never get over is the loss of my sister Sharon. That hurt me even more than Andrew's death. Andrew and I were incredibly close and even though I had only known him a fairly short time, we had a bond that made it feel like we had known one another forever. But Sharon I *had* known forever. She had been through everything with me — the abuse from Mum and her partners and all the difficult times. I miss her desperately still.

I regret that my life with Dean didn't work out and that he was abusive. And sometimes I regret Carl. I regret getting together with him but I know that out of that relationship came my beautiful daughter Dhakota, so I can't really say I regret Carl because it would be like saying that I regret having Dhakota and I don't regret that for a second — I love my daughter to death. But I do wonder if Carl and I shouldn't have just stayed friends and maybe all this hurt wouldn't have transpired.

I regret not making it up with my mum before she died. That might sound strange to people who have made it through reading about my life story up to now. Maybe I am saying that because she is gone and because I can't make up with her I want to. The chances are that if she was still here I wouldn't give a rat's arse about her so maybe regret isn't the right word. I suppose I would have liked the choice to be able to try to make contact with her and find out why a lot of that shit happened. I know I was a shit of a kid, an absolute shit of a kid. And to that extent I have to take blame for what happened in my life and my family, but you don't deal with naughty kids by bashing them up and throwing them out on the street and not even giving them a key to get into their house. I look at Dhakota now and I was a year older than her and I was shoplifting my clothes and walking the streets because Mum kicked me out. Surely I couldn't have been that bad to treat me like that.

I know now that violence breeds violence and that violence did breed violence in myself. I am a prime example of that because all I know is how to react to a situation with violence because that was how I was treated. No one ever treated me calmly they just belted me or kicked or whipped me with a jug cord or held me under the bath water.

I regret that I didn't have a better relationship with my brother Laurie but we are rebuilding that now that Laurie is off the drugs. But my biggest regret with Laurie isn't about our relationship, it is that I was involved in the drug trade. I look at him and think of what drugs did to him and his life and I am ashamed of my dealing in drugs. I have learnt a huge lesson and now I want to set up a foundation called CHANCE and work with Dr Kozminsky to raise money for drug addicts to have rehab and get the naltrexone implants put in. I have seen the benefits of the implants first hand and believe it is the best way to get addicts off the drugs. I have seen the lives saved by the treatment and I believe in it passionately. Maybe if I can get that foundation going it will make up for some of the other shit things I have done in my life because I want to give back to the community now.

I understand the effects of drugs and I know I was involved in that awful business and it is embarrassing to admit that now. But when you are mixed up in something and all the money is coming in and you are living life the way you had never lived it, you don't take a step back and look at the big picture. You are in the middle of a whirlwind and you don't look at who is getting hurt by your actions or who it is affecting. I know I didn't. At the time all you are thinking about is your family and yourself and how best to survive. Then when Laurie and Margaret became addicts and it ruined their lives I realised that this shit happens to all families. And even though I wasn't dealing to Laurie I had to feel partly to blame because I was dealing in drugs and drugs damaged his life so much.

It is hard to say I regret everything that happened through that time, and my time with Carl, because like I said I had Dhakota with Carl. In regard to the murders, I know I could not have stopped them or changed what happened — that was Carl and the boys. Whether I should have stayed around when those murders were happening and the drug dealing was going on, I don't know. Now I would say of course not, obviously I should have got out of there but I also know that at the time it wasn't as simple as that. At the time you don't have that time to think of what is right and what is wrong; you are thrown in the middle of this life and you continue to make the best of any situation. We have to deal the deck we are given. That is the way I have lived my life it is how I will go on living my life.

A lot of people look at the gangster life and think it looks glamorous. I won't lie — for a long time, when we were making money and flying around the world and eating at all these great restaurants and stuff like that, I thought the same thing. But it is all bullshit. It is not glamorous. I have lived it and believe me it is not all you can hope for to end up a lonely wife at home while they are out with their skanks, leaving you to wait by the phone to find out they are dead or arrested. The friends you think you have are not your friends. They are like the life you think you have — it is not real and it doesn't last.

What I think now is that it was all such a waste. It was a shocking waste of life and not just the lives of those people who were killed, or those sitting in jail cells now, but a waste for the rest of us left behind as well. It is a waste for the little girl who only gets to see her daddy on weekends behind prison walls.

POSTSCRIPT

It was just before 1pm on 19 April 2010, and Carl Williams sat quietly at a table in the communal joint kitchen and exercise yard of Barwon Prison's maximum security Acacia unit quietly reading the newspaper. Not for the first time Carl was the subject of the very newspaper stories he was reading. That day's *Herald Sun* had reported that police had paid $8000 in school fees for Dhakota.

A story such as this might only have confirmed in the minds of some in the prison system that Carl was trying to — or had — cut a deal with police to turn informer. But Carl had apparently known for some days this story was coming and he was prepared for it. Besides, he wasn't threatened by the two prisoners with him in the exercise yard — they were mates and he trusted them. Prisoners in Acacia are allowed to nominate one or two other inmates they trust to be able to spend time with in their one-hour-a-day exercise break. Carl then was relaxed and comfortable in the knowledge that the only two prisoners with him that afternoon were friends of his. Seven years earlier, Carl had asked Little Tommy Ivanovic to be Dhakota's godfather but he had been in jail at the time of the christening. 'Little Tommy', a drug dealer, was jailed for 18 years in 2003 for the shooting murder of a motorcyclist. The other prisoner was also someone Carl was at ease around — he was a mate. Carl had lent him clothes.

Slim, fit and looking nothing like the 'Fat Boy' police referred to him as, Carl was relaxed as he sat thumbing through the paper reading the story about him having Dhakota's school fees paid. Whether the story was true and whether indeed Carl was trying to cut a deal and turn informer is largely irrelevant in prison — the perception or belief of a deal was enough to get a man killed. Maybe that perception killed Carl, for at 12.48pm on this autumn day a trusted fellow inmate of Carl's pulled a stem from an exercise bike in the yard, walked up behind Carl and bashed him a number of times in the head. All the while, the other prisoner in the yard — Tommy Ivanovic — was on the telephone.

We know all of this because security cameras filmed the attack and all telephone calls to and from the unit are recorded. The prisoner who attacked Carl, who cannot be named for legal reasons, then dragged Carl to his cell and dumped him there. He was still alive but bleeding heavily from the head. A prison officer had reportedly only been a short distance away the entire time, but was unaware of the attack until prisoners raised the alarm 25 minutes later and another prison officer discovered him in his cell. An ambulance was called at 1.21pm. Three ambulances arrived but the first crew to attend pronounced him dead at 1.32pm.

Carl was 39. Jailed for life for four murders, he was serving a minimum 35 years. But in his case now, life suddenly meant *life*.

News of Carl's death broke quickly in Melbourne. Roberta might have been experienced in dealing with grief and the sudden death of loved ones, but nothing quite prepared her for Carl's death. They were no longer married, but he was in many ways — as she described — her life-long partner. They were best mates that shouldn't have married and they remained close friends right until his death. He was, after all, the father of her child.

Carl admitted in a revealing final interview with Adam Shand — a journalist that Carl and Roberta trusted — that he was enormously reliant on Roberta.

'I will always be connected with her, whether we are married or not,' Shand said that Carl had told him. 'We probably should never have got married, but just stayed best friends. Bert's the one who stuck by me when everybody else just disappeared.'

Indeed Carl and Roberta had stuck close throughout. After the release of the first edition of this book, Roberta and Rob had broken up for a time and Roberta and Carl had spoken of remarrying and even having more children together. It was perhaps just idle talk for soon after Roberta and Rob reunited. It had been a difficult time for both of them as Roberta had battled — in and out of hospital —

with a debilitating blood illness that remained undiagnosed for a long period of time. Rob had also had health problems. These issues had created tensions of their own which had bubbled up in their relationship. But by the time Carl died Roberta and Rob had patched up their differences.

It was Rob who answered the phone that afternoon with the news that shattered Roberta's world. He turned to Roberta and the message was as simple as it was awful: 'Carl's dead.'

'There must be some mistake. Not Carl. The prison would have called me first,' she immediately replied. Roberta later told a women's magazine that her disbelief was compounded by the idea that he was in maximum security being monitored around the clock so he could not possibly be killed under the noses of prison guards. Her thoughts then, typically, immediately turned to her children. How could she possibly tell Dhakota that Daddy had died? Worse still, what if they see it on the news?

She was angry. Fucking angry. Angry at the prison for failing to look after Carl. Angry at the 'maggots' who killed him, the men who had been Carl's 'mates' but turned on him so treacherously. It sent her life into a spin. Roberta suddenly had another funeral to organise. Like Carl — it was big, bold and brash.

Death notices were taken out in the *Herald Sun*.

Dhakota's message read touchingly:

'To Daddy, I will miss you. My dummy aint goin' nowhere so don't you. Nan and Uncle Shane come steal it while I'm asleep. Tell Nan that she is an Indian giver, she gave us you and then she just took you back. Nan can keep you, Uncle Andrew and Uncle Shane in line now.

'Love your one and only — Dhakota.'

Tye, who was denied leave from prison to attend Carl's funeral, wrote:

'When you and Mum first got together we did not see eye to eye. That soon changed and we became close friends and that will NEVER change.'

The funeral was held at St Theresa's Catholic Church in Essendon where his mother, Barb's, funeral had been. But this would not be like Barb's funeral. This would not be like any funeral Victoria had seen. Carl was laid to rest in a $30,000 bronze and 14-carat gold coffin imported from the United States. Michael Jackson had been buried in a similar coffin. The lure of the gold was too much for some evidently, for Roberta noticed on the day of his funeral that a gold cross had been callously stolen from the coffin. About 150 people attended Carl's funeral, where Roberta spoke of her pain at losing her close friend and love.

'I've never tried to excuse or justify Carl's behaviour and have always maintained that the real casualties of the underworld wars are the children on both sides ...' she said.

'I always had a bad gut feeling. He dropped his guard and when he did, a maggot robbed my daughter of her dad. Somebody has to pay for that. My kids are victims. They always were.

'Carlos, you taught me to stand proud and never look down,' she said.

'"Lift your head, Bert," you'd say, and "remember, no one's better than you. Keep your eyes focused straight ahead, be proud, keep going."'

Nine-year-old Dhakota bravely stood before the crowd and read: 'I love my dad a lot and you know what? He loves me.'

A slideshow of pictures of Carl cuddling the kids was shown as songs by Tina Turner ('Simply the Best'), Mariah Carey and Boyz II Men ('One Sweet Day') played.

Later at the graveside at Keilor cemetery a smaller crowd of perhaps 40 stood as the casket was lowered into the ground. Roberta plucked petals from cream-coloured roses and dropped them in gently one after another. The ashes of Carl's mum and brother were lowered in with him, while two white doves were released by his godson and Dhakota. White balloons were also released.

Carl may have died and his body laid to rest, but the story did not end there. The police and authorities had questions to answer — how could this have happened in maximum security? Police had footage of the bashing so they knew how Carl died, but not why. To that end a police operation, Taskforce Driver, was established to explore theories on Carl's death. Victoria's police corruption watchdog, the Office of Police Integrity, was commissioned to review and oversee the police and coronial investigations into Carl's murder.

After his death the *Herald Sun* and *Geelong Advertiser* newspapers reported that Carl had boasted of having visited prostitutes in a motel near Geelong (and near Barwon Prison) to have sex. He was said to have been taken by guards a fortnight before he was killed, to have sex with the two Tasmanian hookers. The significance of the fact the women were Tasmanian was not explained. He had reportedly told a close friend of his intimate encounters, although authorities refused to confirm the liaison.

If true one can only deduce that it was part compensation for Carl's co-operation in some manner with police or prosecutors. Given Carl's conviction on four murders and long jail sentence, it was unlikely authorities would be taking him out of prison to visit prostitutes just because Carl was horny.

Doubts have been raised whether, given the level of planning required to commit the murder, it could have been organised so quickly in response to something such as the suspicions raised by the *Herald Sun* story. However, the story might have further added to perceptions and rumours that already existed, which might have been a reason for Carl being killed.

With the investigation still open, it leaves many unanswered questions that will hang over Roberta and her family. Carl's death, much like his life, has had a lasting influence on Roberta that would never have ended as his body was laid to rest. Now she only wants to know the truth about what happened that day, for closure and to be able to tell her kids.

'I need answers because I have children who will want answers. It's heartbreaking,' Roberta said.

ACKNOWLEDGMENTS

My list of thank yous is a long one, but it comes from the heart ...

I'd like to thank my sister Sharon (God rest her soul), for instilling in me principles and respect. For always being there and showing me what unconditional love is — no matter what the situation.

My four beautiful children, Tye, Danielle, Breanane and Dhakota. Thank you for loving and supporting your mum; for never turning your backs on me, no matter how many times I stuff up, and for being the best kids a mother could love.

To my partner Rob, you're my backbone and my strength. Without you I would never have come this far.

To Rob's family, Santo, Sandra, John, Sharon and Annie, you've accepted me into your family and love me like I belong. Acceptance is your greatest gift and you fill my heart every day with the love of the family that I always wanted. Thank you to my beautiful boys, Lytrell, Chayse and Jackson, who love their Aunty Bert. And Nan, who I love like she were my own.

To my brother Mick for the strong bond that we've developed over the past few years. It has more than made up for the missed ones.

To my sister Michelle for always protecting me, despite our differences.

To my brother Laurie, who has always encouraged me and told me that I can be anyone, or anything, that I want to be. I love you with all my heart, Loz, you're my everything.

To little Breegs, you and your family accepted us and have never judged us, even though we're from such different backgrounds. I love you, kid.

To Michael Gleeson for putting up with me and helping me to write this book.

To Barb (rest in peace), for always telling me that there's nothing that I can't do and for saying to me, 'If anyone can do it, Bert, you can'. I love you, Barb.

To George for always being kind to me and loving and accepting me — even if I am a pain in the arse! I love you, George.

To Lisa, for always being my friend, and her mum and dad, Mary and Al, for always giving me a safe, warm place when I had nowhere to go. I love you.

And last, but definitely not least, to you, Carl, for so many things ... loving all of my children like they were all your own from the very beginning, and making sure that they never went without. And now, you're still there loving them from a distance. We've been through so much together and you've taught me so many things, but the one thing that

I still hold close is the confidence you instilled in me — you used to say to me, 'Bert, don't walk with your eyes to the ground. Hold your head up high and be proud of who you are, no matter what.' You gave me back my life after so many years of abuse. Thank you, from the bottom of my heart.